Ethical Issues in
Developmental
Disabilities

Ethical Issues in Developmental Disabilities

Editors:
Linda J. Hayes
Gregory J. Hayes
Stephen C. Moore
Patrick M. Ghezzi

CONTEXT PRESS
Reno, Nevada

Ethical Issues in Developmental Disabilities / edited by Linda J. Hayes, Gregory
    J. Hayes, Stephen L. Moore, and Patrick M. Ghezzi

Paperback. ISBN 1-878978-15-2

Hardback. ISBN 1-878978-16-0

Distributed by New Harbinger Publications, Inc.

Library of Congress Cataloging-in-Publication Data

Ethical issues in developmental disabilities / edited by Linda J. Hayes, Gregory
J. Hayes, Stephen L. Moore, and Patrick M. Ghezzi.
    207 p. : ill. ; 24 cm.
Includes bibliographical references.
    ISBN-13: 978-1-878978-15-8 (pbk.)
    ISBN-10: 1-878978-15-2 (pbk.)
  1. Developmentally disabled - Services for. 2. Developmental disabilities -
Treatment. 3. Medical ethics.
I. Hayes, Linda J., 1949- II. Title
RC570.2 .E84 1994
174/.2 dc20

95-173951

© 1994 CONTEXT PRESS
933 Gear Street, Reno, NV 89503-2729

Printed in the United States of America

Contributors

Mark A. Adams, M.A., *University of Nevada*

Marcia L. Bennett, Ph.D., *Sierra Regional Center*

Sidney W. Bijou, Ph.D., *University of Nevada*

Jacqueline E. Collins, B.A., *University of Nevada*

Mary Ann Demchek, Ph.D., *University of Nevada*

Debra W. Fredericks, R.N., B.S.N., *University of Nevada*

Patrick M. Ghezzi, Ph.D., *University of Nevada*

William C. Healey, Ph.D., *University of Nevada, Las Vegas*

Gregory J. Hayes, M.D., M.P.H., *University of Nevada*

Linda J. Hayes, Ph.D., *University of Nevada*

Steven C. Hayes, Ph.D., *University of Nevada*

Ramona Houmanfar, M.A., *University of Nevada*

Kenneth R. Huntley, M.S., *University of Nevada*

Donald A. Jackson, Ph.D., *Sierra Regional Center*

Brian Lahren, Ph.D., *Washoe Association for Retarded Citizens*

Duane C. Lord, B.A., *University of Nevada*

David Luke, Ph.D., *Sierra Regional Center*

Stephen C. Moore, Ph.D., *Nevada University Affiliated Program*

Alan Poling, Ph.D., *Western Michigan University*

Ruth Anne Rehfeldt, B.A., *University of Nevada*

Cynthia A. Reinbold, B.A., *University of Nevada*

Stephen L. Rock, Ph.D., *Nevada University Affiliated Program*

Kristi L. Rydeen, M.A., *University of Nevada*

Thomas Scully, M.D., *University of Nevada*

Mark Swain, B.A., *University of Nevada*

Ron Van Houten, Ph.D., *Mount Saint Vincent University, Canada*

About the Conference

This book is the result of the *Nevada Conference on Ethics and Developmental Disabilities*, held in Reno at the University of Nevada in January of 1994. The conferences was part of the Nevada Conference Series, a program designed to bring together applied workers and academics to consider important and controversial aspects of research and practice in psychology and related fields. The *Nevada Conference on Ethics and Developmental Disabilities* was supported by the Nevada University Affiliated Program, the Behavior Analysis Program in the Department of Psychology, the College of Arts and Science, and the College of Human and Community Sciences at the University of Nevada, and by CONTEXT PRESS.

Table of Contents

Preface

This volume is the proceedings of the *Nevada Conference on Ethics and Developmental Disabilities*, held at the University of Nevada, in January, 1994. The conference was a working meeting of the group listed as contributors plus a small but engaged audience, and two consumers of disability services, Cathy Altman and Robb Bussard, who participated in an discussion of these services. We came together to seek our future. To talk about how it ought to be ... and what that meant.

How it *ought* to be, in as much as it isn't yet what it is, is what one *says* about it. Ethics are concerns of this sort, though, more specifically, ethics is an issue of how one ought to *behave*. And how one ought to behave is, likewise, what one says about behavior. In this light, ethics is an issue of how verbal behavior relates to nonverbal behavior.

Talking about how it ought to be, though appearing to describe a future, must still be recognized as occurring in this present. This appreciation does not mean that one is free from the responsibility of discussing the future—nor would one want to be. The future is as rich a source as the past.

Talking complicates matters and ethics is, thereby, a complicated issue to struggle through—to know how one ought to behave. Still, the only way to find out—the only way to become more ethical—is to *practice* ethical behavior. It is to this end that we offer these days of verbal behavior, and its products as this volume.

Linda J. Hayes
Gregory J. Hayes
Stephen C. Moore
Patrick M. Ghezzi

March, 1994

Chapter 1

Ethics, Choice and Value

Linda J. Hayes, Mark A. Adams, and Kristi L. Rydeen
University of Nevada

Ethics is the sort of concept that everyone is familiar with and no one can define. The American Heritage Dictionary defines ethics as "The study of the general nature of morals and the specific moral choices to be made by the individual in his relationship with others." Implied here is the *human* individual for no one would suggest that a horse or a finch or a gnat behaves ethically. Significant also is the *group auspices* of ethical action. The actions of a lone human individual, were such a possibility, would not be ethical. Morals, in turn, are defined in the dictionary as "rules or habits of conduct with reference to standards of right and wrong." Putting all of these considerations together, ethics may be understood as the study of the values and choices of persons operating verbally as members of groups.

This characterization of the topic presents a serious challenge to psychological scientists of the behavioral variety. For what do psychologists have to say about the actions of groups? What do scientists have to say about value? And what do behaviorists have to say about choice?

Behavior in Groups

Let us begin with the problem of the group. How is the individual operating as a member of a group to be understood? How is the sociological concept of the group to be reconciled with a psychological interest in the behavior of an individual? Kantor's (1982) analysis of cultural behavior fields is instructive on this point.

Cultural behavior is conceptualized by Kantor as shared actions with respect to common stimulus functions. In this treatment, engaging in such actions is the criterion for group membership. That is, a psychological group, or in Kantor's terms a "collectivity", is made up of shared acting with respect to stimulating. A psychological group is a collection of interbehaviors, not a collection of organisms, the latter being a strictly sociological matter.

Kantor's analysis of cultural behavior is of some utility in making a scientific analysis of ethics. Hence we will proceed by examining it in the somewhat broader context of Kantor's action classification scheme. The distinctive features of cultural behavior may become apparent by this strategy.

Classes of Action

Universal actions. Kantor (Kantor & Smith 1975, p. 41) argues that the actions of individuals with respect to stimuli may be classified in accordance with the circumstances of their origin in the repertoires of those individuals. For example, some of the actions of individuals are shared among all members of their species as an outcome of their common organismic characteristics and the natural properties of confronted stimulus objects. All humans salivate when lemon juice is squirted into their mouths, for instance. This commonality of action is owing to the natural properties of lemon juice, such as its chemical consistency, and the characteristics of the biological organisms who react to this substance in this way. (Differences across members of the human species with respect their responses to lemon juice are due to the reactional biographies of individuals pertaining to such situations and the circumstances of particular interactions.) Actions having this provenance are called universal in Kantor's system to remind us of the universality of their distribution. The same sort of activity is called unconditioned or unlearned in other systems.

Idiosyncratic actions. Some of what individuals do is acquired over the course of their lives, and some of this activity has its origins in the distinctly idiosyncratic circumstances of those individuals. Such behavior is not shared with other members of the species, except when aspects of other members' life circumstances are accidentally similar. This type of activity Kantor (Kantor & Smith, 1975, pp. 41-42) calls idiosyncratic. For present purposes, it is important to bear in mind that in as much as no two persons may be in exactly the same place at exactly the same time, no two persons have the same history. That is to say, no two persons' idiosyncratic repertoires are the same.

Cultural actions. Cultural behavior constitutes a third class of actions in Kantor's system (Kantor, 1982, pp. 163-164). Cultural actions have some of the characteristics of both the universal and idiosyncratic categories, yet constitute a distinct class. Like universal actions, cultural acts are shared, though not with all members of the species. They are not in this sense universal, having their origins in very different ontogenic circumstances that do not apply to all members of the species.

More specifically, cultural responses are correlated with common or conventional stimulus functions. Such functions operate independently of the natural properties of the stimulus objects in which they inhere, which is what is meant by "conventional" in this context. The commonness of the stimulus functions of a cultural stimulus object, moreover, is not an accidental result of two or more persons reacting in the same idiosyncratic way to them. Rather, cultural stimulus objects have common functions because persons have endowed them with special properties. And, finally, unlike universal actions which occur as an unavoidable ' outcome of the natural properties of stimuli and the biological constituents of organisms, cultural responses are acquired through a culturalization process operating under specific group circumstances.

For example, a voodoo doll is an object that stimulates cultural reactions of fear or wariness on the parts of a particular group of people. The object itself is not harmful in any way however, and fear therefore does not arise as a reaction to the natural properties of a voodoo doll. Rather, fear reactions arise because a functional property of injuriousness has been attributed to this object over the course of a particular group's cultural evolution.

To reiterate, cultural behavior is shared action with respect to conventional stimulus functions arising under specific group auspices. Ethical conduct is of this sort, although it has other distinguishing features still to be considered.

Descriptive Qualities of Cultural Behavior

Kantor further isolates the activities categorized as cultural by articulating a number of other descriptive qualities of this type of event, a number of which help to clarify this concept for present purposes.

Limited distribution. First, cultural behavior is limited in its range of distribution (Kantor, 1982, pp 173-174). For example, particular varieties of religious belief, until recent times, have been characteristic of particular geographic regions.

Conventionality. Second, cultural behavior is artificial or conventional (Kantor, 1982, pp. 165-169). For instance, whether salad is eaten before or after the main course has no basis in biological, environmental, humanistic or rational circumstances. The practice in either case is conventional.

Arbitrariness. Third, cultural behavior is arbitrary in the sense that there are no fixed standards as to its form that are imposed upon it from without (Kantor, 1982, pp. 170-171). It constitutes its own standard. Putting tinsel on a Christmas tree may be characteristic of one psychological group though not of another and there are no independent standards of beauty, or appropriateness, or completeness against which such practices may be measured or judged.

Stability. Finally, cultural behavior is stable. Although cultural behavior is not unchanging or unchangeable, it is considerably more stable than idiosyncratic behavior and this stability makes for suspicion about activities peculiar to other collectivities. That is, there is considerable rigidity about one's own way of doing things which accounts for the strangeness of others' ways of doing them. Eating horse flesh or dog meat or monkey brains seems very strange to one who eats only cows, pigs and chickens and the suspicion goes both ways.

From the standpoint of an individual, we may also see that cultural behavior, broadly speaking, constitutes the most prominent aspect of the repertoires of individuals. It is the dominant repertoire, to which idiosyncratic behavior is subordinated in cases of conflict. It is further imposed upon individuals by members of a sociological group, often without their awareness. And it is what distinguishes an individual as a member of a sociological group in which certain varieties of ethical conduct prevail.

Value

As stated earlier, ethics may be understood as the study of the values and choices of persons operating verbally as members of groups. To this point we have examined what it means to characterize an individual's action as reflecting group membership. We turn now to the problem of value.

It is commonly assumed that values and value judgements are out of reach of scientists. Science can tell us what we *can* do but not what we *ought* to do. Skinner (1971) comments on this issue in his book, *Beyond Freedom and Dignity*. In his words: "Physicists and biologists often agree (that what we ought to do is out of reach of science), and with some justification, since their sciences do not, indeed, have the answers. Physics may tell us how to build a nuclear bomb but not whether it should be built. Biology may tell us how to control birth or postpone death but not whether we ought to do so. Decisions about the uses of science seem to demand a kind of wisdom which, for some curious reason, scientists are denied. If they are to make value judgements at all, it is only with the wisdom they share with people in general" (Skinner, 1971, p. 97). As may be obvious from the tone of this passage, Skinner disagrees with this argument. From his perspective, to make a value judgement, that is, to call something good or bad, right or wrong, is to classify it in terms of its reinforcing effects (1971, pp. 98-99).

Kantor also addresses this issue, arguing that, contrary to popular philosophical notions, "values are not additional or epiphenomenal to circumstances of everyday existence. They are functional in every respect and (are) not to be set beside or above events" (Kantor, 1982, p. 320). What Kantor implies by "functional in every respect" here is that the value of a stimulus object or event is one of its stimulational properties or functions (1981, p. 169). That is to say, "valuing" is just one of the many actions a given object or event may stimulate.

Types of Value Functions

It may be helpful at this point to distinguish between two types of value functions, namely those that are intrinsic to objects and events and those that are attributed to them.

Intrinsic value functions. Intrinsic value functions inhere in the natural properties of objects or conditions. That is to say, some values exist independently of persons' verbal attributions (Kantor, 1981, p. 321). In such cases, the value of an object is a matter of its suitability or utility for particular purposes. For example, to pound a tent peg into the ground, a rock has the value of a hammer. To reach a book on a high shelf, a chair has the value of a ladder. Likewise, we may regard the physicochemical properties of grass or earth as valuable for the construction of a nest by a bird.

Attributed value functions. Attributed value functions of stimuli, as the name suggests, do not have their sources in the natural properties of stimulus objects. They are rather verbally imposed upon stimulus objects by persons, without whom they would not exist or operate. Value functions of this type may participate in idiosyncratic as well as cultural behavior fields, the latter being relevant to present purposes.

Cultural Value Functions

The values implicated in cultural psychological situations are shared stimulus functions, frequently ethnic in nature and origin. That is, they are derived from interbehaviors that originated in earlier periods of psychological contacts with things and events. For example, cultural value functions may pertain to child rearing practices, to the place and roles of children in a family, to the number of children a family ought to have, and so on. In one ethnic collectivity, having many children may be held to be good, while in another it may be viewed as the mark of ignorance. In one collectivity, children are to be seen and not heard, while in another more inclusive practices are thought proper.

Similarly, cultural value functions may inhere in the roles of father and mother. In one family, it is held to be good for the mother to stay home with the children; in another, the mother's career outside the home is valued in much the same way as is the father's. It may be good in one family for the father to assume the role of disciplinarian, while in another, this role is thought best shared by both parents. In one family it may be assumed that the father will bear little or no responsibility for the upbringing of the children, while in another abandonment of the family by the father would be unthinkable. In one collectivity, sexual activity among family members is abhorred, in another it may be regarded as the right of the father to seek sexual favors of the daughter.

Cultural value functions may also pertain to circumstances and conditions of economic, military, political, patriotic and religious significance, among many others. In one collectivity, for example, self sufficiency may be thought right and good. In another, work may be viewed as a drudgery to be avoided whenever possible. Property and possessions may be valued above all else in one family, while in another happiness or loyalty or some other quality of action is held most high. Competition may be fostered in one group, cooperation in another. And so on.

The point we are trying to make here is to suggest that not only do persons share actions as a product of their acquisition under group auspices, but also that some of those actions are valuative. Members of a psychological group, in other words, not only act alike in many overt ways, they also hold the same things and events to be good or right or proper. It is this more subtle verbal and ideational repertoire that we take to constitute "group values" including "family values", from a psychological perspective.

Relativism of Cultural Values

Before going on to discuss what difference it makes to have made this analysis of values, we would like to comment on a difference between our arguments in this regard and those of conservative politicians, lest anyone think we came to the same conclusions. The conservative political argument assumes that it is possible to articulate ultimate and absolute values. Conservatives believe that the valuing acts of individuals may be judged against an absolute standard of some provenance; and as such they may be ordered in terms of their relative goodness. In short, what some value as good is not as good as what others value as good. In fact, what some take to be good is not good at all, its just plain bad. What some take to be right is wrong.

We are making no such claim. Quite the opposite, in fact. As argued earlier, cultural behavior, of which valuing is a type, is arbitrary in the sense that there are no fixed standards as to its form imposed upon it from without. There are no standards of good and bad, right and wrong, against which a given performance may be measured. On the contrary, cultural behavior constitutes its own standard. That is to say, the standards are manifested in and only in the shared actions themselves.

This position is radically relativistic, we admit, and it is not one that is shared widely. Even Skinner was not a relativist of this magnitude. The final argument for Skinner was survival: Actions contributing to the survival of the individual and particularly the culture were held by him to be good or right, those not so contributing, bad or wrong (Skinner, 1971, p. 137). Our argument with this line of reasoning is that in as much as we cannot know in advance what will lead to survival, especially of the culture and its practices, the standard of survival is a facade. There really is no standard operating here.

Like Skinner, Kantor (1982) argues that criteria for evaluating values may be established, describing refinements in cultural conduct as improvements or deteriorations, though he stops short of specifying absolute criteria for such comparisons. From our perspective, though, as with Skinner's (1971) position, unless it is argued forcefully that there are unalienable standards fixed from sources beyond the events under analysis, the standards implied are illusory.

In summary, psychological acts of the cultural sort, including those of valuing, are both arbitrary and artificial, operating without standards imposed from without and having no basis in biological, humanistic, rational or other circumstances. It follows that value is relative. Let us add at this point that value and truth are not synonymous. They are measured against different standards and according to different criteria. Truth has to do with the relation of verbal to nonverbal events. Value has to do with the relation between one set of nonverbal events and another. In short, the problem of value is not solved by applying to it a pragmatic or any other truth criterion, lest anyone wonder why we have not hit upon this solution.

Choice

Ethics, we have argued, may be understood as the study of the values and choices of persons operating verbally as members of groups. We have now examined what it means to characterize an individual's action as reflecting group membership and what we mean by values in this context. We move on now to the problem of choice. What do we mean by choice and what does a behaviorist have to say about it?

For a behaviorist there is no such thing as choice when this concept is approached philosophically. It is not possible to vacillate on this point and stay within a behavior analytic framework. The concept of choice assumes that a number of alternative courses of action are possible at any moment, and in as much as only one action actually occurs at any given moment, an appeal is made to the evidence of what "might have been." Choice implies that something other than what *did* happen *could have* happened, as though what did happen were not the culmination of a history. As argued by Hayes (1988, p. 25), "We cannot speak of what 'might have been' when confronting what is because what is is a point in the evolution of what has been. Had it been otherwise, it would be otherwise. But it is not otherwise–it is as it is." In short, the philosophical category of choice is *ahistorical*, and is, thereby, antithetical to the philosophical position of behaviorism.

The behavioral position on this issue is widely misunderstood. It should not be confused with the position of predetermination or predestination, wherein a creative agent of some sort must be invoked to account for the course or direction of evolution and the end toward which it is assumed to be inevitably moving. Behaviorism, as we understand it, has no use for such an agent because neither a beginning nor an end, and hence no direction, is postulated by the system. Likewise, the view that "what has been is the only thing that might have been" should not be misinterpreted to suggest that what *will be* is known. What *will be* is fundamentally unpredictable.

That behaviorism has no room for the concept of choice as a philosophical category is not to say that the study of choice, as is reported in a substantial portion of the articles published in *The Journal of the Experimental Analysis of Behavior*, is somehow anti-behavioral. Neither is it to suggest that contemporary applied research and practical interest in choice-making by historically disenfranchised groups runs contrary to the behavior analytic perspective in psychology. Not at all. It is rather to suggest that these investigations and interests in choice constitute a different domain. They have little to do with the philosophical category of choice.

They have a lot to do with the concerns underlying the delivery of services to persons who are developmentally disabled, though. Hence it is to these issues that we may more usefully address ourselves.

Choosing as an Event

Let us consider first what we mean by choosing as a field of interaction, as a kind of *responding with respect to stimulating embedded in a setting.* What is the character of this event? What are its participants? Under what conditions does the term "choice" constitute a finer discrimination, a more refined description than mere "responding", and under what conditions is this delineation superfluous?

Let us begin by suggesting that "choice" describes a circumstance of which there is reason to believe that more than one response might be performed with respect to a particular stimulus; or where the functions of more than one stimulus object might be actualized at the same time. All conceptions of choice involve the presence of alternatives in some manner. And while we believe that whatever occurs under these conditions may be attributed to the historical significance of the larger setting in which it is embedded–which is to say, whatever happens, happens–the participation of alternatives in some manner remains an aspect of what choice appears to be. The real problem here is to figure out what it is that prevails as alternatives in events of this sort.

It does not appear to be the choice itself since when these events occur there is only one of them: having done X or having done Y. If not the choice itself, is it the setting or context in which choice occurs? Is it past events? Is it our predictions about future events?

Herrnstein (1970) appears to hit upon *responses* as the prevailing alternatives. He argues that all behavior is choice in the sense that there are always alternatives to the response being measured by the experimenter. Williams (1988) takes Herrnstein to mean by this that the animal is always "deciding" which response to perform. True enough, the interests of the experimenter do not determine the activity of the organism under study. The organism may engage in any of a number of behaviors at any given moment. It might press the bar, but it might also scratch itself, defecate, rear up on its hind legs, and so on.

Nonetheless, to characterize all behavior as choice on the grounds that response alternatives are always available is, at best, superfluous in our view. That is to say, if the circumstances under which one would describe an event as "choice" are indistinguishable from those in which one would say merely "response", then the term "choice" adds nothing.

Analysis of Choosing

But do we really mean to suggest that "choice" is nothing more than mere responding? We think not. Rather, it is the "choosing", the "deciding" act that calls out for analysis in this domain. And in making this analysis, what appears to distinguish choosing from responding in general is *the participation of the anticipated consequences of alternative courses of action*. It is the anticipated consequences of alternative courses of action that can be understood to be prevailing as alternatives in choosing events. This is what is meant in nontechnical terms as "the weighing of outcomes" in choice situations.

The consequences of actions as yet to happen are not, by definition, aspects of the current situation, however. They are future events. How is it that an event not present in a given situation can participate in that situation? This brings us to the topic of implicit behavior.

Implicit behavior. Kantor (1924, pp. 295-315) describes implicit behaviors as actions occurring in the absence of the stimulus objects or events with which they were originally coordinated. Such actions are still coordinated with the stimulus functions of those original objects but the functions at issue inhere in other objects, objects that are present in the immediate situation.

The transfer of stimulus functions from one stimulus object to another in such cases is argued, by Kantor, to have come about by virtue of historical contact of a person with the two stimuli or their respective functions in temporal or spatial proximity. Contact with proximally related stimuli produces a situation in which one stimulus is part of the setting in which actions with respect to a second stimulus are taking place. As a result, one stimulus may give rise to actions originally occurring with respect to the other stimulus object, and vice versa. A similar process is articulated as classical conditioning in which, as a result of temporal proximity, salivation, originally occurring with respect to the food stimulus, comes to be stimulated by the sound of a bell.

Transfers of stimulus functions from one object to another is what Kantor (1924, pp. 295-315) refers to as the development of substitute stimulus functions, the evidence for which is the occurrence of actions in the absence of the stimuli with which they were originally coordinated. Implicit behavior is the name given to such interactions. Implicit behavior is one of the means by which a person's history of interactions is brought to bear in the present situation, as articulated by Kantor.

The proximity of stimuli as a basis for stimulus function transfer in this account has been a source of some dispute, particularly as the account appears to overlook the development of equivalence classes in which stimulus function transfers occur in the absence of proximal relations among stimuli; and also because the account appears to suggest the efficacy of backward conditioning beyond the evidence for this effect. While there is neither time nor sufficient reason to address this issue fully (for a more complete account, see Hayes, 1992) it may be useful to point out that a proximity of actual stimulus objects is not required by the analysis. Once substitutional functions of stimuli have been developed through proximal relations among actual objects, subsequent proximities among the stimulus functions of those objects in their absence is all that is required for subsequent function transfers. To reiterate, the analysis being made here does not depend on stimulus *objects* ever having occurred proximally with respect to one another. Neither does it rely on backward conditioning. Proximity in this analysis, further, does not imply *sequential temporal* relation. Functions transfer under conditions of their temporal concurrence or simultaneity. The operative relation is as such not temporal but spatial; and space is the category in which time extends backward and forward.

Participation of consequences of alternative course of action. Returning now to the issue of choosing, our task was to explain how the consequences of alternative courses of action may participate in the occurrence of choice responding, despite their absence from the immediate situation. The explanation is accomplished by assuming the occurrence of implicit behavior during the confrontation with stimulational circumstances in which a choice eventually takes place. Among the functions of those stimulational circumstances are those coordinated with references to or reflections upon actions one has taken or might take with respect to the objects in question. Further, because actions taken with respect to objects or events tend to be proximal with their consequences, reflecting on alternative courses of action may give rise to actions normally occurring with respect to the consequences of those actions. That is, reflecting on past behavior may serve as a substitute stimulus for implicit valuative and other sorts of actions with respect to the consequences of alternative courses of action. It is by way of such activity that the consequences of action may be said to participate in choice situations despite the fact that as events proper they are not among those making up such situations.

This analysis is not unlike Skinner's analysis of problem solving in which Skinner (1969, p. 133) distinguishes between a problem—analogous to a choice situation in our example, problem solving—analogous to choosing in our analysis, and the solution to a problem or, in our case, the actual choice made in a given situation. The difference between Skinner's analysis and our own is the extent to which Skinner is willing to characterize what in his view is a private problem solving event. He (1969, pp. 136-146) argues, in common sense terms, that problem solving entails the construction and manipulation of discriminative stimuli, among other activities, but does not provide a detailed analysis of the reactional participants of such activity nor its stimulational circumstances. Instead, the nature of the problem solving event is inferred from the eventual solution. As a result, while it may very often be the case that what one decides to do is not what one does—after all, the two are not casually related—cases in which one's decision matches the act taken cannot be distinguished from cases in which it does not in Skinner's system. By failing to analyze the act of choosing per se, the repertorial conditions of the actor cannot be distinguished from his or her motivational conditions. It is for this reason, among others, that we hold it important to focus on choosing as an act.

In summary, choosing in our view is a complex response occurring in a situation distinguished by multiple historical potentialities of action and involving implicit interactions with the consequences of alternative courses of action, terminated by—though not in our view synonymous with—one course of action or another.

Ethical choice. What distinguishes an ethical choice from a choice of any other variety is the nature of the actions occurring with respect to the anticipated consequences of alternative courses of action. When these are *valuative*, that is, when our responses with respect to the anticipated consequences are to find them good, bad, right or wrong, the choosing act is ethical in kind. Choosing as such is not always an ethical matter. That is to say, though one may still be engaged in the act of choosing when the anticipated consequences of alternative courses of action do not stimulate valuative acts in particular, choosing acts of this sort are not ethical in type.

Summary and Conclusion

Let us return once again to our original definition of ethics, namely, that *ethics is the study of the values and choices of persons operating verbally as members of groups*, so that we may review our analytical efforts to this point.

We began with the problem of the group in psychological perspective, arguing that a *psychological* group, unlike a sociological one, was not a collection of organisms but of actions. Specifically, it was held to be a collection of shared, learned actions with respect to common, verbally attributed, stimulus functions. These we called cultural reactions to distinguish them form other types of activity. Cultural reactions were claimed to be arbitrary in character, meaning that they operated without the limits of fixed or accepted standards imposed upon them from without. They rather constituted their own standards. To behave as a member of a group from this perspective then was to behave as other members of the group behave, and to do so for no reason other than that this was what one had learned to do as an accident of having been born into a sociological group who behaves in this way.

Valuing, we argued, was one of the ways we might respond to a stimulus, the value of a stimulus being one of its functions in other words. And we distinguished between intrinsic and attributed value functions, arguing that only attributed value functions were relevant to the topic of ethics. Attributed value functions and the valuing responses coordinated with them—that is, our reactions to things as good, bad, right and wrong—were conceptualized as a type of cultural reaction, having all of the characteristics of cultural reactions in general, including the absence of externally imposed standards of completeness, adequacy, excellence, etc. In short, we argued that values, all values, were relative not ultimate or absolute.

Finally, we examined the issue of choice in this context. Choice situations were said to be comprised of multiple historical potentialities of action as a kind of setting in which a distinct act of choosing occurred. The choosing act was said to involve implicit interactions with the consequences of alternative courses of action, terminated by one course of action or another. The terminal response—the choice— was argued to be the end point in an historical continuity of action, eliminating any suggestion of agency, capriciousness or spontaneity in the account.

An ethical choice, further, was distinguished in part by the nature of the actions occurring with respect to the anticipated consequences of alternative courses of action. When these were valuative, that is, when one's response to anticipated consequences was to think or call or find or feel or perceive them to be good, bad, right or wrong—then the choosing act was ethical in kind. In short, while ethical conduct always implies choice, choice does not always imply ethical conduct.

Verbal Behavior

What remains to be addressed explicitly is the adjective "verbal" in our definition of ethics: Ethics is the study of the values and choices of persons operating *verbally* as members of groups. We have assumed from the outset that only verbal organisms engage in ethical behavior—recall our early assertion that no one would suggest a horse or a finch or a gnat were behaving ethically. Still, the role played by verbal behavior in this domain has not been elucidated. There are two points in the analysis where this repertoire comes in to play.

The first of these is in the implicit interaction with anticipated consequences with alternative courses of action. While it is true that a nonverbal organism may interact implicitly with the consequences of future action, interactions of this sort are relatively undifferentiated or imprecise when compared to this activity on the part of a verbal organism (see Parrott, 1984 and Hayes, 1991 for further discussion.) The argument here is more complicated than we have space to explicate. Suffice it to say that verbal events are more serviceable than nonverbal events as substitute stimuli. In short, a verbal repertoire, while not *necessary* for implicit responses to future events, greatly enhances the precision and thereby the utility of this type of interaction.

A verbal repertoire is not merely useful but is rather necessary for the manifestation of another aspect of ethical conduct, however. Responding to attributed value functions of future events is something only a *verbal* organism can do. The goodness or badness of a stimulus is not one of its intrinsic properties. It is an attributed property and the process by which this comes about as well as the repertoire required to respond to it are verbal in kind. Ethical behavior is not something nonverbal organisms engage in.

Choice in Practical Perspective

The above arguments conclude the theoretical portion of our chapter. It is our plan now to consider some of the problems we face in the applied domain as it relates to the topic of ethical behavior. In other words, we plan to deal with issues of prediction and control in this arena, and to provide some input as to how applied workers might facilitate choice-giving to persons with disabilities.

Changes in the professional community's outlook on people with developmental disabilities have been relatively rapid over the past few decades. Full inclusion as a goal is a revolutionary idea, and at least one of the problems faced by service providers on the forefront of inclusion planning is that not everyone involved values this goal. Not all consumers want to leave their sheltered workshops. Not all families want their disabled members to live independently. Not all neighbors want to share their neighborhoods. Not all employers want to hire disabled workers. Consequently, if we are interested in bringing about changes in the life prospects of persons with developmental disabilities, we must address ourselves to the problem of how we go about changing what people value. Frankly, however, we don't know an awful lot about how to do this.

And what's worse is that even if we did know how to change what people value, valuing, as a variety of cultural behavior, is particularly resistant to change. Recall that one of the defining characteristics of cultural behavior was its *stability*. In short, we may anticipate substantial difficulties in our attempts to change what people value. Moreover, because changes in cultural behavior are slow and pervasive as opposed to rapid and precise, when all is said and done to bring about changes in what people value, it will be impossible to say with certainty that the changes ultimately observed may be traced to deliberate efforts on our parts.

But even this is not the most difficult of our problems. It isn't enough just to figure out how to change what people value. We have to figure out how to make people value particular things—the things that we, as human service professionals, value; and the prevailing value in the human service professions at this time is *choice*. The arguments supporting this value as an absolute are numerous. They range from the rational to the scientific to the humanistic to the evolutionary. From our perspective, however, *no* argument is equal to the task. In our view, as previously argued, all values, including choice, are *relative*.

To figure out how to change what people value nonetheless, and having done so, go on to make them value giving people choices will require more than philosophy has to offer. Likewise, to give people choices and to know that we have done so falls outside of the domain of philosophy. To solve these problems we must look instead to basic research on choice, as has been developed in the animal laboratory, and to the technology of choice-giving as it is practiced in the real world of service delivery. It is to these issues that we now turn, and we may begin by reviewing typical choice-giving practices in applied settings.

Typical Choice-Giving Practices in Applied Settings

Choice-giving practices vary with the verbal abilities of persons served, and we may look at the extremes on this continuum separately.

Practices in Place for Persons with Substantial Verbal Abilities

When verbal abilities are substantial, giving people choices typically amounts to asking them what they want or would like to do. This is how service workers ordinarily make contact with choices in their own lives and how they make them available to their children or others in their charge, hence it seems reasonable to follow the same practice with developmentally disabled people who have only minor verbal deficiencies. And under many circumstances, this means of giving people choices may indeed result in a statement of their genuine preferences for certain things over other things or certain activities over other activities.

Audience control. There are some problems with this practice, however. The first of these is the extraneous control over choices exerted by audience variables afforded by the practice. Very often significant life choices are made in the context of interdisciplinary treatment teams. A developmentally disabled consumer is asked to make a life choice—such as a change in housing, a career decision, or a decision about such personal issues as reproduction or contraception—and to do so in the presence of a large number of professionals and other significant others. Often times, too, the consumer has not been properly prepared for this question and is not in the company of an effective advocate. Under such conditions, we should not be surprised when consumers tell us what we want to hear. This is especially likely when the questions contain the answer, as when a consumer is asked: "You *do want a job* don't you?" or "You *don't want to live in a group home* all your life do you? The obvious problem with this strategy is that what we want to hear may have little to do with the consumer's preference. A more subtle problem is that evoking statements of so-called preference under the control of extraneous variables, may create confusion over genuine preferences such that the person no longer knows what they want. In short, not only do such practices risk not providing choice, they also make choosing more difficult.

Repertoire limitations. Another problem with the "ask people what they want" strategy is that it assumes a repertoire of available answers to this question, from which a consumer may be regarded as selecting one particularly well suited to this occasion. Often times, however, repertoires are more limited than this strategy demands. When, time and time again, a consumer provides the same answer to a question such as what sort of work would they like to do, we should not assume that this is a statement of unwavering commitment to a particular career. It may just be the only answer the consumer is able to make to this question.

Extraneous sources of control. Sometimes choices are made on the basis of extraneous circumstances. For example, a person may choose to quit his job in the community, not because of some dissatisfaction with the job or inability to perform well in it, but because of other circumstances only tangentially related to the job, such as the means of transportation to it, or the fit of the shoes that must be worn on it, and so on. When choice is valued highly and when it is assumed that a simple statement of preference reveals, in an uncomplicated way, what a person's preference truly is, extraneous sources of control over statements in this regard tend to go unnoticed or uninvestigated. In consequence, for want of a larger sized shoe, a person looses an opportunity to hold a competitive job.

The point we are trying to make in all of these cases is that verbal behavior is not so much a tool for communicating one's inner desires as it is a form of behavior controlled by the environment like any other behavior (Skinner, 1957). Verbal statements of preference or choice must be appreciated from this standpoint, in order to avoid disserve to consumers.

Practices in Place for Persons with Inadequate Verbal Abilities

The problem of providing choice to persons who have only minimal verbal repertoires, or who are completely nonverbal, is somewhat more complicated. In such cases we rely on the evidence of what people *are* doing and on affective properties of their reactions to alternatives. Let us consider each of these in turn.

Taking what people do as an indication of preference. It is often reported that a person likes or chooses to do something on the grounds that this is what the person may be observed to be doing most of the time. A person may be said to like music because he is often seen sitting in a room in which music is playing, or he is said to like toast because he eats toast for breakfast every morning. To assume that people tend to do what they like to do or choose to do is not an unreasonable assumption. However, we must exercise some caution here. To take what one does as what one *chooses* to do implies that one might be doing something else. There must be alternatives available to talk about choice. Hence, it might be that a consumer chooses to listen to music or chooses to eat toast, but this can only be asserted if there are opportunities to doing something other than listen to music and items other than toast to eat for breakfast. If these other opportunities are not made available, we can assert only that a person eats toast and listens to music, not that they choose to do so, or even like to do so.

Relying on affective behavior to indicate preference. In our own experience, we have come to recognize certain forms of emotional behavior as indicative of our pleasure and displeasure, and the tendency is thereby established to assume that emotional responses on the parts of severely disabled people are useful indicators of their preferences, likes and dislikes. For example, we recognize certain forms of emotional reaction as excitement, or fear, or anger. We assume that excitement occurs in the context of pleasurable or preferred activity; and that anger or fear occurs in the context of displeasurable and nonpreferred activity.

These assumptions may be workable in understanding our own behavior. However, they may not be so useful in understanding the likes and dislikes of people with severe disabilities for a number of reasons. In the first place, the emotional expressions of people with severe disabilities tend not to be as differentiated as are the expressions of normally developed people. That is to say, it is more difficult to distinguish an expression of fear from one of anger or excitement in such persons. Consequently, too great a reliance on such expressions to indicate preference will inevitably result in interpretations based on our own emotions. In other words, we will tend to interpret an undifferentiated emotional expression as fear if we ourselves are fearful in a given situation; as excitement, if we ourselves are excited. The outcome is to substitute our preferences for those of our charges.

A second complication in relying on emotional expressions to indicate preference on the parts of severely disabled people, is that emotional expressions are not particularly well differentiated in anyone including normally developed people. On the contrary, they are so much alike that naming them when they arise is done in terms of the prevailing environmental circumstances. Agitation is called fear if standing at the edge of a cliff. The same form of activity is called anger, if one has just been knocked down. Jumping up and down is called excitement if a consumer's parents have just arrived to take then home for a visit. But jumping up and down is called fear if a nurse has just arrived to give an injection. In short, emotions are interpreted *in terms of* external circumstances. This is a problem when emotions are being used to evaluate relative preferences for those same external circumstances.

Finally, for both verbally competent and incompetent persons, we take perseveration to be an indicator of choice. For example, we assume that when a person talks incessantly about some thing or event that this measures the strength of their preference for this thing or event. Talking about dogs all the time may not mean that a person would choose to pet a dog were one present, nor to own a dog were this a possibility. It might mean just the opposite: That the person is afraid of dogs, and would hide were one to show up. The talking in this case is a form of self management. It serves to bring about appropriate defensive activity were the referent for the talk to be contacted.

Perseveration is not limited to verbal activity. For example, we may find ourselves staring at a grotesque scene, despite feelings of repulsion. We may be unable to take our eyes off someone whose behavior is irritating to us. Under these conditions we would also not be wise to confuse perseveration with preference.

Developing a Protocol for Choice-Giving

In consideration of the typical practices of choice-giving described above, it would seem useful at this point to develop a set of criteria for choice-giving that would overcome some of the problems associated with these practices. In doing so, we will find it helpful to organize our considerations in accordance with the three-term contingency formulation of operant psychology. That is, we plan to discuss these criteria as they apply to setting the occasion for choice-giving, choice making as a response, and the consequences of choosing. More specifically, we will develop a set of criteria that must be met in order to assert: 1) that we are providing opportunities for disabled people to make significant life choices; 2) that we are teaching them to engage in acts of choosing; and 3) that we are strengthening such acts in their repertoires. In developing these criteria, we will enlist support from research conducted in the animal laboratory, both as it applies to relevant methods and findings. We begin then with some considerations pertinent to setting the occasion for choice making.

Setting the Occasion for Choice Making

Availability of Alternatives

Choice depends, most obviously, on the availability of alternatives: There can be no choice if only one alternative is available. For example, one does not choose to speak English if English is the only language spoken in one's culture. One does not choose to eat with one's hands if no utensils have ever been available. One does not choose to crawl if one has never learned to walk. In short, the opportunity to make choices depends on the availability of alternatives, either in one's repertoire of responses, or in the things around which those responses are organized.

While these two cases—response alternatives and stimulus alternatives—may be reduced to the single case of the interactions of responses with stimuli, it is sometimes useful, particularly in applied work, to focus on one or the other aspect of this interaction at a time. Focusing on response alternatives speaks more to the responsibility of service providers to develop consumers' behavioral repertoires over time, while focusing on stimulational alternatives puts the onus upon providers to make multiple opportunities for already learned behavior available on a given occasion of choice making.

Behavioral alternatives. With regard to behavioral alternatives, choice requires that more than one response is possible in a given situation. A person may choose to be polite or impolite, for example, only if both are possibilities. If a person has never learned to say thank you, not saying it on this occasion is not an instance of choosing to be impolite. Likewise, a person may choose to comply with a request only when they have understood the request well enough that noncompliance could have occurred. Compliance as a choice depends on noncompliance having been an alternative in a given situation.

Stimulational alternatives. The availability of stimulus alternatives as a prerequisite for choice assumes the availability of the repertoires necessary to interact with the stimulus circumstances available. Still, to choose among stimulus alternatives means the alternatives must be simultaneously present. For instance, eating a pear rather than an apple may be considered a choice only when both a pear and an apple are available. One does not choose to eat a pear when a pear is the only fruit available. Similarly, watching television constitutes a choice among activities only when other activities are also available. People are not choosing to watch television when there is no opportunity to do anything else.

As obvious as the availability of alternatives for genuine choice making may seem, the applied literature contains many examples of failures to operate in accordance with this criterion, at least explicitly. Often the repertorial conditions of disabled persons are ignored (e.g., Parsons & Reid, 1990; Dyer, Dunlap, & Winterling, 1990; Mithaug & Hanawalt, 1978).

Conversely, situational alternatives are not thoughtfully manipulated. A common problem in this regard is to overlook consumers' preferences in favor of one's own (e.g., Kennedy & Haring, 1993); wherein most preferred stimulus situations, as judged by someone other than the consumer, are juxtaposed with least preferred situations, similarly evaluated. There are a number of problems with practices of this sort. For present purposes, the most significant problem is that least preferred stimulus situations are very likely to constitute stimulus situations for which adequate behavioral repertoires are missing. There is, as such, only one alternative available in this situation and there is, thereby, no choice taking place in it.

Prior Experience with Alternatives

Choice is not just a matter of alternatives being available, however. They must be available to the person making the choice. The alternatives must be psychologically available to the consumer. This means that for a choice to be made among alternatives, the person making the choice must have had more than mere exposure to those alternatives. It is not exposure but *experience* that is required for genuine choice. Giving a person a choice between a coke and a zook is not a choice if the person has never tasted a zook. Giving a person a choice between going bowling and going bungee jumping is not a choice if the person has never before been bungee jumping.

The problem of engendering experience with alternatives is solved in the basic laboratory by forcing contact with all alternatives. This is usually accomplished by arranging conditions whereby only one alternative is available, and contact with it is made probable by heightened deprivation of the reinforcers available for responding on that alternative. For example, prior to opportunities to choose between two different schedules of food reinforcement, food deprived subjects are confronted with series of trials in which only one alternative is available (e.g., Catania & Sagvolden, 1980). Contact is subsequently arranged with the other alternative in a similar manner.

Experience is a complicated matter, nonetheless. The difference between experience and exposure, as understood in this context, is the difference between participating in an event and observing others participating in that event—the difference between playing a game and watching someone else play a game. Experience means participation, both with respect to the activities involved as well as in the outcomes or consequences of those activities, be they positive or negative. The experience of eating a green apple is not exhausted in the act of taking a bite and chewing—it includes as well the experience of the sour taste. Likewise, the experience of having a job is not just doing the work for which one was hired. The experience of sweeping floors or delivering mail for a living is not just the handling of a broom or the toting of a mail bag, its also the spending of the money earned for doing so. Experience means participation in an event in its entirety.

The applied literature has not fully embraced this criterion. For instance, in an otherwise exceptional study by Kennedy and Haring (1993), profoundly and multiply disabled youth were presented with stimulational alternatives including a computer and a musical keyboard, with no mention of consumers' experience with these alternatives. In this study, choice was measured as relative engagement time across the alternatives, wherein engagement was defined as actively manipulating the choice objects in the appropriate manner. The problem here is that appropriate manipulation of objects depends on more than mere exposure to the objects in question. It depends on prior direct experience with them; and in the absence of this experience, the alternatives are not psychologically available and choice among them cannot be said to have taken place.

Substitution of indirect for direct experiences. Another misstep in the administration of experiences to developmentally disabled people is the substitution of indirect for direct experiences. It is easy to see why this mistake is so readily made. Much of what we know about the world has been acquired indirectly. For instance, though never having been to Madrid—never having experienced it directly—we may acquire a great deal of knowledge about it indirectly by reading books and looking at pictures. In other words, it seems possible to "experience" events not actually encountered. Normally developed adults routinely make choices between alternatives they have never encountered directly, and no one would contest the characterization of such events as choice making.

Developing a choice training protocol for people who are developmentally disabled on the model of indirect learning available to normally developed people is not a sensible practice, however. At least not for most purposes. This is the case because the indirect experiences under consideration here depend for their efficacy on the sophistication of the verbal repertoires of the learners involved. To whatever extent those repertoires are underdeveloped, that is the extent to which such practices will be inadequate in providing substitutes for direct experiences. It goes without saying that underdeveloped verbal repertoires are commonplace among persons with developmental disabilities. Moreover, even for the normally developed adult, there's nothing quite like being there. What one knows about Madrid by direct experience is quite unlike what one knows by way of books and pictures. In summary, genuine and full experience of alternatives in a choice situation means having previously been engaged in direct nonverbal contact with those alternatives in their entirety.

Developing Choosing Behaviors

We have been discussing the conditions under which we find it legitimate to say that a choice has been made. More specifically, we have argued that there must be alternatives to choose among, and the alternatives must be psychologically present for the person making the choice. They must, in other words, be alternatives with which the person choosing has had prior experience. In these discussions, choice has been viewed as an outcome—as the end product of an unspecified act of choosing. We turn now to the act of choosing itself.

Human choice situations are often characterized by a single opportunity for a nonreplicable choice to be made. A person chooses to take a particular job or not take that job, to marry a particular person or not marry that person, to take a vacation in Montana or not to so do. Given this circumstance of nonreplicable selections among alternatives, occurring at particular points in time, an analysis of choosing must focus on the only activity available for analysis, namely that which occurs immediately *prior* to given choices.

Choosing between two alternatives, then, is held to entail acts of comparing and contrasting the two alternatives as to their positive and negative features. Among those features might be: the effort required to engage in one activity versus another; the cost, as measured in time or money, associated with one or the other; the loss of opportunity entailed in selecting one over the other; the relative value of the consequences of doing one versus the other; and so on. These are everyday events for normally developed adults. And they are all highly verbal acts. A baby cannot compare and contrast alternatives in this way because a baby does not have the verbal repertoire with which to do so. And, often times, neither does a person with developmental disabilities.

How then are we to teach people with disabilities to choose among alternatives if they cannot engage in the activities we have identified as being essential to this task? This is a difficult question. And it is not one that has been addressed in the applied literature on choice. In a review of research on choice and related issues appearing in *The Journal of Applied Behavior Analysis* over the past 15 years, not one article mentioned this problem, let alone its solution.

We may approach the problem in two ways. First, we may see it as our task to develop procedures to teach people with only minor language deficiencies to make contact with things and events indirectly through language. Meaningful language is not just emitting conventional sounds or producing conventional marks on a page. It is also responding in other ways associated with those sounds and marks. It includes perceptual and other kinds of implicit activities with respect to the things spoken of (see Parrott, 1984, for further discussion of this issue). Accordingly, a training protocol adequate for the purpose of developing choosing behavior must assess not only the production of linguistic forms but also the occurrence of appropriate implicit activity related to those forms. Procedures designed to measure "meaningfulness" of speech specifically and sensitively have yet to be developed. (One reason for this oversight may be traced to the view that choosing, as an act of the will, occurs spontaneously and without the need of training. To realize the goal of choice for people with disabilities, this view must be overcome.)

To generate choosing on the part of someone with significant linguistic deficits requires a different procedure. A person with little or no language cannot be understood to make a nonreplicable choice at a given moment based on meaningful activity occurring just prior to that choice. The meaningful activity in this situation is linguistic and a person without language is not engaging in such activity. Hence while a person without language may find him or herself in a nonreplicable situation as a result of some activity called choosing, the activity must necessarily be attributed to someone other than the person without language. Finding oneself in a new home, for example, is not a necessary outcome of one's own acts of choosing— one's own acts of deliberation—but may rather be the outcome of such acts on the part of a caretaker. In short, choices among nonreplicable alternatives based on personal prior acts of choosing do not occur for nonverbal persons.

Choice for such persons is not thereby eliminated. It must be reconceptualized, however. The basic literature on choice provides some assistance in this regard. The choice paradigm in the animal research laboratory calls for repeated direct experiences with alternatives, whereupon preferences for one alternative versus the other are measured in the proportion of activity or time allocated to one or the other alternative when both are simultaneously available (Baum & Rachlin, 1969). This procedure sidesteps the problem of making a choice on a single occasion, and does not thereby require, nor require comment on, the linguistic or representational activity ordinarily occurring prior to a given choice.

Strengthening Choosing as a Repertoire

While choice may be viewed as an outcome of a particular act or acts at a particular moment, it may also be understood as a characteristic of a behavioral repertoire. That is, we may not be interested so much in insuring that a particular act of choosing occurred at a particular moment, but rather that a person approaches his or her life circumstances with an ability to make choices. We may, as such, be more interested in strengthening the operant class of choosing than evoking a particular instance of choice. To do so, we must consider the consequences of such acts.

Choosing as a class of responses will be strengthened only when the consequences of particular choices are brought to bear. For example, to strengthen choosing with respect to going to work or being absent from work, the significant consequences of particular choices, namely having money or not having money at the end of the week, must be contacted. These consequences will both strengthen choosing as an operant and allow for differential reinforcement of particular choices. On the contrary, if those consequences are not brought to bear (as when, for example, a parent or guardian makes up for losses of income produced by choosing to stay home from work), subsequent opportunities for choice-making in this regard do not eventuate in genuine choices. This is so because under such circumstances the alternatives are not sufficiently differentiated with respect to their outcomes to make choosing necessary. That is to say, staying home produces the same outcome as going to work; and, as such, there are not two alternatives from which to choose, but rather only one. In short, there is no choice to make.

The Effects of Choosing a Given Alternative on Subsequent Choices

It is one thing to strengthen choosing as an operant class. It is another to strengthen particular choices to such an extent that the class is undermined. In other words, repeated reinforcement of particular choices eventually produces a circumstance in which unchosen alternatives, having been so infrequently and so distantly contacted, are no longer psychologically present. And without alternatives there is no choice. This circumstance is routinely ignored in the applied domain. It is, instead, assumed that when alternatives *appear* to be available, whatever a person is doing is what they have chosen to do despite that fact that appearances may be deceiving. The deception here pertains to the availability of alternatives.

Sensitivity to the effects of choosing a given alternative on subsequent choices is evident in the basic literature on choice. In this arena, continued contact with non-preferred alternatives is maintained by randomly alternating, with a probability equal to .5, on which of two alternatives reinforcement is programmed for a given episode of choice responding (Catania, 1966). This procedure, while allowing for a determination of relative preference for alternatives, as measured in the proportion of responses allocated to a given alternative over multiple episodes, also insures that non-preferred alternatives are routinely contacted and thereby remain psychologically present to responding organisms at the outset of each episode of choice responding.

Eliminating Multiple Sources of Control over Choice Responding

Research on choice in the basic laboratory has identified a number of other methodological problems in the assessment of choice that have implications for practice. Let us turn to these problems and their solutions.

Preventing control over responding in one alternative by reinforcement available in another. The standard procedure for measuring choice in the animal laboratory is to expose animals to concurrent schedules of reinforcement and examine, as choice, the relative rates of responding on the alternative schedules. A concurrent schedule is one in which "two or more responses, of different topography at least with respect to *focus, are capable of being executed with little mutual interference at the same time or in rapid alternation, under the control of separate programming devices" (Ferster & Skinner, 1957, p. 724). The results of these operations are to produce remarkable orderly relations between the choice measure and the relative reinforcement rates on the two alternatives: The proportion of total behavior allocated to either alternative is approximately equal to the proportion of total reinforcement allocated to that alternative (Williams, 1988). This relationship has become known as the Matching Law (Herrnstein, 1970).

One problem with this procedure is the potential for reinforcement available for responding on one alternative having an influence on responding in the other. This occurs as a result of the programming of the schedules in the two alternative. More specifically, the schedules are typically independently programmed, Variable Interval Schedules wherein time to the availability of reinforcement on one schedule may elapse while responding on the other schedule is taking place and vice versa. This means that reinforcement may often be available for the first response occurring after switching from one alternative to the other. The result is to establish a superstitious sequence of responses characterized by switching back and forth between alternatives.

To prevent the establishment of excessive switching, concurrent schedules are usually programmed so as to prevent reinforcement in a given alternative from being delivered immediately following a change over from the other alternative. For example, reinforcement available for the first response to a new alternative may be delayed for a few seconds following a change over. This procedure, appropriately called a Change Over Delay (COD), extinguishes excessive switching from one alternative to another as a result of an adventitious contingency (Catania, 1966). In doing so, the COD sustains the relationship between relative rates of responding and relative rates of reinforcement described by the Matching Law, and its addition to a concurrent schedule arrangement is thereby seen as a procedural refinement. Human choice situations may have similar features, allowing for the maintenance of superstitious responding.

Adventitious contingencies may interfere with the measurement of choice in other ways as well. For example, suppose a developmentally disabled person were given the opportunity to choose between two job sites on the basis of brief exposures to the two alternatives; and suppose that, quite by accident, a friend happened to be present at one of the sites. The presence of the friend might influence the job choice in this case as a form of superstitious behavior, generated by an adventitious contingency. The applied worker must be vigilant about the operation of such contingencies as they may have outcomes for individuals that may prevail over long periods of time.

Eliminating rate manipulations confounding choice measures. Basic research on choice has also identified a related problem. In the basic preparation, choice is measured as the proportion of the total behavior allocated to one alternative relative to the proportion allocated to the other. Behavior, further, is measured in the number or responses occurring with respect to a given operandum within a particular period of time, or, in other words, the rate of responding occurring on a particular operandum. Rate of responding is a conditionable dimension of behavior, though (Nevin, 1979). Hence the rates observed on a particular manipulandum are multiply controlled: they are indicative of both the schedule in effect on that particular manipulandum as well as the relative rates of reinforcement scheduled on the two manipulanda. This situation is exaggerated when the schedules are specifically rate manipulative, as in the cases of Differential Reinforcement of High or Low Rates, but the principle applies in less obvious cases as well. As such, relative rates of responding on two alternatives, in which different schedules of reinforcement prevail, is not an unconfounded measure of preference for one alternative over another.

To overcome this problem, concurrent chain schedules (e.g., Rachlin, Castrogiovanni, & Cross, 1987) have been employed to examine preference. In a concurrent chain schedule, identical initial links of two chain schedules are simultaneously available, and the relative rates of responding in these links is taken to indicate preference for the terminal links associated with those initial links. Because entry into the terminal links on the two chains schedules is available for responding on identical (usually Variable Interval) schedules, the rates of responding in the initial links are not differentially controlled by the schedules in effect in the initial links. These rates, instead, reflect preferences for different terminal link schedules; and the degree of preference, as measured in relative response rates, tends to match the relative rates of reinforcement in the terminal links. As previously mentioned, the Matching Law (Herrnstein, 1970) describes this relation between relative response rates and relative reinforcement rates.

These measurement problems and their solutions are not irrelevant to human choice situations. They suggest caution in interpretation. For example, a greater tendency to talk about one alternative versus another—a human response comparable to animal lever pressing—may not indicate preference for that alternative. It may instead indicate differential reinforcement for talking about an alternative. Suitable modifications of the concurrent chain schedule to fit the human choice situation are thereby recommended.

Escape from Freedom

To this point, we have not questioned the virtue of making choices and have assumed, implicitly at least, that the opportunity to make choices about significant life events ought to be guaranteed for persons with disabilities. But is it the case that people, including developmentally disabled people, would freely choose to have the responsibility of choosing among alternatives in all circumstances? Choosing, we may acknowledge, is not always an easy thing to do. Some choices are very difficult to make, and we may occasionally suffer as a result of the choices we have made. In addition, various forms of coercion may be embedded in what appear to be episodes of free choice.

The development of an ethical and effective protocol for developing and sustaining choice-making among developmentally disabled people depends on how these circumstances are understood and how this understanding is incorporated into our training programs. Let us then consider each of these issues in greater detail.

Choosing Not to Choose

We are often confronted with choice situations in which *immediate* but small, short lived, or otherwise not completely desirable outcomes are pitted against situations entailing larger, longer lived but *delayed* outcomes. For example, under conditions of significant food deprivation, we may confront a choice between eating a candy bar or making a meal. Choosing a candy bar under these conditions is very likely to occur, even though it may represent a poorer choice for a number of reasons, including our well being in the long run.

The long, and sometimes even short term consequences of making poor choices in such circumstances very often results, for normally developing people, in attempts to avoid making choices. We avoid going to places where candy bars are sold, for example, or make it a point to carry no change with which to purchase candy bars from machines, and so on. The appeal, "Get thee behind me Satan", reflects this intention to avoid having to make choices in circumstances where poor choices are very likely to be made.

This phenomenon has not gone unnoticed in the animal laboratory. Hayes, Kapust, Leonard, and Rosenfarb (1981) demonstrated a preference on the part of pigeons for no choice when choosing led, irresistibly, to the selection of a minuscule but immediate portion of grain over a delayed but larger portion. In other words, freedom to choose is not always preferred: animals as well as normally developed persons will, under certain circumstances, do what it takes to escape from freedom. Developmentally disabled people ought to have the same prerogative.

Choosing Early in a Chain of Behaviors

A related issue has to do with *when* choices are made. For example, often humans find themselves in circumstances in which particular courses of action are inevitable given actions taken at earlier choice points. For example, the decision to smoke a cigarette during a period of attempting to quit smoking is almost inevitable given that one has already decided to go out drinking with some friends who smoke. Likewise, the decision to eat the cookies, when on a diet, is not made upon coming across the bag of cookies in one's kitchen. The decision to eat the cookies was made, functionally, much earlier in this chain of events. The decision to eat the cookies was made when the cookies were purchased at the grocery store earlier that day.

To develop useful and appropriate choice-making repertoires in people with developmental disabilities we must understand that what may appear to be choice points are, in fact, not that but rather outcomes of earlier choices. This appreciation will prevent us from exposing disabled people to unrealistic expectations–the expectation that cookies will not be eaten once purchased, that cigarettes will not be smoked once intoxicated, and so on. If we want to bring about responsible choice making in disabled people, we must teach them to identify the true choice points in long chains of activity so that deliberate choosing may be engineered or evoked at the point at which it matters.

Making choices early in a chain so as to impact subsequent behavior in safe, healthy, productive or otherwise beneficial ways, is what we typically mean by self-control, as opposed to impulsiveness. Impulsivity is not an infrequent problem for people who are developmentally disabled, at least partly because of inadequacies of their verbal repertoires. A considerable body of research on this issue (e.g., Rachlin

& Green, 1972; Logue, Smith, & Rachlin, 1985) is available, however, showing that self control—or choosing early in a chain by which there is not a choice at a later time—may be learned as an outcome to repeated experience with the consequences of impulsive choices. That is to say, impulsivity may be both predicted and controlled, and choice-making protocols would be most usefully constructed in accordance with these findings.

Choosing among Good Alternatives

Finally, we turn to the issue of how choice is impacted by the characteristics of the alternatives available from which to choose. We have been operating on the assumption that choice is important because it affords people the opportunity to do what they enjoy doing, as opposed to something they do not enjoy; that they get what they want, not something they don't want. This assumes, as well, that something they enjoy or want is counted among the available alternatives. But what if the alternatives are not good ones? Of what value is choice under such conditions?

It is in this arena that coercion may be dressed up as choice. For example, when a child is given a choice between eating her vegetables and going to bed hungry, or when a developmentally disabled man is allowed to choose between doing his chores or going to his room, few would herald such events as revolutionary steps in the ethical treatment of people. There is little to recommend such events, as they have very little to do with the concept of freedom. They are, rather, simple cases of aversive control disguised in the language of choice.

It is important to recognize the character of such events. Aversive control produces counter-control (Skinner, 1971): the child throws his plate, the man tears his shirt. Failing to recognize a choice between bad alternatives as coercion, may lead us to believe that freedom of choice produces undesirable behavior.

Summary and Conclusion

In developing a protocol for choice-giving that might be used to teach people with developmental disabilities, we have focused on the conditions under which choosing may occur, the response of choosing itself, and the consequences of choices made. We have argued that choosing is possible only under conditions in which previously experienced, and thereby psychologically present, alternatives are available. Choosing as a response was approached in two ways. As a nonreplicable event under a particular set of conditions, choosing may be understood as linguistic and representational activity occurring prior to a choice response. Choosing characterized by prior activity of this sort is not available to persons without language. For such persons, choosing may be understood as selections of one alternative over another over repeated opportunities to make selections, in much the same way as choice is conceptualized in the animal laboratory. Finally, we dealt with choosing as an operant class, arguing that if this class were to be strengthened in an individual's repertoire, the consequences of specific acts of choosing must be contacted in their entirety. Some problems of extraneous sources of control over choosing were also discussed in some detail.

In closing, we wish to return to issues of a more philosophical sort—issues that ought not be ignored in the applied domain if adequate services are to be provided for people with disabilities. While the opportunity to make choices about significant (and even not so significant) life events may be a valuable goal toward which service providers and disabled people alike may be striving, and it no doubt represents an important humanistic development, too great an emphasis on choice in human service delivery systems is not without certain problems. The first of these is the suggestion that people are free to choose and, as such, must be held accountable for their own behavior and its consequences. The second is the impact of this view on the development of the science of behavior and the technology of behavior change.

Let us begin with the first problem, namely that people are responsible for their own behavior in as much as it is freely chosen. This position may be illustrated with a number of examples. For instance, if a person starts a fire at work and is arrested for arson and subsequently goes to jail, this is said to be the person's choice. Likewise, if a woman engages in unprotected sex and subsequently dies of AIDS; the woman can only blame herself. If a person eats too much junk food, and subsequently becomes obese; this is held to be the person's choice. Such is the fate, we would say, of one who has no will power. If a person abuses his children and subsequently looses custody of them, we have little sympathy for him. When people choose to hurt others in this way they deserve to suffer the consequences. In short, when people's behavior is freely chosen, they must be held accountable for it. They must take the blame for their undesirable actions.

It is not only a person's criminal, or dangerous, or careless, or foolish, or impulsive or otherwise inappropriate and undesirable behaviors for which he or she is held accountable as a consequence of an emphasis on choice in society, though. It is also a person's courageous, generous, intelligent, creative, and otherwise *desirable* behaviors for which he or she may be held responsible. Responsibility in this case is measured in personal praise. We praise people for doing good, but only if doing good is a matter of choice. If a person does good because someone is holding a gun to their head, we tend not to praise them for their good deeds. There must be choice involved. A person must *freely choose* to do good for others or society; and when they do so freely choose, we give them a great deal of praise.

For example, if a person risks his life to save an infant from a building collapsed in an earthquake, we call him a hero and publish his picture on the front page of the newspaper. If a person makes an outstanding contribution to science, we give her a Nobel prize. If a person's creative or artistic or athletic performance is exceptionally good, we give him an Oscar or a gold medal. We honor people in these ways only when we believe them to be responsible for their own behavior, though. If we believe, for example, that a person did not appreciate the danger to his own life in saving the infant, we are less likely to give him credit. If a person's contribution to science is stolen or plagiarized or copied from the research notes and findings of another scientist, we strip her of her prize. And if a person's athletic achievement is enhanced by drugs, we have no praise for him or her. Quite the contrary, we ban them from competition. In short, we give praise to people who behave in ways that we cannot easily account for by pointing to some external cause—whose behavior arises from within—whose behavior represents the sheer will and free choice of the person involved.

It stands to reason that we would withhold blame for *undesirable* behaviors when these same circumstances prevail. And this is in fact the case. When behavior may be traced to external causes and is not thought to arise from within, we tend not to blame the people for their behavior. We tend not to blame the arson for his behavior quite so much when we understand that he is mentally retarded. When the child abuser is discovered to have been abused as a child himself, we tend to have greater sympathy for him. There but for fortune go you or I, we think. And when a person's family or society does not teach them the hazards of unsafe sex or the consequences of too much junk food, we are less likely to blame them for contracting AIDS or becoming obese. It is only when in full awareness of these outcomes people willfully engage in behaviors producing them that we find them blameful. Blame, like credit is due to those who *choose* to act in ways deserving of blame and credit. Where there is no awareness of the consequences of behavior, and no choice, we cannot rightly give either credit or blame (Skinner, 1971).

This view of human nature would have us believe that what a person does is up to them. It would have us believe that if we interfere with what a person does—if we force them to do other than what they choose to do—we would be depriving them of the opportunity to earn credit or the right to be blamed. In other words, this view suggests that if we do not allow a person to freely choose what they want to do, then their behavior, no matter how desirable, appropriate, courageous, generous, intelligent, creative—no matter how good it is—the individual cannot be given praise for it. Likewise, no matter how vile, selfish, careless, stupid, or ruthless, without choice, the individual cannot be blamed.

This understanding of human behavior is troublesome. Praise and blame are effective consequences for behavior—effective *causes* of future behavior. Yet to sustain these causes in our analyses of behavior, we must also sustain the belief that behavior is freely willed. In other words, to make effective use of these causes of behavior, we must insist that behavior is not caused but is, instead, freely chosen. The opportunity for control over behavior afforded by the concept of free choice may account for high value placed on choice in our society.

This perspective has profound implications for the practice of behavior analysis, which brings us to the second problem too great an emphasis on choice produces. Attributing all behavior to choice implies that whatever people are doing must be what they choose to do, otherwise they would be doing something else. If a mentally retarded man sits in front of a television set all day, this is what he chooses to do. If a child isolates herself from other children, this is what she chooses to do. And so on.

The problem here is that this argument provides justification for the abandonment of the science of behavior through which we may understand behavior, and the technology of behavior change based on it. The argument goes something like this: We don't need to *understand* behavior nor know how to *change* it because, in as much as people are free to do as they will, what they are doing must be what they *choose* to do; and who are we as behavior analysts to rob them of their dignity by making them do otherwise?

Let us close by saying that choice is a powerful concept, with both very good and very bad implications. As service providers, we should exercise caution in its implementation. As behavior analysts, we would be well to be wary of choice. Choice is a Pandora's box—and we will need to be ready for what shows up when the box is fully opened.

References

Baum, W. M., & Rachlin, H. C. (1969). Choice as time allocation. *Journal of the Experimental Analysis of Behavior, 12*, 861-874.

Catania, A. C. (1966). Concurrent operants. In W. K. Honig (Ed.), *Operant behavior: Areas of research and application* (pp. 213-270). Englewood Cliffs, NJ: Prentice-Hall.

Catania, A. C., & Sagvolden, T. (1980). Preference for free choice over forced choice. *Journal of the Experimental Analysis of Behavior, 34*, 77-86.

Dyer, K., Dunlap, G., & Winterling, V. (1990). Effects of choice-making on the serious problem behaviors of students with severe handicaps. *Journal of Applied Behavior Analysis, 23*, 515-524.

Ferster, C. B., & Skinner, B. F. (1957). *Schedules of Reinforcement.* New York: Appleton-Century-Crofts.

Hayes, L. J. (1988). Philosophical implications of interbehavioral psychology. *The Interbehaviorist, 16*, 23-27.

Hayes, L. J. (1991). Substitution and Reference. In L. J. Hayes & P. N. Chase (Eds.), *Dialogues on Verbal Behavior* (pp. 3-18). Reno: Context Press.

Hayes, L. J. (1992). Equivalence as process. In S. C. Hayes & L. J. Hayes (Eds.), *Understanding verbal relations* (pp. 97-108). Reno: Context Press.

Hayes, S. C., Kapust, J., Leonard, S. R., & Rosenfarb, I. (1981). Escape from freedom. *Journal of the Experimental Analysis of Behavior, 36*, 1-7.

Herrnstein, R. J. (1970). On the law of effect. *Journal of the Experimental Analysis of Behavior, 13*, 243-266.

Kantor, J. R. (1924). *Principles of psychology* (Vol. 1). Chicago: Principia Press.

Kantor, J. R. (1981). *Interbehavioral philosophy*. Chicago: Principia Press.

Kantor, J. R. (1982). *Cultural psychology*. Chicago: Principia Press.

Kantor, J. R., & Smith, N. M. (1975). *The science of psychology*. Chicago: Principia Press.

Kennedy, C. H., & Haring, T. G. (1993). Teaching choice making during social interactions to students with profound multiple disabilities. *Journal of Applied Behavior Analysis, 26*, 63-76.

Logue, A., Smith, A. W., & Rachlin, H. C. (1985). Sensitivity of pigeons to prereinforcer and postreinforcer delay. *Animal Learning and Behavior, 13*, 181-186.

Mithaug, D. E., & Hanawalt, D. A. (1978). The validation of procedures to assess pre-vocational task preferences in retarded adults. *Journal of Applied Behavior Analysis, 11*, 153-162.

Nevin, J. A. (1979). Reinforcement and response strength. In M. D. Zeiler & P. Harzem (Eds.), *Advances in the analysis of behavior: Vol. I. Reinforcement and the organization of behavior* (pp.117-158). New York: Wiley.

Parrott, L. J. (1984). Listening and Understanding. *The Behavior Analyst, 7, 29-39.*

Parsons, M. B., & Reid, D. H. (1990). Assessing food preferences among persons with profound mental retardation: Providing opportunities to make choices. *Journal of Applied Behavior Analysis, 23*, 183-195.

Rachlin, H., Castrogiovanni, A. S., & Cross, D. (1987). Probability and delay in commitment. *Journal of the Experimental Analysis of Behavior, 48*, 347-353.

Rachlin, H. C., & Green, L. (1972). Commitment, choice, and self control. *Journal of the Experimental Analysis of Behavior, 17*, 15-22.

Skinner, B. F. (1957). *Verbal behavior.* New York: Appleton-Century-Crofts.

Skinner, B. F. (1969). *Contingencies of reinforcement.* New York: Appleton-Century-Crofts.

Skinner, B. F. (1971). *Beyond freedom and dignity.* New York: Bantam.

Williams, B. A. (1988). Reinforcement, choice and response strength. In R. C. Atkinson, R. J. Herrnstein, G. Lindzey, & R. D. Luce (Eds.), *Steven's Handbook of Experimental Psychology* (2nd ed.) (pp.167-244). New York: Wiley.

Discussion of L. Hayes, Adams, & Rydeen

Ethical Behavior

Brian Lahren
Washoe Association for Retarded Citizens

In commenting on this paper, the reader should be aware that I have a specific learning disability when it comes to the kinds of argumentation presented by Hayes et al.: I am a Skinnerian. I find Skinner's position on values and choice to be an interesting and sophisticated starting point for engaging the complex philosophical issues presented by choice and valuing. Frankly, I am not well versed in the work of J. R. Kantor and I find the brief treatment of the Kantorian view of choice puzzling at times. The result is that you should consume these comments with more than a few grains of salt.

This paper ambitiously attempts to treat choice and values from a Kantorian philosophical/theoretical perspective while contrasting these views with B. F. Skinner's treatment of the same topics. Although this wide ranging choice of targets is admirable and potentially interesting, it simply cannot be adequately handled in so brief a presentation. The result is that this paper provides, at best, only incidental contact with the complex philosophical issues raised by choice behavior (see, for example, Andrew Oldenquist's "Choosing, Deciding and Doing" in the Encyclopedia of Philosophy, 1972 reprint edition) for a summary of the issues Hayes et al., pass by. The discussion is more developed with regard to J. R. Kantor's view of the topic, but seems thin where Skinner is brought into the discussion.

The Kantorian sections of this paper are the most carefully developed and provide an abbreviated overview of the structure of J. R. Kantor's assessment of the context of valuing and choice behavior. What I find most interesting about this discussion is that while Hayes et al. enter the discussion of Kantor's view of values and choice by discussing "universal actions" (corresponding roughly to reactions to unconditioned stimuli), "idiosyncratic actions" (the product of individual histories), and "cultural actions" (used to introduce the idea that values and choices may be significantly cultural and hence conventional in form) none of this discussion actually addresses where values originate. This is particularly problematic when the discussion intentionally steers one away from the typical Skinnerian move of equating values with reinforcers and reinforcers with observable changes in behavior (i.e., contingencies of survival and contingencies of reinforcement). For example, one is left with the impression that for Kantorians, values materialize rather inexplicably from the arbitrary interaction of idiosyncratic experience and cultural actions. This would be more understandable if one could, without referring to contingencies of reinforcement, explain what it is about the idiosyncratic experiences of individuals or the conventions of one's culture that makes one want to value one thing over another, or choose X versus Y.

The force of the argument is to simply assert that values and choices are behaviors of groups acting verbally and that these behaviors have the descriptive features of limited distribution, conventionality, arbitrariness and stability. Unfortunately, the discussion never identifies a perspective in Kantor which would tie the arena of human values to an empirically demonstrable starting point. It doesn't help to say values come from one's culture if you can't say where one's culture got them in the first place. It seems somewhat counter-intuitive to assume that values are purely arbitrary and that cultural conventions have no contact with biological necessity. Such a position flies in the face of our understanding of our species' place in the evolutionary processes.

I will return shortly to a problem I have with what I take to be mentalism in the analysis of "choosing" in this paper. First, however, I would like to respond more constructively by noting certain similarities between the Kantorian and Skinnerian perspectives in this paper, both of which make contact with the practical realities of value related discussions. This is worth doing since these points of agreement can at least stand as a starting point for a more practical assessment of the roles choice and value statements have in the context of discussions about people with developmental disabilities.

1. Both Skinner and Kantor agree that values are in some sense an aspect of the natural world as opposed to a Platonic world of ideals and *a priori* concepts. Of importance to the topic of developmental disabilities is the implication that valuing and choosing are natural aspects of our behaving and are analyzable and teachable.

2. Both agree that cultural practices represent the field of activity in which individuals acquire the behaviors of judging, valuing and choosing. In other words, values are largely, but perhaps not entirely acquired. Kantor's "intrinsic value function" more or less maps onto Skinner's biological reinforcers. Kantor's "attributed value function" corresponds roughly to Skinner's assessment that social contingencies of reinforcement account for the learned values members of a verbal community share.

3. Both agree that much of our talk about values is conventional and that this conventionality is culturally derived. We simply are taught many of our values in social contexts. However, Skinnerians would disagree that "cultural behavior constitutes its own standard." The Skinnerian view is that cultural practices are the source of some of our values and all of our *talk* about values. Cultures may reinforce or punish behaviors which then come to be described as "good" or "bad" by members of the culture. But, cultures themselves are not the source of the most basic values. Cultures

are merely evolved patterns of interaction which, among other things, mediate punishment and reward, including control of the distribution of the biological necessities through patterns of cultural practice called economic activity. Cultures teach us to talk about things which are good and bad in ways which usefully connect such talk with the culture's reinforcing and punishing practices.

4. Both agree that the *form* of a cultural practice may be arbitrary, although I would suggest that the *functional* import of many cultural practices is far from arbitrary: Whatever local form cultural practices manifest (from valuing monogamy to valuing polygamy), they are constrained by the survival value they impart to their adherents. It is easy to observe cultural values that regulate procreation and distribution of basic biological necessities. This is, after all, what is being debated in our culture's current free-for-all regarding "choice vs. right to life" and "welfare reform." In other words, values are not in all cases truly arbitrary in the sense of being free from any constraint whatsoever. Pure cultural relativity with respect to values would appear to have little survival value.

5. Both recognize that there is no ideal set of values to which all would give their assent. Both are cultural relativists to greater or lesser degrees, depending on the value under discussion.

6. Both agree that the act of evaluation is an inherently verbal behavior.

Hayes et al. move their arguments beyond these points of agreement and begin to align themselves with a more traditional, and, in my mind, more mentalistic and associationistic view of choice. This occurs when the behaviorist view of choice is simply dismissed as not apprehending the real issues of choice. Behavioristic views of choice are dismissed as deterministic such that, by definition, there can in effect be no choices. They also lack an agent who contemplates the consequences of future actions; although there is no lack of nonmentalistic behavioral interpretations (at the same speculative level of discourse) which account for the seeming teleological/intentional quality of choice behavior. The reader is referred particularly to the published work of Willard Day to see some of the most carefully developed behaviorist alternative views.

Defining the choice situation as one in which "It is the anticipated consequences of alternative courses of action that can be understood as prevailing as alternatives in choosing" puts Hayes et al. in the position of finding an internal mechanism for representing these future consequences within an agent who chooses. An inherently mentalistic bit of speculation involves the Kantorian notion of "implicit behavior." By mentalism I refer to the attempt to explain behavior by appeal to events taking place elsewhere, or at a different level of observation than the events for which the explanation is offered. This move then precipitates a mechanistic sequence of internal linking operations involving "substitute stimulus functions" and "subsequent proximities among the stimulus functions of ... objects in their absence." Ultimately the authors lead us to the conclusion that "explanation is accomplished by assuming the occurrence of implicit behavior during the period between the initial confrontation with circumstances in which a choice eventually takes place and the occurrence of that choice response." This, to the extent that it functions as a foray into explanation, is mentalism pure and simple. It is also an interesting blend of elements from the intellectual history of psychology: associationism, act psychology and the usual noncontact with contemporary philosophical distinctions related to choice, purposiveness and ordinary language.

In the end, the philosophical discussions are less helpful than the basic view of choice implied by the points of agreement between Kantor and Skinner:

· If we want people to have values, we must teach them.

· If we want people to choose, we must teach that.

· What are we to teach? Whatever will make our students more successfully adapted to the parts of their culture they will be in contact with.

· Who will choose what to teach? Those who teach and those who pay the teacher's salary. They will do so based on what is reinforcing to them. Ultimately it will be based on their biologies and their histories of reinforcement in their culture.

· Is that good or bad? Who knows. Are the people who are taught to value and choose happier, better neighbors and more self sufficient? Only time and experience can teach us. Choosing and valuing are simply additional behavioral repertoires that we must add to the list of skills to be taught in an individualized approach to helping our friends with developmental disabilities.

Chapter 2

Stages of Moral Development as Stages of Rule-Governance

Steven C. Hayes
Gregory J. Hayes
University of Nevada

Moral development is central to any analysis of human development. In addition, moral behavior includes many forms of behavior that define aspects of developmental disability. Sometimes developmentally disabled persons are kept in restrictive settings because of behaviors such as stealing, aggression, lack of impulse control, and other behaviors that are, in their broadest sense, aspects of moral development.

Surprisingly few behavior analytic approaches to the topic exist. Those behavioral approaches that do exist either deal with the topic quite globally (e.g., Skinner, 1953) or do so in ways that are only loosely related to behavioral principles (e.g., the "learning" chapters in Kurtines & Gewirtz, 1984). The present chapter attempts an analysis of moral behavior in terms of a Relational Frame Theory view of rule-governance.

The Domain of Moral Behavior

The root of the word "moral" means custom or manners, but more seems involved than behaving in a customary and mannerly fashion. We seem to apply the term when a) the action involved is deliberate, b) there are not obvious direct contingencies that would produce the behavior (there may even be notable insensitivity to such contingencies), and c) the action has to do with what is good, right, or proper.

Thoughtful consideration or deliberation seems necessary. If a person accidentally broke up a fight by stumbling and thereby separating the antagonists, it would not be considered a moral action. But if the person acted with deliberation, it might be.

The actions must be insensitive to obvious, immediate, and direct contingencies. For example, we have moral rules about stealing or adultery–activities with obvious direct consequences that might promote them–but we do not have moral rules such as "Thou shalt breath" or "Thou shalt fight when thou art hurt by another." Even if the action appears moral, if the basis for the action can be explained by immediate and direct contingencies it will no longer be a moral act. For example, if a married person declines an opportunity for adultery because the spouse is behind the door with a gun, this may be sensible but it is not particularly "moral."

Finally, moral behavior must involve principles about what is personally or socially good. An Olympic athlete in training may show deliberate actions that are notably insensitive to immediate contingencies, but few would consider such training to be a moral act. Conversely, if such actions have to do with principles about the human value of movement—as in the case of a monk who engages in exercise regimens for spiritual reasons—it may be considered moral.

From a behavioral point of view, these three characteristics all boil down to issues of the generation or application of verbal rules. "Thoughtful consideration" or "deliberation" does so in an obvious way. "Insensitivity" to the effects of direct contingencies is a major impact of verbal rules according to the behavioral literature on rule governance (S. C. Hayes, 1989). "Principles about what is good" are presumably specific kinds of rules.

We will adopt the following as a working definition: Moral behavior is behavior governed by and consistent with verbal rules about what is socially and personally good. If we are to interpret this behaviorally, we are immediately confronted with the question "What is a verbal rule?"

The Nature of Rule-Governed Behavior

Skinner (1957) presented one behavior analytic analysis of verbal behavior, but he did not present *the* behavior analytic account. Indeed, the contemporary basic literature in behavior analysis seems to challenge many of the central aspects of Skinner's theory. For example, the equivalence literature quite clearly shows that tact-like performances emerge readily without the specific history that tacts require. In one recent study (Lipkens, S. C. Hayes, & L. J. Hayes, 1993) a 16-month-old infant taught to orient toward an object when given a name then named the object without explicit training. This naming cannot be a tact because there was no history of reinforcement (generalized or otherwise) for saying the name in the presence of the object.

As a result of such data, a variety of behavioral perspectives on verbal behavior are emerging. Over the last several years we have developed an alternative behavioral account of verbal events and rule-governance (S. C. Hayes, 1989, 1991; S. C. Hayes & L. J. Hayes, 1989, 1992). A detailed review of these topics goes beyond the scope of this article and these other articles are readily available. We have argued that it is possible to learn to derive stimulus relations, and that such an action can be brought to bear on specific stimuli on the basis of contextual cues to do so. The core concept in Relational Frame Theory is that perhaps relating itself is, at least in part, an overarching operant class.

The typical example we have analyzed is stimulus equivalence, but if one is willing to give an operant analysis of equivalence there seems to be no reason to stop there. If equivalence relations can be learned, why not other relations—difference, opposition, comparisons, and so on? Furthermore, precisely what is learned and how is this history brought to bear on a particular instance of responding?

We have argued that three things are learned: contextually controlled generalized mutual entailment, contextually controlled generalized combinatorial entailment, and contextually controlled generalized transformation of stimulus functions (S. C. Hayes & L. J. Hayes, 1992). It is this last characteristic that provides an interpretation of rule-governance under the general rubric of Relational Frame Theory (S. C. Hayes & L. J. Hayes, 1989). As a practical example of a transfer of functions, suppose a child is trained that the written word D - O - G is called "dog" and that the word D - O - G goes with actual dogs. We may say that the child has had two relations directly trained: D - O - G dog and D - O - G "dog." Later the child plays with a dog for the first time and enjoys it—we may suppose that dogs have become discriminative stimuli for approach or eliciting stimuli for emotional responding directly through play. Now, upon hearing his mother say "dogs" from another room the child may smile and go to the other room even though a dog is not visible and the child has no direct history of reinforcement for any of these activities in response to the word "dog." Based on the relational frame account, the word "dog" has acquired similar functions as actual dogs not through a direct history, but indirectly through its participation in a relational frame with dogs.

In our analysis of verbal events, the word "verbal" is used as a technical term to qualify functions that depend upon derived stimulus relations, or what we term "relational frames." A relational frame is a specific type of arbitrarily applicable relational responding: responding that shows the contextually controlled qualities of mutual entailment, combinatorial entailment, and transfer of functions; is due to a history of relational responding relevant to the contextual cues involved; and is not based on direct non-relational training with regard to the particular stimuli of interest. Thus, when the word "dog" has discriminative-like functions, not due to direct training but to derived stimulus relations, the word "dog" is functioning as a verbal stimulus by our definition.

Rules as Verbal Antecedents

Viewed this way, a rule may be functionally defined as an antecedent verbal stimulus. A dog might be taught to get slippers when the master says "slippers" but the command is not functioning as a rule for the dog, since there is no reason to suppose that it has these discriminative functions based on derived stimulus relations.

Often, verbal antecedents of this kind will alter the functions of other stimuli. For example, if I say "when the bell rings get the cake out of the oven" the functions of the actual oven, bell, and cake may be altered by the rule do to the transformation of stimulus functions in terms of the underlying relations. Function altering, however, is neither a defining characteristic of rule-governance, nor a technical account of the process involved. Instead, if this approach is correct, the behavioral process of framing relationally explains both why verbal events are different from nonverbal events, and why verbal events can so readily serve as function altering stimuli.

Our interpretation of rule-following is speculative, but does not stray far from what is already known. Even if Relational Frame Theory is incorrect, the empirical phenomenon of equivalence alone would support much of the analysis. Skinner's definition of rules (contingency specifying stimuli) may be harmonized with the current view if we take the word "specifying" to refer to the presence of functions based on derived stimulus relations. His view of verbal behavior (behavior based on trained social mediation) may be harmonized with this account if we suppose that the training involved is the training need to establish relational frames and socially conventional stimuli participating in them.

The Types of Rule-Following

It is one thing to deal with the meaning of a word or sentence. It is another to explain why rules are followed. The two are not synonymous. One can understand the sentence "stand up now and wave your arms" based on the derived relations sustained among the terms and the conventional relations they involve. For example, "stand up" and the act of standing are in an equivalence class, while "stand up now" establishes the current applicability of a previously learned temporal relation. Very likely, however, few readers stood up and began to wave, even though the conventional relations were previously established and the relations among the terms were correctly derived. The rule was "understood" but not followed. To explain rule-following, additional contingencies need to be specified. There are at least three distinct types of rule-governed behavior organized by the contingencies that motivate action with regard to the particular antecedent verbal stimuli involved (S. C. Hayes, Zettle, & Rosenfarb, 1989).

Pliance. Taken from the word compliance, pliance is behavior due to a history of socially-mediated consequences for a formal correspondence between antecedent verbal stimuli and relevant behavior. When a rule functions this way, it is said to function as a ply.

Suppose a parent tells a child "Clean up your room or you'll never find your toys." If the child cleans up the room because in the past the parent or other rule-givers have followed such statements with differential socially-mediated consequences for following or not following the stated rule, it is an instance of pliance. For example, the parent may look in later and say "I thought I told you to clean up this room? No toys for you when I go shopping today—they would only get lost in this mess!" or, conversely, may find the room clean and say "What a good job you did! I'll buy a new toy for you when I go shopping!" A history of these kind of consequences are functionally involved in pliance.

Note that if the child refuses to clean the room to produce socially-mediated consequences for rule-breakage, this is still an instance of pliance because the unit is a functional one, not a formal one. This might occur, for example, when a child has been ignored when complying but is given a great deal of negative attention for failing to comply. The child may actual prefer negative attention over being ignored. We may call this "counterpliance" to remind ourselves that the form of the rule and the behavior do not match, but it is the same functional unit as pliance.

Tracking. Named so as to connote following a path, tracking is behavior due to a history of a formal correspondence between antecedent verbal stimuli and the contingencies contacted by the form, frequency or situational sensitivity of the relevant behavior. A rule functioning in this way is termed a track.

A simple case might be the advice "The way to get to the bathroom is to go to the end of the hall and turn right." When the listener's behavior is brought under control of the rule because of a history of a correspondence between such rules and the contingencies engaged by emitting the behavior suggested, this is tracking. If the person goes down the hall and to the right and locates the bathroom there and later on such rules are followed because of a history of such experiences, the relevant rules are functioning as tracks.

Note that if the person given such advice *avoids* the walking to the end of the hall, it may still be tracking. The person may have a phobia of public bathrooms, for example. The key issue is not the history of a correspondence between the rule and behavior, but the history of a correspondence between the rule and the contacted contingencies for specified behavior.

The contingencies engaged by tracking are natural, but like pliance they may also be socially mediated. The distinction between the two types of rule following has to do with the functional source of the consequences contacted. For example, a person may be told how to attract members of the opposite sex, and may track this advise and succeed socially. In this case, however, the source of any socially-mediated consequences that result are not for rule-following per se, but for the form, frequency, or situational sensitivity of the emitted behavior. Holding all such factors constant, if the person had engaged in the same behavior (defined by its form, frequency, or situational sensitivity) because of shaping, modeling, or random variation it would have led to the same consequential effects. Thus the contingencies engaged are not for rule-following per se, as they are in pliance.

Augmenting. A third unit of rule-following is augmenting, to suggest a changed or heightened state of affairs. Augmenting is behavior due to antecedent verbal stimuli that alters the degree to which events function as consequences. A rule functioning in that way is termed an augmental.

There are two types of augmenting. *Motivative augmenting* is behavior due to antecedent verbal stimuli that temporarily alter the degree to which previously established consequences function as reinforcers or punishers. This is the original sense in which we used the term augmenting. We described it before behavior analysts had developed an adequate technical vocabulary for such motivative effects, but the motivative augmental maps directly on to Jack Michael's concept of an "establishing stimulus" (Michael, 1982). A motivative augmental is simple an antecedent verbal stimulus that functions as an establishing stimulus.

A simple example may be the statement: "Two all-beef patties, special sauce, lettuce, cheese, pickles, onions, on a sesame seed bun." If the person hearing the commercial has had Big Macs before and if the local McDonald's is open 24 hours a day, there seem to be no contingencies that could lead to pliance or tracking. We have argued earlier (S. C. Hayes et al., 1989) that such commercial statements often function as motivative augmentals by supplying some of the stimulus functions of consequences via a transfer of functions through derived relations—a verbal effect much like reinforcer sampling.

The second type is *formative augmenting*, which is behavior due to antecedent verbal stimuli that establish given consequences as reinforcers or punishers. Formative augmentals are to conditioned reinforcement as motivative augmentals are to establishing operations. The difference between conditioned reinforcement is that formative augmentals have their effects because they are verbal stimuli—that is, because they participate in relational frames.

A simple example may be the statement "Bueno means bon, and bon means good." If "good" was already a reinforcer, and "bueno" now functions much as "good" did earlier, then "bueno" is a *verbal* reinforcer, and the statement that formed bueno as a verbal reinforcer is a formative augmental. In this usage, verbal reinforcement is a technical term: it connotes events that function as reinforcers because of their participation in relational frames.

In more complex forms of formative augmenting, a relational network is established that links given consequences to an abstract pattern of ascribed verbal qualities. For example, justice, dignity, sexism, or freedom are highly abstract terms that are not in equivalence classes with single physical items, but describe an entire pattern of derived relations among events. Once these abstract "goods" and "bads" are established, they can be used to change the consequential effects of other events. For instance, coercing sexual favors may lose its directly reinforcing effects because it is "unjust" or "sexist." This is not simply a matter of using such terms as conditioned punishers or reinforcers because their effects seem in part due to their participation in sets of verbal relations and these sets seem to establish many of the functions of such terms.

Formative augmentals raise a thorny theoretical difficulty that is also raised—but is easier to solve—in the case of motivative augmentals. Motivative effects seems to suggest that the future can cause events in the present. For example, in the case of an establishing stimulus, sometimes it is said that the effectiveness of future reinforcers has been changed. This is a dangerous idea, since it attacks the functional definition of a reinforcer. The solution is to claim that what is strengthened is behaviors that *have in the past* given rise to a given consequence—establishing operations become a type of setting factor. But the same issue is more difficult to solve in the case of formative augmentals in certain instances. When a consequence is actually contacted that was made effective via derived relations, the original rule that established the consequence is a formative augmental, and we need not appeal to the future to explain the present. But what of the case when the effects of a formative augmental may be immediate, but the new "consequence" has not been contacted? For example, "Zig-zigs are great! You can earn them by doing x." How can we explain it if the person now does "x"? Are "zig-zigs" reinforcers, even before they are contacted?

In this case, formative augmentals permit other forms of rule-governed behavior that had lead to consequences in the past. What the formative augmental permits is the functional substitution of consequential terms in the track or ply. For example, "Earn them by doing x" probably functions as a track. The "great things" that will happen if such a rule is followed could be known consequences, but the formative augmental "zig-zigs are great" permits "zig-zigs" to be substituted. The general issue of verbal incentives seem to yield to such an interpretation.

The types of rule-governance are summarized in Table 1. A body of literature exists supporting the pliance/tracking/augmenting distinction. In the case of pliance and tracking, the usual form of this research is to present verbal rules and to manipulate the conditions under which the relevant behavior can occur (see S. C. Hayes et al., 1989 for a review). For example, because socially mediated consequences for rule-following per se can only occur if a) the rule itself is known to the verbal community, b) it is known that the individual contacted the rule, and c) whether or not the rule is followed can be monitored. Rule-governed behavior that shows notable sensitivity to these variables is likely to be pliance; behavior that does

---

Table 1

Types of Rule-Governance

Pliance:

Behavior due to a history of socially-mediated consequences for a correspondence between antecedent verbal stimuli and relevant behavior

Tracking:

Behavior due to a history of correspondence between between antecedent verbal stimuli and the contingencies contacted by the formal and situational properties of the relevant behavior

Augmenting:

Behavior due to antecedent verbal stimuli that produce a change in the capacity of events to function as reinforcers or punishers

Motivative Augmenting:

Behavior due to antecedent verbal stimuli that temporarily alter the degree to which previously established consequences function as reinforcers or punishers

Formative Augmenting:

Behavior due to antecedent verbal stimuli that establish given consequences as reinforcers or punishers

not can often be described as tracking. A number of studies have shown these separate effects (Barrett, Deitz, Gaydos, & Quinn, 1987; S. C. Hayes, Rosenfarb, Wulfert, Munt, Korn, & Zettle, 1985; S. C. Hayes, Brownstein, Zettle, Rosenfarb, & Korn, 1986; S. C. Hayes & Wolf, 1984; Rosenfarb & S. C. Hayes, 1984; Zettle & S. C. Hayes, 1983). Formative augmentals (S. C. Hayes, Kohlenberg, & L. J. Hayes, 1991) and motivative augmentals (S. C. Hayes & Ju, 1993) have been demonstrated in the basic laboratory.

Moral Development and Rule-Governance

The distinction between pliance, tracking, and augmenting provides a working model of moral behavior. We will first describe that model, show why it emerges from our behavioral view of rule-governance, and finally compare it to other models of moral development.

There are six basic kinds of moral behavior that emerge from the pliance/tracking/augmenting distinction: three when we focus on the role of the listener and three when we focus on the role of the speaker. These can be arranged into a usual sequence of their initiation based on normative contingencies. As new forms of moral behavior are added, old forms seem typically to continue, at least to some degree. Thus the theory of moral development that emerges from these views is somewhat like stage theories of moral development, but a) the sequence involved emerges from the contingencies and is not inherent, and b) new forms of moral rules do not eliminate old.

Group 1. The Role of the Listener

The first group of three kinds of moral behavior involve the individual as listener. We argue that when pliance, tracking, and augmenting involve conventions about what is good, they define three kinds of moral activity, and that they typically emerge in sequence.

Type 1. Pliance. Moral pliance involves following rules about what is good or proper because the verbal community differentially consequates rule-following per se. This kind of moral behavior involves compliance (or rebellion) to achieve social ends produced by rule-following (or breakage).

At the level of content, moral pliance is instantiated by rules such as "Don't hit your sister, or else" or "No peeing outside, you little barbarian." At the level of process, moral pliance involves the implicit (and often explicit) rule "Do it because I said so."

Moral pliance seems to occur before other forms of moral activity. Unlike tracking, pliance adds new reinforcers and punishers to those contingencies already present. Children, for example, are told "no" and deviation from the rule is often immediately punished ("I told you no!"). This relatively tight contingency may be necessary to establish rule-following in the first place. In addition, pliance is most likely if a speaker is manding, and all mands imply a state of reinforcability in the speaker, by definition. Thus, there are immediate reasons that the verbal community will establish pliance—it pays off directly for the verbal community.

Acquiring moral pliance requires only consistent rule-givers who control and contingently deliver important reinforcers. If, however, the consequences of rule-breakage are too severe, or if the benefits accrue primarily to the rule-giver, counterpliance is likely as the rule-follower works to undermine the situation.

Type 2. Tracking. Moral tracking involves following rules about what best produces existing reinforcers and punishers for the individual. This kind of morality involves instrumentality, but because it is usually not necessary to develop rules about situations in which reinforcers are direct, immediate, and predictable, moral tracking increasingly emphasizes long-term and probabilistic consequences of action as individuals develop. Examples of moral tracks might be "People won't like you if you lie" or "If you don't share, Susie won't want to come over anymore" or "If you use drugs you will ruin your health." The implicit rule is "How can I do what gets me reinforcers or avoids punishers?"

Because tracking relies on existing consequences, it is a form of rule-following that is readily available to verbally competent persons. The key issue is the degree to which tracks predict the actual contingencies. Acquiring a history of correspondence between the rule and the contingencies requires only frequent, accurate descriptions of the world, beginning with relatively short-term and highly likely situations, and gradually becoming more long-term and probabilistic. Children in verbally emaciated or extremely unstable environments may have a difficult time acquiring tracking, and may instead appear to be impulsive or to have low self-control.

Type 3. Augmenting. Moral augmenting involves the acquisition of and motivation to obtain increasingly abstract reinforcers and punishers, based on systems of verbal relations. Augmenting begins with the establishment of important verbal consequences such as "being a good boy" particularly as "good boy" comes to have more functions than mere conditioned reinforcing functions because of the verbal relations sustained between it and other, largely verbal events ("A good boy is kind, helpful, ..." etc.) Over time these verbal consequences become more and more abstract as individuals work to be "right" or "fair" or "honest" or "free."

Formative augmentals are the more important kind in the area of morality, because they establish new consequential functions through verbal means (i.e., through relational frames). It seems likely that this form of moral behavior is the most difficult of those in Group 1, because it is such a highly verbal process. It seems reasonable to assume that verbal events and rule-governance can proceed most easily when engaging in such activities produce new or more reliable means to existing consequences (as in pliance or tracking)–only after such a verbal repertoire is well established can increasing abstract events acquire consequential functions. In addition, some verbal consequences may compete with existing consequences. For example, being honest may lead to punishment. If augmenting is well-established, the verbal consequence may still completely outweigh other consequences. Because it is verbally complex, and may even compete with direct contingencies, moral augmenting seems likely to emerge last among the Group 1 activities.

Group 2: The Role of the Speaker

In this second group of moral actions, what is primarily at issue is the role of the speaker. Thus, we are not simply concerned with following rules, but with how sets of rule systems can be established that will be followed. These social concerns lead to rules that in turn may be followed by the individual–so the role of the listener is still involved–but it is the focus on support for rule systems that define this group of moral activities.

Group 2 forms of moral activity may emerge before at least some forms of Group 1 activities (particularly augmenting), but in general they should emerge later. Pliance, tracking, and augmenting are listener forms of activity. They are functional units of rule-following. Speakers thus cannot reliably produce plys, tracks, and augmentals–whether given verbal formulae function in these ways has to do with the history of the listeners involved rather than the form of the speech per se. This means, in part, that there is an inherent looseness in the contingencies surrounding Group 2 activities, and thus more extensive histories seem needed to establish, say, a concern for tracking than tracking itself. In addition, a concern for systems that support rule-following is itself an abstract verbal consequence–thus, the most abstract and complex form of Group 1 moral behavior seems at least somewhat assumed in all Group 2 activities.

Type 4. Social Concern for Pliance. Moral behavior of this kind is oriented toward the establishment of pliance in others or in the social group as a whole. In a sense, pliance itself is the "good" that is specified by this kind of moral activity. It is involved with such issues as "How can we establish law and order?" or "How can I get my children to mind me?" or "The youth of today need to do what they are told."

There is a reason that this kind of moral activity is listed first among Group 2 activities: the contingencies that lead to a concern about pliance in the speaker involve states of deprivation or aversive stimulation for the speaker. The typical reason speakers mediate reinforcement for pliance is that rule-following produces consequences that are directly valued by the speaker. When a parent tells a child not to fight with a sibling, part of this statement may be due to the aversive effects produced by such fighting. Similarly, a concern over law and order may be due in part to the very direct aversive effects of lawlessness and disorder. For these reasons, a social concern over pliance seems most likely to emerge first. This type of moral behavior is a matter of caring that people care about socially mediated consequences for rule-following.

Type 5. Social Concern for Tracking. Moral behavior of this kind is oriented toward the establishment of tracking in others or in the social group as a whole. It is concerned with such issues as "How can we eliminate self-destructive behavior in our youth?" or "How can we get people to think in terms of the long-term consequences." It also can involve a concern for the social consequences of action, but not those due to immediate aversive events. Rather, at this level the concern is over the utility of a social contract in which working for the good of others eventually pays off for all. A social concern for tracking emphasizes long-term and probabilistic consequences of action simply because it is only in these conditions that there is usually a need for tracking in the first place.

This kind of moral activity is likely to emerge after a social concern for pliance because the benefits for the speaker are less direct and are more long-term. It may benefit me if our youth were more concerned with what is beneficial in the long run, or were less self-destructive—but such benefits may not be something I notice immediately. Furthermore, this kind of moral behavior requires experiencing that reinforcers for others are like those for you (e.g., the "golden rule"), otherwise supporting tracking in others might simply lead to more effective criminals or psychopaths. This type of moral behavior is a matter of caring that people care about following rules to achieve long-term or probabilistic consequences. There is little reason to be concerned about this issue in the absence of rules.

Type 6. Social Concern for Augmenting. Moral behavior of this kind is oriented toward the establishment of verbal consequences in others or in the social group as a whole and increasing the motivation of others to work toward such consequences. It is concerned with such issues as "How can we establish a society that seeks justice?" or "How can we raise our consciousness about poverty and racism."

This kind of moral activity is likely to emerge last for two reasons: first, the verbal consequences that are involved are often based on entire verbal networks of events. This kind of verbal activity is complex and abstract, and requires considerable verbal histories to occur. Second, the contingencies that lead to such concerns about the behavior of others are themselves quite abstract. This type of moral behavior is a matter of caring that people care about abstract verbal consequences. This consequence (that people care about abstract verbal consequences) is not a direct, existing reinforcer—it can become important only through complex sets of verbal relations. Unlike types 4 and 5, this type of moral behavior does not necessarily produce existing reinforcers of any kind for the individual. Indeed, for example, if justice become more generally important within a social group, taxes on those with resources might increase, restrictions on various economic activities might increase, and so on. That is, if the verbally constructed consequences involved are more widely adopted, existing reinforcers might be less likely, not more likely. Abstract and concrete consequences may be in direct competition. This is not true in the case of pliance or tracking, nor of the Group 2 variants of those forms of rule-governance.

Summary

We have argued that basic behavioral work on rule-governance provides a rational structure within which to analyze moral behavior. We have distinguished six types of moral activity arranged into two general groupings. We have argued for a typical sequence within these groups, and a rough sequence between the groups, based upon the normative contingencies (rather than fixed developmental stages) and the complexity of the behavior (especially the verbal behavior) involved. The stages of rule-governance and thus of moral behavior are summarized in Table 2.

While there is some empirical basis for the pliance/tracking/augmenting distinction, the application of these concepts to moral behavior is purely theoretical. Because behavioral theories of moral development are so sparse, such an exercise seemed useful on its own terms, even if very tentative. We wanted to find a way to begin to examine the plausibility of this analysis, however, and settled on the following strategy. The second author, who teaches in the area of ethics and is not well-versed in behavioral psychology, selected six major moral theorists who represented a range of views about moral development. This was done without first knowing the behavioral theory that was being applied. Only when these theorists had been selected and described did we then attempt to relate the current theory to these other theories. Our logic was that if a focus on behavioral processes could produce a theory that helped illuminate or explain perspectives that emerged from a study of moral behavior itself, the utility of this process approach would more viable.

Table 2

A Rule-Governed Account of Levels of Morality:

Categories and Examples

Group 1: Rule-Governance

Pliance

I have to do what Mommy tells me.

Tracking

How can I do what gets me reinforcers?

Augmenting

I want to be a good person.

Group 2: Support for Systems of Rule-Governance

Social Concern for Pliance

How can we establish law and order?

Social Concern for Tracking

How can we eliminate self-destructive behavior in others?

Social Concern for Augmenting

How can we establish a society that seeks justice?

Six Representative Theories of Moral Development

We give thumbnail sketches of each of six important theories below, and attempt to analyze each in terms of the modern behavior analytic work on rule-governance. The descriptions of these theorists, in line with the purposes of this exercise, were edited only for length, not content. Thus, no attempt was made to describe them in ways that would make easier an analysis in terms of the concepts of rule-governance.

Emile Durkheim

A late-19th-century French sociologist, Durkheim noted three essential aspects of the internalization of values and the development of morality. First, there is a need for discipline and authority, which he argued allowed individuals to restrain more basic drives, to adhere to the laws of society, to cooperate with others, and to create an environment in which significant autonomy was possible. Through authority and discipline came the implanting of norms, rules, and habits by influential adults. Secondly, moral development depended on attachment to a social group. Finally, personal autonomy and self-determination, which gave the notion of moral action meaning, could emerge only within a social and normative context. In Durkheim's view, any notion of autonomy as absolute and without societal context was dangerous and illusory (Durkheim, 1961).

Analysis. Durkheim is claiming that it is only through discipline and authority exerted within a social group that the individual can come to work toward his or her own ends. This viewpoint can be understood by focusing on Group 1 moral activities. It seems that Durkheim is emphasizing the importance of pliance to the eventual establishment of "autonomy." The concern over autonomy, while superficially inconsistent with a behavioral point of view, seems to involve both tracking and augmenting—doing that which works best for the individual (tracking) and furthermore coming to determine one's own goals and values (augmenting). Of course, in a behavioral view, self-determination is itself to be analyzed in its social/verbal context—but that seems also to be Durkheim's point. The primacy of pliance was also emphasized in our viewpoint.

Sigmund Freud

Through his well-known concepts of id, ego, and superego, Freud posited that only through guilt, conscience, and repression could morality arise and social interaction take root. Without the repression of libido and more basic urges, life would be dominated by an anarchistic, dog-eat-dog reality; morality would have no place in day-to-day activities. Thus moral development demands that we learn and accept the need for restraint. To maintain society, such restraint, mediated by the superego, is inculcated into the young by parents, teachers, and other adult authority figures. Through the suppression of individual autonomy, a pro-society morality emerges (Freud, 1961).

Analysis. Freud's view also seems to emphasize Group 1 activities, especially pliance and tracking. The conflict between the id and superego can be viewed as a conflict between direct reinforcers and arbitrary social reinforcers for rule-following. Pliance puts both into conflict—were there no conflict there would be no need for rule-governed behavior in the first place. Ego functions involve successful day-to-day living—the domain of tracking.

Alfred Adler

Adler, in breaking with Freud's views, postulated an inborn desire for coopera-tion as a primary force in human development. Such a desire permitted individuals, seeking to move beyond the inferior and powerless state of childhood to a position of superiority, to develop a deep sense of social interest. It is this sense of social interest which thus tempers the inevitable excesses that power and authority over others would otherwise generate (Adler, 1928, 1964, 1978).

Adler and his principal followers measured the maturity of individuals and societies by the standard of social interest. Moral development then was fundamen-tally determined by the extent to which an individual and the culture-at-large allowed their desire for cooperation to emerge (Dreikurs, 1971). In its mature form, such a desire would create a just and egalitarian society. Individuals, however, could not simply be relied on to discover their desire for societal cooperation. Appropriate moral development also required the influence of adults, who were charged with redirecting a child's motivation and behavior toward more mature, socially appropriate ends. Adult input, at the same time, needed to avoid the excesses of authoritarianism. Heavy-handed repression of individual autonomy was unneces-sary; the inborn desire for cooperation will result in maturation of both the individual and society via more gentle and egalitarian means (Adler, 1978; Dreikurs & Soltz, 1964).

Analysis. Adler adds Group 2 concerns, defined both by Adler and ourselves in terms of social interest, to Freud's Group 1 focus. As with Adler, in its "mature" (i.e., most complex) form, the issue in Group 2 morality is a just and egalitarian society. We agree as well that adult intervention is required (e.g., pliance is important), but that the excesses of authoritarianism should be avoided (e.g., pliance is only one, fairly basic, form of moral behavior, and if it is done to excess counterpliance may emerge).

Robert Sears

Sears' behavioral model of moral development (Sears, Maccoby, & Levin, 1957) relied on attractive incentives, satisfying consequences and punishment for bad behavior. Moral development required both negative and positive modeling, but positive models were emphasized, especially from the mother. Further, in order for behavior to be directed appropriately, punishment for wrong behavior needed to be very consistent. The child learned that actions had consequences. Several methods were employed to evolve conscience and standards of self-control: the intervention of adult authority figures, especially in halting actions which unfairly impacted others or which may have been harmful to the child; the fear of punishment or the expectation of reward; and the desire for personal, internal control (including the desire to avoid circumstances which would lead to guilt or shame.)

In Sears' view, conscience evolved based entirely on learned behavior. Once a level of internal control was achieved, actions need not be motivated by fear of punishment—the child would continue to act consistent with learned behavior in the absence of external controls or monitoring. The process of internalizing values based on experience began at a very young age and continued into adulthood, although Sears considered the years prior to adolescence most important (Sears et al., 1957; Sears, Rau, & Alpert, 1965).

Analysis. Like Freud, this interpretation is focused on Group 1 activities. Once again, we see a sequence from the intervention of authority figures (pliance) to the fear of punishment (both pliance and tracking), to the desire for personal control (tracking and augmenting). Sears emphasizes that punishment needs to be very consistent for higher forms of moral activity to emerge—in our terms, pliance is probably foundational and requires consistency.

Jean Piaget

Piaget believed that cognitive and moral development proceeded in tandem. The progression of moral development followed certain prescribed steps which Piaget claimed were innate, basically invariant, hierarchical and which applied universally across cultures. These steps were nonetheless impacted by social factors, which could significantly alter the rate of development or determine the level of development ultimately achieved.

Drawing data from his well-known clinical interview technique, Piaget described personal moral development as a process of moving from "heteronomous morality," in which the young child's decisions were based entirely on an overriding respect for adult authority, to "autonomous morality," in which an increasing sense of personal autonomy emerged (Piaget, 1962).

The very young child was seen as strongly focused on self (egocentric), which limited his cognitive ability to appreciate other points of view beyond his own and to accept rules arising from social interaction. Once able to acknowledge the problems produced by such a limited focus, the child, assuming continued social interaction with peers and others, then naturally moved in stepwise fashion to a more and more egalitarian focus, emphasizing cooperation (Piaget, 1962).

Analysis. There are two major points here, both of which are readily analyzed from our point of view: the move from concern over adult authority to personal autonomy, and the move from an egocentric to a social focus. Point one reiterates the sequence from pliance to tracking and augmenting; points two emphasizes the emergence of Group 2 activities.

Lawrence Kohlberg

Perhaps the most influential of modern moral development theorists, Kohlberg's work was empirically based and multi-cultural in nature. From his studies he concluded there were universal stages of moral development, which were consistent across cultures. These stages, shown in Table 3, ranged from the most primitive in which rules were obeyed in order to avoid punishment, to mid-level stages in which a child (or adult) conformed in order to avoid disapproval or acted in accordance with the belief that right behavior meant doing one's duty and adhering to the rules of society, to a stage in which morally correct acts were a function of conscience in accordance with universally applied ethical principles (Kohlberg, 1980; 1983).

Kohlberg objected to efforts to implant the norms of the majority in a society in the young and others. Rather, he viewed the goal of moral education as facilitating the process of individual moral development by stimulating "the 'natural' development of the individual child's own moral judgment and capacities, thus allowing him to use his own moral judgment to control his behavior" (Kohlberg, 1980, p. 72).

If development is stimulated rather than imparted via fixed rules, the child will naturally move to higher stages of moral development. He insisted his studies, which covered a variety of cultures in addition to the United States (e.g., India, Britain, Honduras, Taiwan, Mexico's Yucatan region, Israel, and Canada) demon-

---

Table 3

Kohlberg's Stage Theory

Preconventional Level

"Responsive to cultural labels, but interprets these in terms of the physical consequences of action or the power of those who enunciate the rules"

1. Orientation to punishment, obedience, and power
2. Instrumental exchange - conforming to obtain rewards

Conventional Level

"Maintaining the expectations of the group is valuable in its own right, and efforts are made to support and justify this order"

3. Interpersonal conformity - the "good boy" orientation
4. Orientation to law, order, authority, and duty

Postconventional Level

"Effort to define moral values that have applicability apart from the authority of groups or the individual's identification with them"

5. Social contract orientation
6. Acts of conscience in accord with universal ethical principles

---

strated an invariant sequence of development that was not subject to the whims of cultural relativism. Each stage represented an organized system of thought, and individuals functioned at a specific stage at least the majority of the time regardless of the moral dilemma presented. Each stage in Kohlberg's theory represented a more evolved form of judgment because, in his view, each step came ever closer to meeting what he termed the prerequisites of morality: impersonality, universalizability, ideality, preemptiveness, and the like (Kohlberg, 1980; 1983).

Analysis. Kohlberg's Stage 1 and 2 (see Table 1) correspond fairly closely to pliance and tracking. His Stage 3 (interpersonal conformity) does not have a clear parallel in our theory, though it could be interpreted as a form of pliance that emerges when peers and not parents become the relevant mediators of reinforcement. Our Type 3 (augmenting) does not seem to be clearly delineated in his system. His Stages 4 through 6 map fairly closely on to our Types 4 through 6, however. That is, his "law and order" stage looks rather like our "Social concern for pliance" activity; his "social contract" stage looks something like our "Social concern for tracking" activity; and his "universal ethical principles" stage seems to overlap with our "Social concern for augmenting" activity.

Of all the theorists reviewed, Kohlberg seems to be most similar to the perspective developed here. This is reassuring, because Kohlberg's theory is by far the most empirically driven of those reviewed. Kohlberg, being heavily influenced by Piaget, takes an organicist, developmentalist perspective, however, in which stages are their own explanation. Our approach is explicitly historical and contextual. We do not have any stages, though there are certain expected sequences that emerge from normative environments and behavioral complexity.

Conclusion

Table 4 shows a comparison between our perspective and that of these six theorists. Our rule-governed interpretation does not apply with equal force to all the theorists reviewed (in the spirit of the exercise, all were included here) but in many areas there is a clear relationship. This relationship seems surprising. These six theorists represent a wide range of sociological, cognitive, behavioral, psychoanalytic, and developmental theories. Furthermore, the present theory was neither developed from the moral development literature nor primarily from the field of moral behavior. We did not examine the nature of moral judgement and then abstract principles to describe moral development per se—instead we attempted a simple and unambiguous extension of our existing theory of rule-governance, developed over the last decade within the basic human operant literature, to the complex topic of moral behavior.

The development of basic principles that would allow an analysis of complex human behavior has always been one of the major promises of a behavior analytic approach: If a direct extension of a contemporary behavioral perspective makes contact with many of the distinctions made by moral theorists and the data they collect, it suggests that the extension is not arbitrary and that the underlying analysis has scope.

How Moral Development Should be Trained

According to the present analysis, morality should be trained both by increasing basic relational abilities and by moving persons through the increasingly complex contingencies involved in the six types of moral behavior this theory describes. Basic relational abilities are those that enable rule-generation and rule-understanding. According to the present view, these would be increased by (among other approaches):

Comparison of Relevant Theories of Moral Development

Hayes	Kohlberg	Adler	Piaget	Durkheim	Sears
Pliance	Punishment and Obedience		Hetero-nomous Morality	Discipline and Authority	Behavior Modeled and Directly Consequate
Tracking	Instrumental Exchange	Suppression of Id Impulses	Autonomous Morality	Attachment to a Social Group	
Augmenting	Interpersona Conformity			Personal Autonomy	Sense of Internal Control and Internalized Values
Establishing Pliance	Law and Order				
Establishing Tracking	Social Contract	Sense of Social Interest			
Establishing Augmenting	Universal Ethical Principles				

a) increasing the number and flexibility of learned relational frames, such as before-after, opposites, many different kinds of comparisons, cause-effect, and so on.
b) training increasingly subtle and flexible contextual control over these relational actions. If the theory is correct, this should include training both in the arbitrary control of stimulus relations and in their control by properties of related events (that is, in learning to apply an inherently arbitrarily applicable response non-arbitrarily).
c) training in the combination of relational frames.
d) training increasingly subtle and flexible contextual control over the transformation of stimulus functions through relational frames.

Moving though the six types of moral behavior should be increased by training experiences that create pliance, tracking, and augmenting, in the case of Group 1 activities, and by training experiences in the training of Group 1 activities in others. In the case of Group 2 behaviors:

Pliance should be trained by consistent and moderate discipline, reasonable and regular requests for help, clear statements of rules, monitoring of behavior, provision of functionally positive and social mediated consequences, the development of social praise as a generalized reinforcer, and by a consistent relationship between rules and positive socially mediated consequences for rule-following.

Tracking should be strengthened by stating rules accurately and frequently, by relating listener behavior to natural consequences, by stating accurate rules about consequences the listener cares about, by building increasingly complex descriptions of natural consequences as listener behavior is successfully regulated, and by allowing the natural contingencies to apply.

Augmenting should be increased by constructing futures often and accurately, by describing consequences in detail shortly before they are contacted, by linking other forms of rule-following to specially constructed futures, and by building increasingly elaborated sets of relations increasingly abstractly related to existing positive consequences.

Many of these recommendations are quite speculative. They are tightly linked to the underlying theory, however. If they were shown in general not to hold, the present approach to moral behavior should be cast aside.

What is Different About this Approach?

From a behavioral perspective, what seems to be missing from existing theories of moral development is not the basic outline of moral development as a phenomenon but rather a clear relation between these facts and a set of basic psychological processes. The present approach begins with a historical, contextual, and functional approach to verbal relations and rule-governance. These basic phenomena lead directly to a theory of moral development. The theory provides a clear rationale for typical sequences of moral development and a set of recommendations about how to train such behavior.

The advantage of an analysis rooted in basic principles is the scope of the resulting account. Theoretical analyses based on specific domains tend to have fairly good precision but limited scope. What does Kohlberg's theory suggest about the effect of instruction on sensitivity to changing contingencies, for example? What does Kohlberg's theory suggest about the nature of verbal events? It is silent, or nearly so, on these questions, and for good reason. Kohlberg's theory, after all, is of moral development per se, not of meaning, understanding, intelligent behavior, language, and related phenomena. Relational Frame Theory is, first and foremost, an approach to these broader topics but it also provides an approach to moral behavior. If such a stretch is shown to pay off, it increases its utility as a parsimonious and coherent account of human verbal behavior.

References

Adler, A. (1928). *The nervous character: Fundamentals of a comparative individual psychology and psychotherapy* (4th ed.). Munich: Bergmann.

Adler, A. (1964). *Social interest: Challenge to mankind.* New York: Capricorn.

Adler, A. (1978). *Cooperation between the sexes: Writing on women and men, love and marriage, and sexuality.* New York: Norton.

Barrett, D. M., Deitz, S. M., Gaydos, G. R., & Quinn, P. C. (1987). The effects of programmed contingencies and social conditions on response stereotypy with human subjects. *Psychological Record, 37*, 489-505.

Dreikurs, R. (1971). *Social equality: The challenge of today.* Chicago: Regnery.

Dreikurs, R., & Soltz, V. (1964). *Children: The challenge.* New York: Hawthorn.

Durkheim, E. (1961). *Moral education: A study in the theory and application of the sociology of knowledge.* New York: Free Press.

Freud, S. (1961). *Civilization and its discontents.* New York: Norton.

Hayes, S. C. (Ed.). (1989). *Rule-governed behavior: Cognition, contingencies, and instructional control.* New York: Plenum.

Hayes, S. C. (1991). A relational control theory of stimulus equivalence. In L. J. Hayes & P. N. Chase (Eds.), *Dialogues on verbal behavior* (pp. 19-40). Reno, NV: Context Press.

Hayes, S. C., Brownstein, A. J., Zettle, R. D., Rosenfarb, I., & Korn, Z. (1986). Rule-governed behavior and sensitivity to changing consequences of responding. *Journal of the Experimental Analysis of Behavior, 45*, 237-256.

Hayes, S. C., & Hayes, L. J. (1989). The verbal action of the listener as a basis for rule-governance. In S. C. Hayes (Ed.), *Rule-governed behavior: Cognition, contingencies, and instructional control* (pp. 153-190). New York: Plenum.

Hayes, S. C., & Hayes, L. J. (1992). Verbal relations and the evolution of behavior analysis. *American Psychologist, 47*, 1383-1395.

Hayes, S. C., & Ju, W. (May 1993). *Verbal establishing stimuli and verbal reinforcers.* Paper presented at the meeting of the Association for Behavior Analysis, Chicago.

Hayes, S. C., Kohlenberg, B. K., & Hayes, L. J. (1991). Transfer of consequential functions through simple and conditional equivalence classes. *Journal of the Experimental Analysis of Behavior, 56,* 119-137.

Hayes, S. C., Rosenfarb, I., Wulfert, E., Munt, E., Zettle, R. D., & Korn, Z. (1985). Self-reinforcement effects: An artifact of social standard setting? *Journal of Applied Behavior Analysis, 18,* 201-214.

Hayes, S. C., & Wolf, M. R. (1984). Cues, consequences, and therapeutic talk: Effect of social context and coping statements on pain. *Behaviour Research and Therapy, 22,* 385-392.

Hayes, S. C., Zettle, R. D., & Rosenfarb, I. (1989). Rule following. In S. C. Hayes (Ed.), *Rule-governed behavior: Cognition, contingencies, and instructional control* (pp. 191-220). New York: Plenum.

Kohlberg, L. (1980). Stages of moral development as a basis for moral education. In B. Munsey (Ed.), *Moral development, moral education, and Kohlberg.* Birmingham: Religious Education Press.

Kohlberg, L. (1983). *Moral stages: A current formulation and response to critics.* New York: Karger.

Kurtines, W. M., & Gewirtz, J. L. (1984). *Morality, moral behavior, and moral development.* New York: John Wiley.

Lipkens, G., Hayes, S. C., & Hayes, L. J. (1993). Longitudinal study of derived relations in an infant. *Journal of Experimental Child Psychology, 56,* 201-239.

Michael, J. (1982). Distinguishing between discriminative and motivational functions of stimuli. *Journal of the Experimental Analysis of Behavior, 37,* 149-155.

Piaget, J. (1962). *The moral judgement of the child.* New York: Collier.

Rosenfarb, I., & Hayes, S. C. (1984). Social standard setting: The Achilles' heel of informational accounts of therapeutic change. *Behavior Therapy, 15,* 515-528.

Sears. R., Maccoby, E., & Levin, H. (1957). *Patterns of child rearing.* Evanston, IL: Row, Peterson.

Sears. R., Rau, L., & Alpert, R. (1965). *Identification and child rearing.* Stanford, CA: Stanford University Press.

Skinner, B. F. (1953). *Science and human behavior.* N.Y.: Free Press.

Skinner, B. F. (1957). *Verbal behavior.* N.Y.: Appleton-Century-Crofts.

Zettle, R. D., & Hayes, S. C. (1983). Effect of social context on the impact of coping self-statements. *Psychological Reports, 52,* 391-401.

This article was supported by a grant from the National Institute of Health, National Institute on Drug Abuse, grant number DA08634.

Discussion of S. Hayes and G. Hayes

Morality Framed as Rule-Governance

Kenneth R. Huntley
University of Nevada

Hayes and Hayes' paper is provocative and replete with complex analyses of even more complex phenomenon. The reader who is not familiar with this material would be well advised to read the original sources (see citations in Hayes and Hayes' chapter) and then reread this paper before fully appreciating (or even understanding for that matter) the breadth of what is being presented. The scope of this review is restricted to commenting on Hayes and Hayes' contention of the relevance of rule-governance for moral development.

Rules, Morality, and Contingencies

In addressing the issue of moral development, a first step is in examining the conditions under which we emit these terms. With morality, however, the controlling variables appear to have an added dimension of complexity. The recognition of this complexity is seen in Skinner's (1974) analysis of the subject:

In an operant analysis of the stimulus control of verbal behavior, we can identify the referent of abstract terms, but terms like "morality" and justice" raise an additional problem. It can be solved by recognizing that the behavior we call moral or just is a product of special kinds of social contingencies arranged by governments, religions, economic systems, and ethical groups. We need to analyze those contingencies if we are to build a world in which people behave morally and justly, and a first step in that direction is to dismiss morality and justice as personal possessions (p. 251).

The development of morality is, essentially, a process by which the social environment arranges certain contingencies of reinforcement (e.g., a system of values, morals, etc.) under which a person behaves morally because of that particular environment. Skinner (1974) stated, "Man is perhaps unique in being a moral animal, but not in the sense that he possesses morality; he has constructed a social environment in which he behaves with respect to himself and others in moral ways" (p. 246). Accordingly, moral development may be either contingency-shaped by direct contact with the contingencies of reinforcement or may be occasioned by rule-governed behavior. In most, if not all cases, it is probable that moral development is a product of both types of contingencies.

Hayes and Hayes' papers takes an important second step in examining the relevance of rule-governance as a descriptive and instrumental tool in developing morality in individuals with developmental disabilities. The multiple sources of control which account for rule-governance are suitably accounted for by their distinctions between plys, tracks, and augmentals (Hayes & Hayes, this volume). These terms are used to distinguish important patterns of variables which seem useful in accounting for the development of morality in individuals. The relevance of rule-governed behavior to moral development was similarly recognized by Skinner (1974):

> An "important determinant of moral behavior and a major component of character development" is said to be "willingness to follow rules," but a person "wills" to follow a rule because of the consequences arranged by those who state the rule and enforce it" (p. 197).

There are many reasons why this kind of analysis of morality is fundamental. Rule-governed behavior allows the individual to readily engage in behaviors that might otherwise take quite some time to develop. Hence, even though a person may not know what morality means in the sense of having never been reinforced for acting in ways we call moral; they may act in ways we might call "moral" by means of merely following a rule. This would be close to what Hayes and Hayes describe as pliance. Another reason they might follow the rule is because of the consequences that have been stated in the rule. In this instance, the rule-following is most likely an instance of tracking. Finally, a particular rule may alter the reinforcing effectiveness of certain events. The augmental is described in this way.

We are faced with a problem, however, in sustaining the behavior over time and under conditions in which the person or persons either stating or enforcing the rules are no longer around. In different contexts, a person may be less inclined to act morally if their behavior has been completely rule-governed up to this particular point. In essence, what we want is to have moral behavior become contingency-shaped under positive reinforcement. The question then becomes one of how we might best accomplish this. This problem is further compounded by a feature of rule-governance that in some cases is helpful and in others is an impediment, specifically, that rule-governed behavior is often reported to be insensitive to its consequences. This so-called insensitivity may be useful initially in generating novel instances of moral behavior. A case in point is a child given the rule "you need to share your toys with your cousin" and, as a consequence, shares his/her toys with another for the first time. Rule-governance becomes problematic when the variables accounting for following the rule are no longer present or when the rule-follower is insensitive to the consequences occasioned by his/her behavior. For example, going back to our original example with the child who had shared his/her toys on a previous occasion. Now, at some later time, the child refuses to share his/her toy with the cousin, either due to the rule-giver no longer being present to provide and/or enforce the rule or that the child's behavior was not differentially reinforced by the affection the cousin provided when given a toy.

One solution to this dilemma is just to allow the individual to come into contact with the contingencies directly without benefit of rules. This solution, however, could be problematic to individuals with developmental disabilities. It may in fact be the case that moral development always involves rules of one type or another, especially in light of the complex social environment that western civilization has created and that we find ourselves in. Another, and perhaps more practical consideration, would be to give rules that were in fact sensitive not only to the contingencies arranged by the rule-giver but also sensitive to the immediate effects the behavior has on others. This type of rule-governed behavior may be described a kind of conditional rule, a sort of if-then statement operative in the situation under which it is to be followed and sensitive to its effects upon others. How conditional these rules would need to be remains to be seen. Research has shown that rules may be contingency-shaped so that, indeed, they make the rule-follower more sensitive to the contingencies of reinforcement. Nevertheless, further research investigating this subject matter is warranted.

In summary, Hayes and Hayes provide the theoretical foundations for a naturalistic analysis of moral development. In doing so, they further extend the principles of behavior analysis (e.g., rule-governance) to yet another important aspect of complex human behavior. The stage is set for empirical research in the basic labs and in applied settings on analyzing and investigating the application of rule-governance in the development of morality, both for individuals with and without developmental disabilities. One of the goals of science is prediction and control; another is understanding. Both of these goals are equally suited to the task at hand. Let us begin.

Reference

Skinner, B. F. (1974). *About behaviorism*. New York: Alfred A. Knopf.

Chapter 3

Ethical Issues Concerning Persons with Developmental Disabilities: A Developmental Perspective

Sidney W. Bijou

University of Nevada

I am going to talk about the ethical issues related to the treatment of children with developmental disabilities by their parents and by associated child-care providers. Included among the latter are baby sitters, child care workers in various settings, and teachers, all of whom parents trust to take care of their children. Although viewing their child-rearing practices in ethical terms may seem an affront to parents of children having some kind of disability, nonetheless, in light of the history of the treatment of such children in institutions, and what is currently happening to many disabled children in their homes, a close scrutiny of parental child-rearing practices seems justified. The long and sad history of children may be thought of as having gone through three distinct phases. I won't go into the details here, but will mention only the highlights.

During the middle ages, developmentally disabled children were considered odd, evil, weird, and even possessed of the devil. They were subject to ridicule, seclusion, incarceration, and punishment. During the next, more humane period, which began in the middle of the nineteenth century, they were looked upon as patients in need of treatment in special hospitals, which ultimately became large state institutions. These institutions were usually located in rural, even remote, areas. The third phase was ushered in with the human rights movements of the 1970s. Questions began to be raised by various socially conscious groups as to whether developmentally disabled persons were receiving the kinds of treatment human beings deserved. As a consequence, legislative and judicial agencies began to spell out in clear-cut terms the rights of developmentally disabled persons and simultaneously, to prescribe accountability procedures. The word was out: the road to "normalization" required institutions to provide rights that would create a "homelike" environment for all institutionalized persons with developmental disabilities. In his book published in 1980, Amary listed 44 specifiable rights for such persons. There is little doubt that the number of rights is even greater now.

The human rights phase is still incomplete. There remains the formidable task of working out personnel selection procedures and accountability mechanisms to ensure that every institutionalized developmentally disabled person actually receives the full benefit of these rights. When this goal is achieved we may feel assured that when a developmentally disabled person is turned over to the state for care, he or she will in fact receive the most humane and socially beneficial treatment.

We turn now to the treatment of developmentally disabled children reared in their own homes. Unquestionably, some families rear their developmentally disabled children in ways that promote their potential development and prepare them to function as adequately as possible in society. Then there are parents who for some reason or another, provide a less than adequate environment for their children's development and social adjustment. And finally, there are parents who neglect their developmentally disabled children and subject them to abuse ranging from mild to life-threatening. A newspaper recently reported a study that showed that developmentally disabled children are far more often abused by their parents than non-developmentally disabled children.

Generally, social service agencies intervene only when parental behavior inflicts visible damage or injury to the child. As an expression of outrage over this situation, laws are being enacted to punish anyone, including parents, for assaulting children. Our main concern is with parents who actively or passively deprive their developmentally disabled children of opportunities to develop and to acquire personal and socially desirable skills to the extent of the child's capacity. Paradoxically, we are now approaching a situation in which society is more preoccupied with actualizing the rights of developmentally disabled children reared in public institutions than with safeguarding the rights of these children brought up in their own homes.

I would argue that parental behavior that hampers a developmentally disabled child's development and future social adjustment is unethical because such behavior exacerbates and often compounds a child's disability (Bijou & Dunitz-Johnson, 1981). I would also argue that it is to society's advantage to help parents who are guilty of such deprivation, because in the long run, a well-brought-up developmentally disabled child will not only lead a more satisfying life, but will be less of a burden and may, in some way, even make a contribution to society.

This stance gives rise to two obvious questions: 1) How would one know that a parent is guilty of unethical behavior? And 2) What could be done to help parents learn acceptable, ethical, child-rearing practices? The answer to the first is that doctors, nurses, teachers, baby sitters, and others who have contact with the child or family would be obliged to notify the appropriate agency as soon as they suspect or witness this behavior, just as is required now in instances of any child abuse. To make this approach work, extensive public education would be required to deal with the rights and needs of developmentally disabled children.

The answer to the second question (i.e., what can be done to help these parents?): is intervention by trained personnel in the nursing, medical, educational, psychological, and social-work professions. Their aim would be to teach parents how to treat their child in ways that enhance their development and ultimate welfare. A variation of a model developed and practiced internationally by the Portage

Project would be appropriate (Shearer & Shearer, 1972). The variation required would involve helping parents deal with any personal problems they may have.

In this group we would expect to find parents who are limited in ability and education, parents who must function day in and day out under stress because of economic, emotional, and social problems. We would also find parents who solve their problems by the abuse of drugs or alcohol, and parents who are grossly disorganized or disturbed. A by-product of intervention of this kind would in all likelihood result in a reduction or prevention of many cases of child abuse. A program such as this would not infringe on the parents' right to rear their child according to their preferred life style. Rather, it would serve to assure that within any family structure, conditions would be present that would enhance the child's development and future welfare.

The remainder of this presentation will be devoted to a discussion to the kinds of parental behaviors toward children with disabilities that might be viewed as unethical during the infancy, early and middle childhood, and the adolescent periods. However, I will not deal with ethical issues concerning a decision to abort an abnormal fetus (e.g., a Downs syndrome) or to withdraw life supports from a severely malformed neonate.

Infancy (Birth to 18 Months)

Two ethical issues may arise in the infancy of a developmentally disabled child. One pertains to the decision to institutionalize a malformed neonate. The other refers to the parental treatment of a developmentally disabled child during the infancy period.

Decisions to Institutionalize a Malformed Neonate

In the past the problem of whether or not to institutionalize a neonate having obvious serious disabilities was solved by simply doing so on a physician's recommendation. These recommendations were presumably based on the two-fold assumption that the infant would not develop according to the parent's expectations and that rearing a developmentally disabled child would be an extraordinary burden to the parents and other members of the family.

History has taught us that such a dual assumption is not always warranted. First, significant advances in behavioral and medical science have indicated that many developmentally disabled children develop better than we once thought possible, and second, many adults have become sensitive to the rights of persons with developmental disabilities and consider it a challenge to rear a developmentally disabled child as an integral member of their family.

From an ethical point of view, it would seen that the decision to institutionalize a deformed or high-risk neonate should take into account not only a physician's recommendation, but also a number of additional factors:

1. The nature and severity of the physical disability.
2. Current knowledge relating to the probable development of a child with a particular developmentally disabling condition.

3. The attitude of parents and other members of the family about having a developmentally disabled child in the family.
4. Availability of supportive systems in the community.
5. Religious attitudes about rearing a developmentally disabled child.
6. Quality of care that can be expected from an institution to which the infant would be sent.

Rearing an Infant With Developmental Disabilities

Parents of an infant with developmental disabilities, like parents of a normal infant, have the responsibility of caring for and treating their baby in ways that maximize his or her health, development, and potential for social adjustment. What are considered to be good parenting practices during the infancy period are well known and have been described in various ways. Basically, the biological aspects consist of providing an infant with all the necessities for survival which include adequate nutrition, protection from harm and extreme environmental variations, sanitary living conditions, and ample opportunities for sleep and rest. The humane aspects consist of caring for the baby in the context of love, affection, abundant verbal stimulation, and encouragement for advances in personal and social development.

Parental practices that approximate these requirements would be considered ethical, those that fall short, unethical. In the following discussion, I shall refer to the child with developmental disabilities simply as "the child" in order to avoid repeating the modifying term.

Early Childhood (18 Months to 5 Years)

In the early childhood years it is incumbent on the parents to make certain that the gains their child made during infancy are maintained, and that they assist the child to achieve, in so far as possible, the developmental tasks usually associated with this period. This responsibility extends to those part-time persons selected by the parents to care for their child, e.g., baby sitters or preschool teachers.

Ethical issues focus on behavior that "over-helps" or "under-helps" the child to achieve such personal tasks as learning to walk, using the toilet independently, dressing and feeding oneself, and engaging in simple forms of conventional communication. They also include social tasks such as learning to control one's aggressive behavior, respecting the property rights of other, playing cooperatively, and caring for others.

In general, both over-helping and under-helping a child are considered unethical because they limit the child's chances of developing according to his or her ability, and because they tend to create behavior problems that may well compound the disability. Over helping deprives a child of opportunities to learn by doing and makes him or her the recipient of reinforcers without even attempting acceptable or approximately acceptable responses. Such treatment often results in over-dependence and the "spoiled-child" syndrome. Feelings of guilt, misplaced compassion, or ignorance of the long range consequences generally account for such parental behavior. In addition, if parents perceive and treat their child as being sick and keep shopping around among "experts" for the "right" diagnosis, they invariably do things for him or her that the child is capable of doing. These parents have a tendency to believe that they will discontinue those practices when their child gets better.

Under-helping a child to learn the requisite personal and social skills means not only that advances in development are not being responded to in a positive manner, but that occasions for development are not being provided. Such parental neglect is often associated with personal problems or ignorance of the needs of a developing child.

Middle Childhood (5 to 12 Years)

In middle childhood the ethical issue centers on the parent's behavior with respect to helping their child, a) to adjust to school, b) to join a small community of peers, and c) to participate as a member of his or her family to the extent of his or her ability (Schulman & Mekler, 1985).

Although some of the control of their child will now be in the hands of teachers and school counselors, the parents are still responsible for seeing that the school does more than place their child in a special class and allow him or her to merely occupy a seat and mark time, a practice often called "keeping the child warm". They should insist that the school allow them to participate in drawing up the most suitable educational program plan (e.g., Individual Education Plan, I.E.P.) and see to it that the plan is actualized and maintained.

In addition, the parents may find that they must also help their child make a social transition from home to school, i.e., from the one-to-one relationship he or she has been receiving at home to the formal group relationships that are part of most school systems.

A child is sometimes unable to become a member of his peer groups because of special difficulties or physical limitations. In this case, parental understanding and guidance are essential in helping the child to accept the fact that in making contact with others, he or she, like other children in the group, must follow rules, particularly in relation to controlling aggressive behavior, respecting the property rights of others, and sharing in work and play situations. In other words, a handicapped child must adhere to the moral code of society just as a non-handicapped person does.

Finally, it is the parent's continuing responsibility to help their child become a participating member of the family, within the limits of his or her ability. Over-and-under helping with home obligations deprives the child of the opportunity to learn essential social skills, along with the feeling of being an equal, accepted family member. In contrast, specifying exactly what behaviors are required and what the contingencies are for not complying, has the effect of allowing the child to feel that despite his or her limitations, he or she is loved and a truly accepted family member, treated as an equal with the other siblings.

Adolescence (12 to 18 Years)

Like typical normal adolescents, adolescents with developmental disabilities will probably have difficulties making adjustments, particularly social adjustments, during the teen years. Despite the loss of some of their control to the adolescent peer group, the parents are usually the best source of guidance and support. Both the adolescents and the parents face at least three challenges.

The first challenge is helping the adolescent to select a vocational training program that is commensurate with his or her ability and interests, as prescribed by law. This requires the parents and adolescent not only to seek out an appropriate program, but to work constructively with instructors, counselors, and in some cases, community agencies such as the local chapter of the Association for Retarded Citizens.

The second challenge is helping their child accept family membership and its responsibilities. Here the parent may encounter some difficulty because it is easier to be righteous and dogmatic rather than to be understanding and tenacious about stating rules and describing consequences.

The third challenge is that of helping the adolescent adjust to the heterosexual peer group. Because the social situation is inherently complex, this may be the most difficult task of all. The social complexity is apparent when one takes into account the current sexual morality with regard to teenagers (and even younger adolescents) in respect to sexual intercourse, gender role models, teenage pregnancies, single parent families, drug and alcohol abuse, and with ever increasing teenage violence.

Summary and Conclusion

I have taken the position that the parents of children with developmental disabilities have a direct as well as an indirect responsibility to rear their children in ways that enhance their development and potential for social adjustment. Some parents meet this obligation. Others do not. I am concerned with the latter group, a concern justified in light of the history of treatment of institutionalized children with developmental disabilities and current accounts of neglect and abuse by their parents and other adults.

According to this view, the behavior of parents of children with developmental disabilities is considered unethical when it fails to provide the child with the basic biological and psychological needs or because it "over-helps" or "under-helps" a child to achieve the developmental tasks of infancy, early childhood, middle childhood, and adolescence. Over-helping or under-helping a child to grow and develop are viewed as unethical or immoral because these behaviors deprive the child of acquiring abilities, skills, and attitudes that are the essential ingredients of psychological development.

In a sense, I have proposed a "bill of rights" for the child with developmental disabilities reared in his or her family. Twenty years ago such a proposal might not have seemed necessary or appropriate. Today, it is both.

References

Amary. L. B. (1980). *The rights of the mentally retarded-developmentally disabled to treatment and education*. Springfield, IL: Charles C. Thomas.

Bijou, S. W., & Dunitz-Johnson, E. (1981). Interbehavioral analysis of developmental retardation. *The Psychological Record, 31,* 305-329.

Schulman, M., & Mekler, E. (1985). *Bringing up a moral child*. New York: Addison-Wesley.

Shearer, M. S., & Shearer, D. E. (1972). The Portage Project: A model for early childhood education. *Exceptional Children, 36,* 210-217.

Skinner, B. F. (1978). *Reflections on behaviorism and society* (pp. 33-47). Englewood Cliffs, NJ: Prentice-Hall.

Discussion of Bijou

Developmental Disabilities, Change, and Culture: Improving Circumstances for Children

Mark A. Swain

University of Nevada

Bijou discusses the general history of the treatment of persons with developmental disabilities. He especially reminds us of the less than adequate treatment of children with such disabilities. The tenor of his chapter reminds me of J. R. Kantor's treatment of the concept of the tragedy. Kantor regarded a tragedy as the thwarting of some known class of event continuum (Kantor, 1983, p. 37). Put simply, something that is cut short, or truncated, before its potential is actualized is a tragedy. From a developmental point of view, we may understand that nothing is more tragic than the thwarting of the development of a child. For the child has the most to lose because the child's years are few, and given adequate circumstances most children will likely remain alive and psychologically active for many years to come.

In my view, we continue the tragedy when we explicitly or implicitly adopt guiding tenets which are confused and unmanageable. This occurs, for example, when we adopt guiding philosophies which confuse a proper working philosophy or set of guiding principles with a doctrine that specifies some sort of "ultimate circumstances" such as total inclusion, complete choice, or a no risk life. This, we may understand as an attempt to achieve or approximate idealist conditions; or we may consider it an overcorrective reaction to the shortcomings of the past. However, if the current generation of service providers is going to make a meaningful impact upon the conditions of these children, a careful analysis of their situation will be necessary. In particular, it will be important to design a system which functions to facilitate the development of children, rather than a bureaucratic system which simply functions to maintain itself. This is no small task. It will involve a careful and systematic application of virtually all that is known about the nature of individual and group behavior, not to mention an ongoing experimental analysis of the system.

This brings us to an important consideration. How does the professional community address issues relating to the quality of life of children with developmental disabilities? That is, how do we provide effective services to these children without initiating policies which further their estrangement from the "normal" population by removing opportunities to encounter the type of developmental reinforcement contingencies which shape socially important repertoires of behavior? This, I understand, to be Bijou's main concern throughout his chapter.

By definition, developmentally disabled people need certain measures of assistance. Of course, the assistance required varies considerably across individuals, some needing very little assistance, others needing extensive services. As Bijou notes, we have seen that over the years the circumstances in which we have provided these services have drastically changed. These changes are especially apparent since the influence of the human rights movement of the 1970s. The movement toward "normalization" required a rethinking of common conventions associated with the care of developmentally disabled people. This included the dismantling of large institutions which provided impersonal and uniform "care" for the developmentally disabled population which was (and is) as diverse as the so-called "normal" population. How then, do we now provide assistance which is cost effective, tailored to individual life-circumstances, and free from policies which drastically "over" or "under" help individuals?

Toward a Solution

Bijou offers *one piece* of the answer to such an approach. In order to avoid the problems of the past, we must look to the current circumstances, the trends, the pertinent history relevant to how we encourage people and arrange environments to maximize potential development and thus avoid the tragic outcomes of the past. By observation of lifestyles and examination of public records, Bijou finds it necessary to directly address the home circumstances of the developmentally disabled child. This does seem necessary, due to the de-institutionalization of many persons with developmental disabilities, as well as the many young children that are now never institutionalized, but instead, remain in the home. This provides us with a certain paradox: while it is necessary to thoroughly address the home situations of these individuals, it is this "invasion" into the home which will likely meet with considerable resistance. If this type of system were introduced, it is this issue which would generate the most controversy and simultaneously be the focal point of real change. How then, would such a system work?

Changing Cultural Practices

The implementation of an effective system which has as its goal to improve the home environments of developmentally disabled children would necessarily involve changes at the level of cultural practices. In fact, Bijou's description (present volume) of the treatment of developmentally disabled persons is itself a historical analysis addressed at the cultural level. The questions addressed in this discussion, as well as the Bijou chapter, all concern how we as a culture are going to "manage" those with developmental disabilities. This is indeed a complex issue for which the answers with regard to implementation are not obvious. However, some answers do inhere in what is already known about the science of human behavior. While it is beyond the scope of this discussion to address this issue in appropriate detail, I will mention some important considerations. First, however, I will consider the concept of culture and how developmentally disabled individuals fare in typical Western cultural circumstances.

Consistent with our present purposes we may understand culture as those interactions associated with variables arranged by other people which affect the psychological interactions of individuals (see Skinner, 1953, p. 419). As such, cultural interactions are ubiquitous, and to a large extent establish the organization of our psychological activity in a variety of circumstances. What is unique about many developmentally disabled persons is the degree to which cultural variables determine the frequency of these types of events at great expense to individual behavior. For instance, it is not uncommon that cultural practices would determine: 1) where a developmentally disabled person will live; 2) who the individual will live with; 3) the type of education received; 4) types of job opportunities; 5) financial circumstances; 6) the extent to which there is contact with non-disabled people, etc. Of course, these practices are complex and will depend (in part) on such things as the functioning level of the individual and family circumstances. Nonetheless, few would argue that the developmentally disabled population is not subject to social controls which far exceed those prevailing for the general population. Herein lies the central challenge to the system recommended by Bijou and considered within this discussion. Improving the home situations of developmentally disabled children would require that the general population relinquish some of their control over the lives of those with developmentally disabilities. For example, parents and caretakers would need to cooperate with agencies overseeing activities occurring within their homes. It is this issue which demands the most attention by those interested in changing cultural practices. What the children need in terms of behavioral home services is much less of a problem. This technology is readily available to those interested in the improvement of developmental contingencies (Bijou, 1993, Martin & Pear, 1978).

Conclusion

In order to avoid problems associated with the by-products of controlling practices (see Skinner, 1953, pp. 297-449), any attempt to implement a plan of the type advocated by Bijou would require careful and systematic implementation of techniques based on what is known about the nature of human behavior. A program of this magnitude would necessarily require governmental involvement, private interest group activities, efforts from representatives of the developmentally disabled population, along with other social institutions interested in the improvement of conditions of children with developmental disabilities. The creation of several agencies overseeing the project would likely reduce the possibility of excessive control practices by any one agency (Skinner, 1953, p. 440), thereby also reducing the magnitude of counter-control activities. Beginning efforts would likely involve the engineering of reinforcing contingencies designed to increase the likelihood of desired parental/caretaker behavior until such time that other more "natural" consequences could function to maintain the practices. The ultimate goal of such an effort would be to establish better developmental circumstances for children with developmental disabilities as standard cultural practices.

References

Bijou, S. W. (1993). *Behavior analysis of child development*. Reno, NV: Context Press.

Kantor, J. R. (1983). *Tragedy and the event continuum*. Chicago: Principia Press.

Martin, G., & Pear, J. (1978). *Behavior modification: What it is and how to do it*. Englewood Cliffs, NJ: Prentice-Hall.

Skinner, B. F. (1953). *Science and human behavior*. New York: Macmillan.

Chapter 4

Competence

Patrick M. Ghezzi and Ruth Anne Rehfeldt
University of Nevada

This paper is organized around several themes—observations, really—which we have put down in two parts. The first part addresses two questions: How can we know what competence is? and Why *must* we know what competence is? The second set of observations deal with how our views on competence bear upon services provided to people of all ages and levels of development, with an emphasis on children and their teachers and parents. A third and final part summarizes the discussion, and offers some conclusions related to the themes developed in the second part of the paper.

What It Is and Why It Matters

In his concurring opinion in the Supreme Court decision in Jacobellis v. State of Ohio (1964), Justice Potter Stewart wrote, " I can't tell you what pornography is, but I know it when I see it." It is tempting to view competence in the same well-known light, but a moment's thought reveals that we can, and indeed, we *must* know what is meant by competence.

How can we, and why must we, know what competence is? As to this first question, we can begin to know what competence is by taking a moment to examine a simple circumstance in which we might apply the term. On the occasion of being asked to recommend a physician, we reply, "Dr. Smith is highly competent."

What this common example reveals is that one person is asking another to make a judgement about someone who provides a service to others. In this example, we were asked to judge a physician's services. We might have used an example where we were asked to judge a lawyer or a teacher, a carpenter or a hairstylist.

The point behind this is that, first, it is with regard to a person's performance that we ordinarily speak in terms competence, and second, that we ordinarily attribute competence only to certain people. These people are professionals who sell, build, or repair things, or who cure, treat, care for, educate or otherwise provide some sort of service to others.

There are some obvious exceptions to this service-to-others aspect of competence. We might be asked, for example, to judge the social competence of a student, or to judge whether or not a defendant is competent to stand trial. In these and a handful of other cases, a person obviously is being judged, but not on the basis of his or her performance of a service.

For present purposes, we shall simply set aside these sorts of exceptions and agree to proceed on the assumption that when we speak of competence, we are referring to one person's judgement of another person's performance in his or her capacity as one who provides a professional service to others.

One thing to note about competence is that when we invoke the term, the tendency is toward qualification. That is, we might say, for example, that "Dr. Smith is a *highly* competent physician" but that "Dr. Jones is *minimally* competent." From a functional point of view, these sorts of "autoclitic" interactions (Skinner, 1957) inform the person who has solicited our judgement as to its "strength" or "intensity." Presumably, this would then have some bearing on whether or not the person, in the short-term, acted in accordance with our judgement, or in the longer-term, sought our judgement on future occasions.

That this tendency toward qualification is strong, but at the same time is apt to be quite narrow, is evident when, for example, we say simply that, "Dr. Marx is competent." Our audience probably would want more from us, for instance, some elaboration, as in, "Can you tell me more?" or some clarification, as in, "What do you mean, *competent*?" In short, our audience would seek some qualification, with an eye toward evoking from us a definite positive or negative judgement. Ordinarily, we give our audience its due. But, in the event that we persist in offering the nondefinitive, "Dr. Marx is competent," our audience likely would understand us to mean that Dr. Marx is just an "average physician," which nowadays is a fairly negative judgement.

The point behind this is that although it seems reasonable to suppose that there would be many shades of competence, in everyday interaction the situation is more black and white. That is, as one who might benefit from the judgement of others, anything short of a strong positive judgement is ordinarily understood as a fairly negative judgement.

If what we seek, and ordinarily obtain, from others is a firm positive or negative judgement of competence, and, barring that, we understand the judgement to be negative, then we may have good reason to question the widespread practice of establishing competency requirements. After all, what these requirements establish are *minimum* standards of competence. But, as we have just seen, to say that a person is "minimally competent," or simply is "competent," is, in the eyes of our audience, to bestow upon that person a fairly negative judgement.

A related issue to note about competence is how relative it is. It is relative in the sense that what is judged as competent by one person might not be judged as such by another person, or by the same person at a later date or in a different setting. As consumers, we often respond to this relativity by "shopping around" for services, by getting a "second opinion," and so forth. As providers, we do what we can to gain a consensus, say, through advertisement, as to the quality of our service. But we realize that "shopping around" does not ensure competent service, and that "truth in advertising" can be a misnomerous proposition. Thus, we maintain various institutions that, on the one hand, inform consumers as to what they can expect, and, on the other hand, restrain providers from unsubstantiated claims to competence.

There is another sense in which competence is relative. For example, what is judged in western cultures as competent medical service in 1994 differs greatly from what it was in 1894. At that time, a competent physician was a "saw bones" who literally did just that. Today's physician is trained in a different kind of medicine, is held to a different professional standard, and is judged as competent on entirely different criteria. Presumably, and hopefully, the same could be said about the physician of the future, or for that matter, tomorrow's lawyers, educators, and maybe even parents.

Let us turn now to the second question, "Why *must* we know what competence is?" There are basically two answers to this question, one focused on the individual, the other focused on the culture, and both focused on the benefits to each.

As individuals, it is plainly clear that we benefit by being on either end of a service that has been performed in a highly competent fashion. That is, benefits accrue to those who receive and to those who provide top quality service. Needless to add, individuals who either provide or receive poor service can claim no benefits. Instead, benefits accrue to individuals who avoid giving and receiving shoddy services. In short, it is in our best interest, in the sense of interacting most effectively in the world, to know what competence is in relation both to ourselves and to others.

Benefits accrue as well to a culture that insists both on informing consumers as to the adequacy of a service that they can expect to receive, and on requiring those who offer a service to show that they are competent to do so. Consumer protection agencies, better business bureaus, and a vast assortment of review and examining boards are examples of how a culture weds services to institutions that foster honesty and accountability and penalize deception and irresponsibility. Furthermore, universities, colleges, trade and professional schools provide specialized training to persons who will one day provide a service to others. The mission of these institutions is to convey to the public, through their graduates, what presently constitutes competent performance within any given service profession. The union of these two aspects of a culture–consumer information and protection, and educational practice and supervision–represent both what is highly valued *in* a culture, and what is highly valuable *to* a culture in terms of its continued growth and prosperity.

What we have said to this point is that we can begin to know what competence is by looking at the circumstances in which people refer one another to competence. What people are talking about are judgements as to the performance of someone who provides a professional service to others. As the interaction unfolds, it is not unusual to see that one person is bent on evoking either a definite positive or negative judgement from the other person. That person usually obliges, but when he or she does not, the other person is likely either to conclude that a negative judgement has been given or that a judgement must be sought from someone, or somewhere, else. But in the end, a judgement of competence is a relative matter, subject to the tide of progress and to the vagaries of interpersonal interaction and individual experience. Knowing this, and at the same time knowing that for our own benefit and for that of the culture, we *must* agree on what competence is, we have established institutions to which we can turn for a trustworthy judgement of competence, for protection from deceptive claims to competence, and for learning how to perform a service in ways that others will judge as competent.

Issues and Implications

Let us now turn to the second set of observations pertaining to how competence bears upon services provided to all people, but especially to all children.

Many people believe that what this country stands for—its "ethos"—is reflected in the Constitution, and that on its pages lie the blueprint for what we, the people, value in ourselves and others. The Preamble to the Constitution contains the words *justice, welfare, posterity*, and *tranquility*. If you ask someone to identify an institution that they would associate with each word, you might get something along the following lines. Justice might evoke the legal establishment, and welfare, in the sense of well-being, might bring to mind the medical/health care establishment. It is perhaps a stretch to presume that posterity might evoke the educational establishment, and yet, what is important about that institution must include the idea that succeeding generations benefit by learning about the contributions made by preceding generations (Skinner, 1968). It is perhaps an even greater stretch, particularly among parents, to say that tranquility might bring to mind parenthood and family. But here again, what is important about this institution must include the idea that children and parents alike thrive in circumstances free from economic hardship, personal distress, and other agitations which threaten the security and serenity of family life (Whaler & Dumas, 1989).

What does all this have to do with competence? The point we develop below is that as we move from those people who have day-to-day contacts with children to those who do not, there is a corresponding increase in the lengths that we go to training people to provide competent service, and to holding these people to certain standards and sanctions. In other words, we seem to require more from those who have the least contact with children, and less from those who have the most contact.

To place this point on firm ground, let us return to the four institutions mentioned above. The legal profession is comprised of attorneys, some of whom are dedicated to the important work of protecting, advancing, and otherwise advocating for the rights of children with disabilities. Generally speaking, these people have very little contact with the children they represent. Instead, the bulk of their time is spent in contact with other attorneys.

With that in mind, consider what we require from an attorney. The path to legal practice ordinarily begins in pre-law, passes through law school and clerkship, ending finally in studying for and passing the bar exam. Those who survive the rigors of this progression presumably are in a position to serve the public in ways that would be judged competent. In the event an attorney is charged with not performing legal services in competent ways, he or she may have to face a panel of judges who have the authority to go as far as forbidding that person from ever again practicing law.

The point here is that these elaborate educational preparations and systems of standards and sanctions all are aimed at ensuring a lifetime of providing competent legal service to youngsters with whom there has been little, and sometimes no, personal contact.

Something similar to this characterizes the medical/health care establishment. For example, a pediatrician ordinarily sees a school-age child once or twice a year for just a few minutes each visit. Children with disability might see their pediatrician on a more regular basis, and may even spend more than a few minutes with them on each occasion. Yet, whatever time they do spend with their doctor is minuscule when compared to the enormous amount of time an individual spends in preparation to practice medicine. That path begins in premed, passes through medical school and internship, followed finally by residency. In the end, the person presumably is in a position to serve the public in ways that would be judged competent. The individual who fails to perform medical services in competent ways faces institutionalized sanctions ranging from a mild reprimand to losing a medical license.

The educational establishment is very different from the legal and medical establishments. Take public school as an example. Teachers are in contact with children roughly six hours a day, five days a week, nine months a year for 13 of a child's first 18 years. Not only is this an enormous amount of time, but it is also an enormous responsibility that in many respects eclipses the responsibility given to physicians and attorneys.

With this is mind, one would think that the depth of training given to teachers would be similar to what is received by physicians and attorneys, and further, that the sorts of institutionalized standards and sanctions which keep those professionals in line with respect to performing their services in competent ways would be in place as well for teachers. Needless to say, this is not how things are in education.

In most states, the path to becoming either a regular or special education teacher ordinarily begins and ends after only a few years of course work, a few months of student teaching, and a few hours of certification exams. In other states, teachers can become certified after a year's supervision without having taken any education courses at all. In short, we do not require very much from prospective teachers, other than asking them to spend an extraordinary amount of time with children and to assume primary responsibility for their intellectual and social development.

What types of standards and sanctions are there for teachers? What happens when a teacher is judged as failing to perform educational services in competent ways? Can a teacher be sued for malpractice? Generally speaking, there are no standards and sanctions; nothing *really* happens to teachers whose competence has been unfavorably judged; and, no, a teacher cannot be sued—at least successfully— for malpractice. Teaching is a privileged occupation, wherein teachers literally are given a license to teach however they want, and to be accountable to no one for most of what they do.

It is a gross understatement to say that this is not an ideal situation. Something must be done to bring the teaching profession in line with the tremendous importance that is attached to it. In short, we must elevate teaching from its present status as a mere occupation to an authentic, legitimate profession. We should require teachers to be as skilled in creating an effective learning environment as surgeons are in wielding a scalpel or attorneys in working a courtroom. And, just as there are standards and sanctions for those professionals, so too should we have the same sorts of institutions for teachers.

The fourth and final institution is parenthood. Parents are the ones who spend the most time with their children, and it is the parents who are most responsible for a child's overall growth and development. Unfortunately, many parents today are ill-prepared, and some even contra-prepared, to raise their children in ways that would be judged by others as competent, that is, attentive, nurturing, supportive, instructive, and so on. Needless to add, there are no institutionalized parenting standards beyond what passes for intuition and common sense, nor are there any institution-alized sanctions other than those attendant to child neglect, endangerment, and abuse.

A few comments about parenting seems in order in light of what was said earlier about competence. What services do parents provide, and to whom do they provide them? Can we speak in terms of competent parenting, and if so, on what basis are we to judge this activity?

The short answers to these questions are that parents do not provide a service as do, say, doctors and lawyers, or carpenters and hairstylists. Parent training is not exactly a fixture of our culture, which is one reason why there are no institutionalized parenting standards and sanctions. Moreover, it is difficult to identify a consumer in the parent-child relationship. As a child matures, however, at some point he or she may rightly be called a consumer in the sense of being able not only to accurately judge competent parenting, but to elect do something about a negative judgement of parenting. Recent and highly publicized cases in which a child has asked the court for what amounts to a "divorce" from a parent illustrates this point. One might say that the culture is the consumer prior to the point at which child is capable of legal activity of that sort, but this argument seems to us to be easier to articulate than it is to defend. In any case, despite the ancient adage that "there is no greater service to man, and to mankind, than parenthood," service is probably not the right term for what a parent does.

Parenting is an activity that is routinely discussed among ourselves. We pass judgement all the time on our own parenting, on the parenting of our parents, and on the parenting of friends, relatives, and even strangers. It is easy to talk about this as a competence issue, which, in fact, is precisely what psychologists do when they speak in terms of assessing functional and dysfunctional parenting (Kendziora & O'Leary, 1993). That literature, together with the basic and applied literatures on child development, parent-child relations, etc., has evolved to the point where it is now possible not only to teach parents and prospective parents *about* child-rearing, but *how* to rear children. It is, of course, this same body of empirical work to which we would turn for guidance in establishing standards for effective parenting.

If we ever get around to owning up to the primary contributor to many of today's social problems, we might see that what is needed in this country is something along the lines of Hawkins' (1974) universal parenthood training. Our recommendation would be to speak in terms of *compulsory* parent training. A network of Parent Training Academies, fashioned after highly successful programs such as the Portage Project (Shearer & Shearer, 1972) but expanded to include a wider range of development and ages, could be wedded either to the educational establishment or to the medical/health care establishment. Whatever their name and configuration, the focus of these academies would be prevention, and their mission to provide parents and would-be parents with more and new opportunities and incentives for learning how to optimize the emotional, social, moral, and intellectual development of their children, from infancy through adolescence and beyond.

Summary and Conclusions

By way of summary and conclusions, competence is one of those "slippery" terms that nevertheless can be harnessed to the interpersonal interactions and institutionalized practices of people who provide and receive some sort of professional service. Interpersonally, competence is a judgement call; culturally, it is also a judgement call, but one that is backed by standards and sanctions.

Competency standards and sanctions attendant to the legal and medical establishments are welcome features of a culture. But, an imbalance is struck when so many resources are devoted to perpetuating competence in these professions, while so few resources are devoted to building competence among teachers and parents. After all, teachers and especially parents are the ones whose days are filled with the lives of children, and it is upon their shoulders that we have placed the enormous responsibility for ensuring that these lives are not wasted. If children, as the saying goes, are a nation's most precious natural resource, we should be doing all that we can to elevate education to a legitimate profession, and to move parenting far beyond the haphazard and unregulated practice that it is today.

A final thought is that we do much to protect ourselves from ourselves, but do little to pursue the sorts of things that would make it unnecessary to be so protected in the first place. Physicians do their best to protect our bodies from the ravages of our destructive lifestyles, and attorneys do their best to protect our civil rights from the bane of our intolerance and hostility toward each other. But a competent teacher, thoroughly versed in the fields of child development, learning, instruction, curriculum, and classroom management, and held to the standards and sanctions of a coherent profession, together with a parent, trained to a standard of excellence in the ways of child-rearing, could help shift the balance of medical and legal practice away from reparation and litigation toward preventing disease and advocating for human rights.

It is a virtual certainty that what we have proposed and implied in terms of teacher and parent competency training, standards, and sanctions will not happen in our lifetimes. But if it never does happen, or if it happens too slowly, or happens without sustained input from behavior analysts, this culture, like this morning's shower water, will eventually end up in the sewer.

References

Hawkins, R. P. (1974). Universal parent-hood training: A proposal for preventative mental health. In R. Ulrich, T. Stachnik, & J. Mabry (Eds.), *Control of human behavior: Behavior modification in education* (pp. 187-192). Glenview, IL: Scott, Foresman.

Jacobellis v. State of Ohio, 378 U.S. 184, 84 S.Ct. 1676, 12 L.Ed.2d 793 (U.S. Ohio, 1964).

Kendziora, K. T., & O'Leary, S. G. (1993). Dysfunctional parenting as a focus for prevention and treatment of child behavior problems. In T. H. Ollendick & R. J. Prinz (Eds.), *Advances in clinical child psychology, Vol. 15* (pp. 175-206). New York: Plenum.

Shearer, M. S., & Shearer, D. E. (1972). The Portage Project: A model for early childhood education. *Exceptional Children, 36*, 210-217.

Skinner, B. F. (1957). *Verbal behavior.* Englewood Cliffs, NJ: Prentice Hall.

Skinner, B. F. (1968). *The technology of teaching.* New York: Appleton-Century-Crofts.

Whaler, R. G., & Dumas, J. E. (1989). Attentional problems in dysfunctional mother-child interactions: An interbehavioral model. *Psychological Bulletin, 105*, 116-130.

Discussion of Ghezzi & Rehfeldt

The Skills to Make Competent Decisions

Duane C. Lord
University of Nevada

Competence is by no means an easy issue upon which to reach agreement. There are few, if any, universal standards of competence which can be applied across all situations. In their paper on competence, Ghezzi and Rehfeldt have elected to share observations on how we can begin to know what competence is, why we must know what it is, and how this pertains to services delivered to all children, including those with developmental disabilities.

In addressing the question, "How can we know what competence is?" Ghezzi and Rehfeldt note that there are two ways in which we go about forming judgements of competence, each with its own drawbacks and limitations. The first is to seek out and rely upon the judgement of another individual, presumably one with some experience or expertise in the area of concern. The second is to rely upon the judgement of a cultural institution established to insure some minimal level of competence in a specified area of expertise. What both of these approaches share is a reliance upon the judgement of others in determining competence. As Ghezzi and Rehfeldt so keenly observe, the two approaches differ most in our ability to determine the "strength" or "intensity" of the judgement being offered.

In the case where we seek the judgement of an individual, we also seek some qualification of the judgement being rendered to provide us with both a measure of relative competence for the person being judged, as well as an measure of the certainty of the judger. If asked to recommend a physician and I reply, "Dr. Smith is highly competent", I am implying that he is *more* competent than some other unnamed physician despite the fact that both have met similar competency requirements. I am also giving an indication of the "strength" of my belief in my judgement regarding Dr. Smith.

The other approach to determining competency relies upon the judgement of social institutions rather than individuals. In general, institutions charged with the responsibility of judging the competency of professionals avoid relative measures of competency and opt for the establishment of minimum standards. Ghezzi and Rehfeldt note that a judgement of "minimally competent" is considered by most to be a fairly negative judgement and questions the widespread cultural practice of establishing competency requirements. Why then, do these institutions engage in such practices? One answer may be that the minimal competency standards for most professions are set by the professions themselves. While a judgement of "less than average" competency by other professionals in the same field would provide consumers with a relative standard upon which to base decisions, it would be disastrous to the profession in question. How many people would return for a second visit to a doctor with a medical license on the office wall certifying that he or she was "below average in competency"? The establishment of minimum competency standards by cultural institutions can thus be understood as a guild issue designed to protect professionals as much as to protect consumers.

Ghezzi and Rehfeldt's answer to their second question, "Why must we know what competence is?" addresses the benefits which accrue to individuals who interact effectively with the world by knowing what competency is, and the benefits which accrue to a culture which provides information regarding competency to consumers while requiring those who deliver a service to show that they are competent to do so. They conclude that in the end, individual judgement of competency is subject to the vagaries of interpersonal interactions and individual experience and that for our own benefit we have established institutions to which we can turn for trustworthy judgements of competence. This conclusion has three basic flaws. First, it ignores the problems related to the minimal competency standards established by these institutions which the authors earlier questioned. Second, there is the question of the trustworthiness of judgements rendered upon professionals by peers with a vested interested in the effect of those judgements on their profession. Finally, it suggests that accepting or rejecting the judgements of institutions as opposed to individuals avoids the vagaries of interpersonal interactions and individual experience.

It is this last issue which deserves special consideration. Whether I rely upon the judgements of another individual or upon those of an institution, I still bring to the situation my history of interactions with one or the other and my own individual experience. In the end, we make our judgements as consumers not on basis of the actual competency of a provider with whom we have had no previous experience, but upon our idiosyncratic history with the individuals or institutions whose advice we have sought. Thus one must not only have access to the information required to make a judgement of competence, but must likewise have the skills to make competent decisions regarding competency.

Ghezzi and Rehfeldt's second set of observations pertain to how competence bears upon services provided to children and states that their central point is that there is an inverse relationship between the amount of formal training required by our culture and the degree of responsibility for a child's development. There are two issues which bear on competence. The first is adequate training, and the second is accountability. Here the authors focus on the two institutions most responsible for a child's development; education and parenting.

Although Ghezzi and Rehfeldt imply that teachers do not receive adequate training, they are in fact required to meet the minimum competency standards of the "trustworthy" institutions the authors cite earlier. The critical issue for education is one of accountability. As a culture, we have only just begun to address this issue in the form of vouchers which would allow parents to select schools which provide the most competent educational services to their children rather than being forced to send their children to schools where the teachers have merely been certified as minimally competent and are not held accountable for their performance. Presumably, in such a free market system, schools would be forced to recruit adequately trained teachers and then hold them accountable for their performance.

The school voucher system requires an even greater degree of competence on the part of parents who, as the authors point out, receive no formal training and are held accountable only in the limited areas of child neglect, endangerment and abuse. Their proposal, calling for compulsory parent training, addresses only the issue of formal training, and then presumably only to the degree of meeting minimal standards. While it clear that some parents are ill-prepared or even contra-prepared to raise their children in ways which would be judged as competent, most parents perform adequately despite their lack of formal training. There probably exists an even greater number of parents capable of making competent judgements regarding the needs of their children but who lack the power or control within our culture necessary to carry them out. Embarking upon a program of universal compulsory parent training without addressing the social issues over which parents have no control would probably do little to "insure domestic tranquility".

In summary, we can begin to know what competency is when we have access to unbiased information regarding the relative performance of individuals or institutions. We must know what competency is and have ourselves acquired the skills to make competent judgements in order to benefit as individuals and as a society. Most importantly, for children to derive benefits, parents must not only know what competency is and have the skills to judge services accordingly, but also be afforded the opportunity to execute those judgements as well.

Chapter 5

Inclusion in Childhood Services:
Ethics and Endocratic Oughtness

William C. Healey

University of Nevada, Las Vegas

This paper discusses perceptions and results of some scientific inquiry regarding the ethics and social philosophy of delivering services to children with developmental disabilities, primarily in schools.

My basic premise which was supported, in part, by the November report on Special Education in *U.S. News and World Report* (Shapiro, 1993) is that both the educational ethics and social philosophy governing services provided seem to wallow in a state of undifferentiated mush, routinely resulting (at best) in pervasive decisions to offer cheapest possible minimalism and (at worst) decisions based on unethical motives: thus, the origin of the title which contends that persons with ultimate authority for approving decisions regarding appropriate services too often act out their power from an unprincipled foundation of endocratic oughtness (to be defined further).

To help prepare the potential critics of this paper, a fundamental set of succinct definitions serves to frame my discussions of educational philosophy, ethics, education and two critical criteria for developmental disability services.

Educational philosophy is a set of individual or group beliefs regarding the constructs of education. Such beliefs can be summarized as high-level principle and/or policy that guides, requires, or directs educational practices and, thereby, affects not only the organization of schools but the lives of people in them. However, few contemporary philosophers would consider their role to be one of providing directives. They seem to prefer the Lochian role as spectator and/or commentator in a ballpark of knowledge! In fact, Plato described the philosopher as the spectator of all time and existence. To be a detached ponderer also can be the role of a sociologist, journalist, or even a special educator. Since leaving the schools and taking refuge in academe, I have become less diplomatic but more detached and philosophical as a spectator of the ethics games determining the delivery of services to children with disability. Special educators, as philosophers, become distinctive by asking such Socratic questions as, "What do you mean?" and "How do you know?" Thus, one seeks the analytical understanding of concepts and the rational justification of beliefs. Special educators, as ethicists, become distinctive when they make choices affecting children's lives. To consider whether or not children ought to have a right to schooling is different from theorizing about or studying how they learn best.

An additional view is that the discourse of the educational philosopher and ethicist necessarily intertwines the theoretical and practical questions (Beloff, 1962). This necessity derives from an observation that educational issues involve judgments about worthy things. To hold this latter view is to ensure the *application* of ethics to the resolution of issues in education.

Ethics is a branch of philosophy concerned with analysis and justification of actions regarding practical, not theoretical, questions. Practical questions consider what ought to be or concern reasons for action.

The resolution of educational issues requires value judgments based on ethical concepts and practices that involve morality (Candee & Kohlberg, 1984) and require a precise definition of education. While central and peripheral uses of the term "education" exist, we need to find the essence that binds both uses.

Education is the understanding of knowledge transmitted in a morally acceptable manner; meaning that, to be educated, persons must be changed for the better while learning interrelationships thought to be valuable and, generally, based on a moral code. Another view is that education provides for worthwhile achievements that are morally unobjectionable or mediated. Education includes trying as well as succeeding.

Unfortunately, many educators, politicians, and parents believe that the aims of education have normative characteristics as an extrinsic end. The concept that *individualization* and *diversity* in achievement are realities that should be valued morally and ethically (as well as protected) in education seems to be lost. Yet, preambles to school policy manuals speak mindlessly of "individual" and often "maximum" potential. Most people probably believe education to be ethically appropriate and worthwhile when it develops the majority's intellectual skills and social character. Unfortunately, the economics and politics of education in this democratic society were designed to support group, not individual achievement (Schlesinger, 1992). Therefore, the proper ethical questions that ought to be explored regarding the decisions and activities of educators are two, subject to specific circumstance: "What is your purpose?" and "What is your motive?" For example, are school board members ethical when their unstated motive for appointment or selection is one of higher political gain, or when one board member buys the land identified confidentially by the superintendent as a future school site. More specific to developmental disabilities, are ethics in education ignored when a young blind child, according to research, typically needs intense instruction in Braille to become competent but will only receive one-half the number of hours needed in his/her designated placement (Huebner, 1989; Sowell & Wardell, 1987)?

The genesis of the point of view in this paper preceded the enactment of The Education for All Handicapped Children's Act, 1975 (PL 94-142), but was reinforced greatly when long-standing, generally covert local issues became overt after being articulated nationally at repetitive oversite hearings on the Act. I shall discuss examples that are not exceptions but are broadly representative, especially among school personnel.

For children with disabilities, educational philosophy has derived from a set of emerging principles and moral values that, redundantly, have been violated or have not represented shared beliefs and commitments, thereby prompting questions for ethicists. Examples abound:

1. The principle of zero reject meant that no children with disability (regardless of type or severity) would be exempted from the right to appropriate educational service. Yet, court records document a multitude of children excluded from school or the usual and customary experiences for children, such as schooling with peers. More subtly and not generally known, Public Law 94-142 outlawed service waiting lists. In return, schools with long-standing lists of children waiting for services simply dropped their traditional service of conducting screening programs to identify all children with signs of disability. They, thereby, could subsequently avoid having to add services for all children in need and, by not screening, eliminate waiting lists in a protective act to be in compliance with the law. Such decisions helped to ensure that new children with special needs would not be identified, certainly not in the numbers previously listed.

2. Using tests with demonstrated problems of validity and reliability continues to violate the principle of non-biased, accurate assessment, and yet the practice is perpetuated to the point of serious ethical practice abandonment.

3. The principles of appropriate educational services based on a team consensus of individual needs have died in the hands of multiple school administrators who have told IEP teams to provide services *available*, not services *needed*. This practice was so widespread and well-known that it evoked a formal policy statement from the U.S. Office of Special Education Programs. That statement admonished all service providers who were receiving federal funds to provide the services that evaluators and IEP team members (by consensus) determined were necessary, regardless of their existing availability. If such were not feasible, the primary care-providers were responsible for seeing that necessary services were made available through referral to an appropriate provider.

4. The local retort to the ethical principle of providing "full services" frequently has resulted in a resounding counter-ethical question, often from school board members, of "How can we agree to provide all services needed for approximately 10% of the school population if that act would bankrupt the school, thus depriving 100%?" Of course, if the board's stated position of avoiding bankruptcy for the general good were not rooted in *fact*, then we could claim another breech of ethics.

5. Now we come to the current "societal principle" recently inferred from new law regarding persons with disabilities, which is the movement toward "full inclusion". Perhaps the Americans with Disability Act (ADA) best represents

the principle and elaborates it as a goal for implementation. The inclusion movement in preschools and schools is a natural extension of the goal emanating from the ADA. However, some persons who could be considered zealots are misusing the principle and the goal, seemingly, to do what Kant admonished us to do, which was act toward humanity as an end, never as a means. However, seeking to accomplish the end (which is full inclusion) without evaluating how worthwhile benefits are derived and how unnecessary negative consequences are prevented in achieving the end is to me an unethical decision. Ends ought not be chosen simply because they are means for the individual or group to achieve endocratic power, if not premature praise for accomplishing an end that has unknown effects. Call this the fallacy of misguided correctness.

Class conscious officials who strongly influence service delivery practices have beliefs based on no philosophy or a flawed philosophy regarding persons with disability and their needs, such as schooling. A number of school personnel and others would extend the right to schooling only to some children, not all (Healey, 1990). In fact, the history of education in the United States is replete with examples of exclusion for children of difference, including race and disabilities.

Use of a somewhat dangerously simplified theoretical construct (in adherence to restrictions on length of this presentation) may help to explain why persons responsible for human services may have questionable principles and commit unethical acts.

Ethics is a powerful mental conviction that gives internal orders based on a set of moral principles dealing with good and bad and/or duty and obligation. For example, some human service providers have criteria for determining preferred or proper professional standards and practices. Arieti (1972) called this internal ruling "endocracy" (for the Greek words *endon* and *kratein*: to rule from within). As young children, we, initially learn to trust people. People, also, teach us that we must do certain things. These external expectations or commands become "a duty" for which we are responsible. As this external duty becomes internalized, it transfers from an objective command to a subjective phenomenon because of psychological processes that now convert the command to an internalized imperative attitude. We refer to this attitude as the tendency to obey, and philosophers generally would identify the tendency as a sense of "oughtness." Thus, oughtness psychologically tells one that s/he wants to do something because s/he must do it. The previously external command is now subjectivized as an internal endocratic power; and if you fail to do what you feel you ought, you learn to experience guilt (which you later may learn to suppress). Finally, endocratic oughtness is the human dimension that enables one to commit to an end that is not achievable immediately, such as becoming pregnant to give birth nine months later or creating plans to be completed in ten years.

The fact that inclinations toward duty, morality, or oughtness requires complex psychological processes has little to do with their validity or their perpetuation. Although they begin at an interpersonal level, they get played out in later years on impersonal stages. School, religion, law, culture (organized society) all can reinforce or erode the trust learned at an early age (Kohlberg, 1978). An internal sense of oughtness or inner dictate related to a basic instinct (i.e., survival) may become more important than a principle of action. When this happens, the sense of selfish independence may cloud and, subsequently, overrule the content of principle or morality. At that point, one's actions may not only become undesirable and constitute self-promotion or self-protection, the psychological sense of oughtness may become divorced from one's earliest concepts of goodness. The values of principles are overpowered by less than rightful actions. Some people grow to accept behavioral habits of life and action not driven by moral principles but by such characteristics as fear (usually of being ostracized), self-promotion, lack of knowledge and/or analysis of consequences, and denial of probable effect.

The "truth" becomes a lie. Unfortunately, decisions regarding the acceptance and proper "inclusion" of persons with disabilities are made too often by persons whose moral integrity has become flawed and/or who may be lacking in appropriate experiences. Unlike the overanxious inclusionists, they are unable to apply Kant's teaching that any act to treat humanity, whether in your own person or that of another, ought always be as an end and never as a means only (Kant, 1940). Therefore, one can argue that oughtness is valid only when coupled with actions that derive from high-order concepts of just and good principles (e.g., justice).

Actions based on bad endocratic motives can create consequences of horror in degrees seldom seen from other human behavior. Any persons who permit themselves to be possessed by self-serving endocracy act blindly, often confusedly, toward proposed actions of perceived correctness or appropriateness that others consider the good thing to do in spite of contra-opinions. Endocracy is considered good when associated with good principles of action, which must be connected by reason and logic that achieve the moral imperative identified by people of the same group, or better yet, all humanity. Unfortunately, individuals and groups of people can be observed as yielding unthinkingly to such "in" movements as "full inclusion" of all persons with disability. Some do this without questioning ethical motive or knowledge of the advocates or criteria for demonstrable benefit.

Neither Freudians nor neo-Freudians have been enlightening when explaining ethics and ethical behaviors. Twisting of thought, for example, undoubtedly, led Hitler to a distorted concept that he ought to achieve "greatness" for the Third Reich through the commission of barbarous behaviors. We are capable of unpredictable thoughts and actions because of the myriad of personal experiences we encounter over time with symbol systems, concepts, and behaviors that have negative and positive effects on self. Ethics, the study of moral behavior, is determined by our relationship to others within a cultural framework. Self-protection, self-gratification and self-aggrandizement are clearly not ethical aims.

Few "full inclusion" advocates, including principled special educators, would dispute the moral desirability of the inclusion principle or the practice of inclusion as an ethical educational aim. However, one ought to return to the arguable definition of "education" as the intentional transmission of what is worthwhile (Peters, 1967); because attention ought to be focused not only on the *manner* of education, but also on the *matter*. We need to create an environment in which the included child and peers can grow socially and learn through worthwhile experiences at an appropriate, individualized rate. An ethical obligation exists for inclusion theorists and enthusiasts to study and document these outcomes. For example, serious scientific inquiry ought to turn to setting and evaluating the *criteria* for both social growth and worthwhile learning. At the end of a child's formal education, and along the way, an obligatory professional achievement ought to be obtaining answers for the questions of "What criteria best depict the benefits and detriments of inclusion?" and "What criteria for worthwhile learning has the included child met?" Worthwhile here simply means leading to an improved quality of life for the individual as well as humankind—a concept not without controversy. For instance, some deaf persons contend that full inclusion with hearing children and not deaf peers is discriminatory and inappropriate (Nover, 1993). To the degree that such a placement for a deaf child could be determined to be a deliberately inappropriate placement for learning, such a decision ought to be labeled as unethical.

If or when we detect unethical behavior, it ought to be described overtly, not covertly. Such behavior most often is seen in persons quietly characterized as flashing two faces, drifting in the direction of the prevailing wind, or posturing to protect a significant body part. Thus, humanity now is conditioned to expect, and too often sanctions by its inaction, a subgroup who have grown from the womb to become expert endocratic educational technocrats devoid of ethical principles. This segment of the population ought to be named the "steadfast of standardless conduct," or the unethicists. These people ought not be employed as educators or other specialists who provide services for persons with disability because their motives and behavior do not permit them to model three critical criteria for education.

Educational worthwhileness offers three characteristics: a) freedom and commitment to live out an ethical life; b) the provision of opportunity to develop individuality; and c) full acceptance of the laws of nature, something many technicians who don the cloak of "educator" either have not thought about, do not understand, or refuse to accept. Educators (as ethicists) ought to be compelled to address such questions as "What ought I do to help each individual have a good life?" Neither all educators nor society in general have been willing to practice the most ethical way of living nor have they set such a goal as the highest aim of education or life. To be ethical is to ensure dignity, justice, and love while eliminating pain, including evil and intrapsychic suffering, when such anguish is not of nature but, especially, is inflicted by one person unto another. So long as any educators, as potential leaders in the society, reject full inclusion of all individuals and fail to serve them in a *manner* and with the necessary *matter* required to achieve endocratic power and pleasure in living, then those educators ought to be dismissed into the ranks of the truly bigoted among society and ought to be placed in programs serving the antihuman and unethical.

Yet, a more positive preventive prescription could and, perhaps, ought to be articulated. Humans, primarily, learn by trail-and-error. When punishment exists for making errors, they eventually learn that punishment often can be avoided through cover-up, deceit, hypocrisy, subterfuge, and breaking of ethical codes (Dil & Fuller, 1983). Perhaps we ought to find productive options to punishment for mistakes and fully implement the three characteristics of educational worthwhileness among all humankind. This ought to be done, especially, in setting criteria for educators who will all be providers of service for persons with disability. Such providers ought to delight in demonstrating an endocratic integrity and respect for others that is recognized universally as the purest of ethical thinking and caretaking. To have living an ethical life be a primary aim of education raises two final questions, which are, "Ought such an ideal be reached?" and "Will it ever be?"

References

Arieti, S. (1972). *The will to be human*. New York: Quadrangle Books.

Beloff, J. (1962). *The existence of mind*. New York: Citadel Press.

Candee, D., & Kohlberg, L. (1984). The relationship of moral judgment to moral action. In L. Kohlberg (Ed.), *Essays on moral development: Vol. 2. The philosophy of moral development*. San Francisco: Harper and Row.

Dil, A., & Fuller, B. (1983). *Humans in universe*. New York: Mouton.

Healey, W. C. (1990). *School administrator's attitudes toward the provisions in Public Law 94-142*. Unpublished manuscript.

Huebner, K. M. (1989). Shaping educational intervention for blind and visually impaired learners in response to social change. *Re: View, 21*, 145-152.

Kant, I. (1785). *Fundamental principles of the metaphysics of morals* (pp. 22-23). London: Longmans Green.

Kohlberg, L. (1978). Revisions in the theory and practice of moral development. In W. Damon (Ed.), *New directions for child development: Moral development*. New York: Wiley.

Nover, S. (1993, December). *Our voices, our vision: Politics of deaf education*. Paper presented at a meeting of the Council of Education for the Deaf, Washington, DC.

Peters, R. S. (1967). *Ethics and education*. Palo Alto, California: Scott, Foresman.

Schlesinger, A. M. (1992). *The disuniting of America: Reflections on a multicultural society*. New York: W. W. Norton.

Shapiro, J. P. (1993, December 13). Separate and unequal. *U.S. News and World Report*, pp. 46-60.

Sowell, V., & Wardell, K. T. (1987). Outreach teacher training programs: Rural delivery of services on site. *Journal of Visual Impairment & Blindness, 81*, 14-18.

Discussion of Healey

Holding Inclusion to a Higher Standard

Stephen L. Rock

Nevada University Affiliated Program in Developmental Disabilities

In Healey's article, "Inclusion in Childhood Services: Ethics and Endocratic Oughtness", he identifies a variety of ethical issues in special education. He describes ethical conflicts where frequent or common practices in special education deviate from the principles of the Individuals with Disabilities Act (IDEA, previously Education for All Handicapped Children Act, 1975). Healey cites several examples: school districts that find ways to exclude children in spite of the principle of zero reject; use of assessment instruments and practices that discriminate against members of racial and cultural minorities in spite of the principle of nondiscriminatory testing; and others. His final example raises the central theme of the article: advocating for full inclusion of children with disabilities with their peers without disabilities when the benefits of inclusion are assumed. Healey goes on to discuss the dynamics of individuals exhibiting unethical behavior. He attributes unethical behavior to unprincipled endocratic oughtness, going along with the crowd or "perceived correctness or appropriateness that others consider the good thing to do in spite of contra-opinions." He states that "Unfortunately, decisions regarding the acceptance and proper 'inclusion' of persons with disabilities are made too often by persons whose moral integrity has become flawed and/ or who may be lacking in appropriate experience."

Healey accurately identifies a number of very real ethical problems in special education practices. He is also accurate in that very often in the day-to-day practice of completing paper work, balancing budgets, working to meet the needs of all the children in a classroom, and attending meetings, some administrators, special educators, and others forget the basic principles upon which quality special education is based and is addressed through IDEA. We should, as Healey suggests, respond strongly and overtly to unethical behavior. However, those of us involved in preparing special educators and other human service professionals must also assume our responsibility. University programs must do a better job of preparing educational professionals to advocate for and defend high quality education and services.

While Healey points out some important ethical problems in special education, in his discussion of endocratic oughtness as it applies to advocates of inclusion, he seems to makes several assumptions that are not tenable about the current state of special education services and the movement toward inclusion of individuals with disabilities. In criticizing those who advocate for inclusion because they have not considered whether students with disabilities and without disabilities will "grow socially and learn through worthwhile experiences at an appropriate, individualized rate," he implicitly assumes that this is always occurring in noninclusionary special education programs or appears to hold inclusion to a higher standard. On the contrary, several large scale studies have examined the effects of special education services and have generally found mixed results or no difference between those who received services and those who did not. Healey also assumes that people are "yielding unthinkingly to such 'in' movements as 'full inclusion' of all persons with disability." While inclusion is beginning to become more popular at the national level and with the media, at the local level parents and special educators advocating for inclusion are most often in the minority, frequently are ostracized for their position, and are thought to be unrealistic idealists (a terrible thing for a teacher?). Healey also suggests that proponents of inclusion have not evaluated "how worthwhile benefits are derived" or asked questions such as "What criteria best depict the benefits and detriments of inclusions?"

These are questions that consistently must be asked and answered with careful consideration to ensure the quality and appropriateness of any human service program. Inclusionary special education programs are no different. However, while there are still many questions that need to be addressed in assessing an inclusionary model of special education services, there has been considerable discussion and investigation into these issues, and there is evidence to support the practice of inclusion. Students with disabilities who are included in regular education demonstrate: a) increased likelihood of integration in future environments, b) decreased rates of inappropriate behavior and increased rates of social initiations, c) improved personal appearance, d) increased social interactions and social responsiveness, e) enhanced skill acquisition and generalization, f) increased parental expectations for child's future, g) increased proportion of IEP objectives attained, h) improved attitudes of community employers, i) increased employment in supported or competitive employment jobs, and j) increased normalized living arrangements (Halvorsen & Sailor, 1990). Further, in Oberti v. Board of Education of Borough of Clementon School District (1993) and Board of Education, Sacramento City Unified School District v. Holland (1992), in addition to a January 1994 ruling in the latter case not yet referenced, the court found that there was sufficient evidence to support placement of children with severe disabilities into general education classrooms. In Oberti, the court felt that the original intent of the law was to maintain children with disabilities in the general classroom to the greatest extent possible. Schools district must clearly explore and exhaust ways to support methods of supporting the child in the regular classroom before moving to more restrictive environment.

Finally, Healey suggests that for something to be educationally worthwhile that it leads to: a) freedom to live an ethical life; b) development of individuality; and

c) acceptance of natural laws. Education should provide not only the manner but the matter to achieve these goals, and educators should determine how we may help each person achieve these goals. These criteria address critical ethical issues in services to people with disabilities. Unfortunately, Healey spends too little time discussing the criteria and their implications for special education programs. Several important questions are left unanswered such as, "Who determines if these criteria are met?" and "What is the role of the individual with disabilities in choosing?" In establishing any criterion for evaluating programs for individuals with disabilities, it is critical that the role of individuals with disabilities and their families be clearly stated. Too often in our efforts to help, we have disenfranchised individuals with disabilities and their families, because as professionals we knew best. Increasingly, individuals with disabilities are demonstrating that if given the opportunity to make real choices about their own lives they can be much more independent and productive than was ever imagined. The criteria of natural laws is especially vague and open to a variety of interpretations. If it means there are natural limits that must be respected, it is disturbing. Children with disabilities and their families have consistently rewritten laws of nature when they have ignored the best professional advice and warnings about the natural limitations of disabilities. Children with Down Syndrome, who were expected to die before adolescence and ruin their families' lives, are adults who live independently, work, and make their families very proud and glad they didn't listen. Children walk who were told they would never crawl, children read who were told they would never attend school, and adults have their homes when they were told they would always be institutionalized. To inhibit the potential of any individual because of arbitrary, preconceived limitations of a disability is clearly unethical.

Within a limited space, Healey raises some very critical and complex ethical issues, not often discussed, in providing appropriate educational services to students with disabilities. Individuals with disabilities, their families, and professionals from a variety of disciplines need to discuss the ethical and lifelong implications of the decisions made in providing special education services in both segregated and inclusionary settings.

References

Board of Education, Sacramento City Unified School District v. Holland, 786 F.Supp. 874, 73 Ed. Law Rep. 969 (E.D.Cal. 1992).

Halvorsen, A. T., & Sailor, W. (1990). Integration of students with severe and profound disabilities: A review of research. In R. Gaylord-Ross (Ed.), *Issues and research in special education*, Vol. 1 (pp. 110-172). New York: Teachers College Press.

Oberti v. Board of Education of Borough of Clementon School District, 995 F.2d 1204, 83 Ed. Law Rep. 1009 (3rd Cir. N.J. 1993).

Chapter 6

The Right to Effective Behavioral Treatment

Ron Van Houten

Mount Saint Vincent University

In May of 1986 the Association for Behavior Analysis (ABA) established a task force on the Right to Effective Behavioral Treatment (Van Houten et al., 1988). This task force was charged with examining client's rights as they apply to behavioral treatment. Although the scope of this work was to include the entire range of behavioral services it was to be specifically weighted toward the area of developmental disabilities. The composition of the task force included seven prominent behavior analysts each of whom had conducted extensive research in the area of developmental disabilities.

The task force identified seven specific client rights. One of these rights concerned a general human right: the right to services whose overriding goal is the individual's personal welfare. Another right affirmed the client's right to treatment by a competent behavior analyst. This right is essentially one to be addressed by professional organizations regulating the practice of behavior analysis. The four remaining rights related to the actual practice of behavior analysis.

In this paper I would like to discuss those client rights pertaining to the practice of behavior analysis. These rights include the right to a therapeutic living environment, the right to behavioral assessment and ongoing evaluation, the right to a behavioral curriculum that teaches functional skills, and the right to the most effective behavioral treatment procedures available. In each case these rights affirm a commitment to our roots in radical behaviorism and reflect our unique way of viewing the relationship between people and their environment. This presentation is based on my understanding of the these rights. Although the membership of ABA has endorsed these rights, the interpretations presented in this paper are the sole responsibility of the author and do not represent the official position of the Association for Behavior Analysis.

The Right to a Therapeutic Living Environment

Favell and McGimsey (1993, p. 27) state "the definition of an effective treatment environment must be *functional*, specifying how its individual aspects and composite milieu actually effect the behavior of the individuals." Thus the characteristics of a therapeutic living environment should be empirically determined. All to often the characteristics of an ideal environment as suggested by advocates are based on philosophical rather than empirical arguments. For example, some feel that all leisure materials should be age appropriate. However items that are not judged age appropriate may better reinforce the behavior of those using them and may also be more effective at teaching functional skills. The pressure to be politically correct should not overshadow what should be our major concern, the client's interests.

Favell and McGimsey (1993) also suggest that time spent engaged in activities is a good measure of environment acceptability. They suggest that the environment cannot shape behavior unless the individual engages in behavior. High level of social behavior and high levels of nonsocial, environmental manipulation are necessary conditions in order for differential reinforcement to elaborate one's repertoire, and studies have shown that high levels of engagement are inversely correlated with the occurrence of problem behaviors (Horner, 1980).

Although high levels of engagement are desirable, I suggest that the environment also meet the following criteria: 1) The environment should reinforce behavior which is predominantly socially mediated, or mediated by complex environmental contingencies that involve the manipulation of common mechanical and electronic devices; 2) The environment should shape diversity in behavior; and 3) the environment should shape a high percentage of fine motor behaviors.

The first criterion insures that the environment does not predominantly support simple behavior maintained by sensory consequences such as rocking, hand gazing, etc. Instead, the environment should support behavior that is mediated by other people or the products of technology. These behaviors are likely to tie into teaching contingencies and environmental shaping. The second criteria is that the environment support diversity. A diverse repertoire allows an individual to adapt to a variety of environments and would be supported by a variety of reinforcers reducing the likelihood of satiation. The third criteria recommends the design of an environment that supports the development of fine motor behavior. The value of fine motor behavior in many complex activities is evident, however, and environment that supports the development of such a repertoire must also be one that will respond to approximations and shape relevant behavior. The use of computers that could differentially respond to different clients could perhaps provide such a responsive environment.

Favell and McGimsey (1993) also state that an acceptable environment is the least restrictive alternative. They point out that access, proximity, or scale do not define a least restrictive setting. They state that measures of restrictiveness should be based upon changes in the client's behavior rather than assumptions and ideals. If a change in environment does not lead to greater freedom of movement or an increase in behaviors associated with reinforcement, it would be difficult to argue that it is less restrictive. Indeed all issues of this kind should be argued on the basis of these data.

The Right to Behavioral Assessment and Ongoing Evaluation

An important facet of a behavioral assessment is the determination of the function of a behavior, or the identification of the reinforcers maintaining it. Such an analysis is termed a functional analysis. Although the methodology involved in performing a functional analysis is not yet an exact science, Iwata, Vollmer, Zarcone, and Rogers (1993) have proposed that we classify behavioral function along two dimensions. These dimensions are positive vs. negative reinforcement and socially mediated vs. automatic or nonsocially mediated reinforcement. Iwata et al. (1993) use the term positive and negative reinforcement in the traditional way, and they use the term automatic reinforcement in the same manner as Skinner (1953). This arrangement is diagrammed in Figure 1 below.

There are three types of systematic and empirical functional analysis: 1) Those based on the systematic variation of establishing operations (Michael, 1982); 2) those based on differential reinforcement; 3) and those based on omission training or the use of a DRO schedule. A diagram of a functional analysis based on the

Figure 1

Classification of Behavioral Function

	Positive Reinforcement	Negative Reinforcement
Socially Mediated	Banging Head Produces Attention	Tantrum Produces Task Termination
Not Socially Mediated	Slapping Face Produces Noise and Vibration	Pinching Skin Produces Endorphins

Figure 2

Functional Analysis
Based on Establishing Operations

	High Attention	Low Attention
High Demand	1	2
Low Demand	3	4

Results

High in 1 + 2, Low in 3 + 4 = Socially mediated negative reinforcement

High in 2 + 4, Low in 1 + 3 = Socially mediated positive reinforcement

High in 1 + 2 + 4, Low in 3 = Socially mediated pos. + neg. reinforcement

High in 1 + 2 + 3 + 4 = Suspect nonsocially mediated reinforcement
(further testing with a high and low stimulation condition would follow)

In all functional analysis the conditions tested must be related to conditions
in the natural setting. Not any task or type of attention will do.

systematic variation of establishing operations is presented in Figure 2. Carr and Durand (1985) performed such an analysis to determine if the function of the behavior problems of four behaviorally delayed children were maintained by positive reinforcement in the form of attention, negative reinforcement in the form of escape from a teaching task, or a combination of the two. Although this analysis successfully determined the function of the behavior for each of these children, it was incomplete because it did not cover the case where the behavior continued to occur under high attention and low demand. It is usually assumed that the behavior under this condition is maintained by other socially mediated reinforcers or some form of automatic or nonsocially mediated reinforcement. The addition of further testing with a high and a low stimulation condition while the client is alone would help to test whether automatic reinforcement is a major factor maintaining a behavior but it does not address the issue of negative automatic reinforcement. Perhaps an additional condition that involves the systematic addition of endorphins would address this question because it is assumed that such behavior is negatively reinforced by endorphin production that reduces aversive stimuli resulting from a disease.

This type of functional analysis can be very useful, but like all functional analyses has two potential problems. First, if you do not test conditions relevant to why the behavior occurs in the natural setting you will not get useful results. For example, if the type of attention varied under the high and low attention condition was not the type maintaining the behavior, or if the type of sensory stimulation provided under a high sensory stimulation condition was not the type maintaining the behavior, the results of the functional analysis would not be useful. Second, if powerful reinforcers were introduced in the functional analysis that were not present in the person's natural environment, you could detect a false positive relationship. This is why it is essential that the behavior analyst test potential reinforcers present in the natural setting that are strongly suspected of being important in maintaining the behavior. The difficult facet of conducting a functional analysis is determining what reinforcers you will set the analysis up to test. It is essential that the behavior analyst have the necessary clinical skills to identify the most probable potential reinforcers maintaining a behavior problem.

The second and third type of functional analysis involve the use of differential reinforcement procedures. The second type involves comparing conditions where the response produces the suspected reinforcer with conditions where the response does not produce the suspected reinforcer. The diagram for this type of analysis is presented in Figure 3. If the behavior occurs frequently when it is followed by a suspected reinforcer, such as attention, but not when it is not followed by attention, we can assume the behavior is being maintained by attention. Similarly, if the behavior frequently occurs when it is followed by the termination of a particular activity such as speech therapy, but does not occur when the activity is not terminated, we can assume the behavior is maintained by escape from speech therapy. Again the model gets into trouble when one attempts to identify automatic

Figure 3

Functional Analysis
Based on Differential Reinforcement

	Response Does Not Produce Stimulus	Response Produces Stimulus
Response Terminates Stimulus	1	2
Response Does Not Terminate Stimulus	3	4

Results

High in 1 + 2, Low in 3 + 4 = Socially mediated negative reinforcement

High in 2 + 4, Low in 1 + 3 = Socially mediated positive reinforcement

High in 1 + 2 + 4, Low in 3 = Socially mediated pos. + neg. reinforcement

High in 1 + 2 + 3 + 4 = Suspect nonsocially mediated reinforcement
(further testing with a sensory reinforcement present versus
sensory extinction could follow)

sources of reinforcement. The addition of a contingent sensory reinforcement condition vs. a sensory extinction condition would be of assistance in determining if the behavior is maintained by automatic positive reinforcement. Determining if it is maintained by automatic negative reinforcement might involve the use of an endorphin antagonist to produce an extinction condition.

The third type of functional analysis involves the use of omission training and is presented in Figure 4. Experimental control is determined by comparing conditions associated with the presumed reinforcer made contingent upon the behavior with the presumed reinforcer delivered when the behavior does not occur. It is less clear how this method could be employed to test for sources of potential automatic reinforcement.

Figure 4

Functional Analysis
Based on Omission Training

	Response Starts DRO Interval for Stimulus	Response Produces Stimulus
Response Terminates Stimulus	1	2
Response Starts DRO Interval for Stimulus Termination	3	4

Results

High in 1 + 2, Low in 3 + 4 = Socially mediated negative reinforcement

High in 2 + 4, Low in 1 + 3 = Socially mediated positive reinforcement

High in 1 + 2 + 4, Low in 3 = Socially mediated pos. + neg. reinforcement

High in 1 + 2 + 3 + 4 = Suspect nonsocially mediated reinforcement

The three methods of functional analysis illustrated here are all highly structured. Functional analysis can also be performed in a less formal manner. Examples of less structured methods include the use hands on assessment, the use of sequence analysis, the use of interviews, and the use of behavioral checklists. Although these methods can be helpful, some data indicated that the use of behavioral checklists (Zarcone, Rodgers, Iwata, Rourke, & Dorsey, 1991) and descriptive or sequence analysis (Lerman & Iwata, 1993) can be unreliable. The degree of functional analysis required before implementing a treatment is related to the likely consequences of operating under the wrong assumption. If there are no serious consequences expected, it may be more cost effective to proceed with the most likely hypothesis and perform a more formal analysis only if the chosen intervention fails to work. If however, the consequences of operating under the wrong assumption could be harmful it would be wise to perform a formal functional analysis before proceeding.

There are a number of ways that assuming the wrong hypothesis could lead to harmful results. First if the behavior is severe and action is required immediately, assuming the wrong function would delay solving the problem. Problems that could lead to serious consequences such as injury, or loss of a placement need to be addressed rapidly. Second, assuming the wrong function could lead to the use of a more intrusive treatment than would otherwise be necessary. The use of an intrusive and ineffective treatment could produce new problems and might even decrease sensitivity to an effective treatment. Third, the use of ineffective treatment procedures can decrease the likelihood that staff will follow through when a new treatment plan is developed following a formal functional analysis.

The degree of functional analysis required is also related to the overall time lost in performing the analysis. Early demonstrations were labor and time intensive lasting weeks or months. In recent years more efficient functional analysis procedures have been developed. These procedures can often reliably determine the function of a behavior in a single afternoon (Wacker & Steege, 1993), or even in a one hour session. For example, the data in Figure 5 shows the results of part of an analysis performed to determine the function of face slapping that did not vary with task difficulty or when attention was made contingent upon slapping or when a DRO on slapping was in effect. In order to test the hypothesis that this behavior was maintained by its sensory consequences, a vibrator placed near the area that the boy slapped was turned on and off during alternating five minute periods. The results clearly revealed that the behavior only occurred when the vibrator was switched off. These data provided reasonably good evidence that face slapping was maintained by its automatic consequences.

As functional analysis procedures become more efficient, their use should become more universal. A major drawback is the individual input required. It is not likely that a functional analysis will prove successful unless relevant discriminative stimuli, setting events, and reinforcers are included in the analysis. Such an analysis needs to be tailored to each individual case and cannot follow the same cookbook style for different individuals.

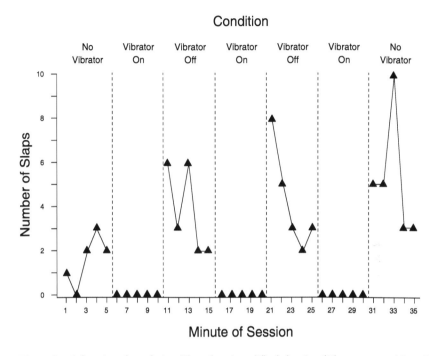

Figure 5. A functional analysis of face slapping. The behavior did not vary with task difficulty or when attention was made contingent upon slapping or when a DRO on slapping was in effect. This figure shows, however, that it did vary with the presence of vibration near the area that the boy slapped, leading to the conclusion that face slapping was maintained by its sensory consequences.

Identification and categorization of precursor stimuli also plays an important role in treatment (Rolider & Van Houten, 1993). Stimulus conditions may serve as discriminative stimuli, eliciting stimuli, or setting events. A complete analysis will involve the identification of those stimuli relevant to the problem at hand. Once relevant discriminative and eliciting stimuli have been identified they can be removed and then systematically reintroduced or faded in (Carr, McConnachie, Levin, & Kemp, 1993; Rolider & Van Houten, 1993).

The client also has the right to have treatment decisions based on empirical data. In each case the efficacy of the treatment plan should be evaluated based on data. If the treatment does produce an acceptable change, further analysis and treatment alterations should be initiated until an acceptable change occurs. The effects of the treatment should also be monitored over time and changes should be considered if the behavior begins to return to pretreatment levels. Additional functional analysis may be required at this point because behavior constantly evolves, as may its function, in response to changes in the environment.

The Right to a Behavioral Curriculum that

Teaches Functional Skills

An individual has a right to programs that teach functional skills. This right stipulates that people have a right to programs that will provide them with repertoires that will be useful in their daily living. From a behavioral perspective functional behaviors are socially acceptable ways to increase the probability of positive and negative reinforcement in ways that will not lead to punishment, or being placed in a more restrictive setting. Before selecting behaviors the therapist should identify how the acquisition of the behavior will benefit the client. Because treatment resources are finite, the highest priority should be assigned to teaching pivotal skills that will, when changed, result in collateral changes in other behaviors as well (Koegel & Frea, 1993).

In order to teach functional skills the therapist needs to examine the contingencies in the natural environment and insure that the topography of the response to be taught will actually be reinforced in the natural setting. Day and Horner (1990) have also documented the importance of response efficiency in determining whether a behavior will be maintained. Behavior that is involves a high response cost is not likely to be emitted if an inappropriate alternative behavior is concurrently available that is easier to emit. Factors pertaining to response cost include how effortful the behavior is, how much time it takes to emit the behavior, how long it takes to produce reinforcement, and the schedule of reinforcement associated with the behavior (Horner & Billingsley, 1988).

Carr, et al. (1993) also recommend teaching appropriate behaviors that will access the same reinforcers that are currently maintaining problem behaviors. If attention maintain inappropriate behavior, teach the person more acceptable ways to obtain attention. If the person engages in problem behavior to get help, teach the person more appropriate ways to request help.

Setting events can also play an important role in treatment. A setting event is a stimulus-response interaction that will change a subsequent stimulus response relationship (Bijou & Baer, 1961; Kantor, 1959). Examples of important setting events are schedule changes, factors that will interfere with sleep, and serious disruptions. Setting events can be altered as part of a treatment plan (Kennedy & Itkonen, 1993) or clients can be taught functional behavior that will alter setting events that are related to problematic behavior.

The Right to the Most Effective

Behavioral Treatment Procedures Available

The right to effective treatment is to a great extent the right to data based decision making. Treatment selection, should be based primarily on the scientific literature and the persons documented response to various treatment options that have been used in the past. Axelrod, Spreat, Berry and Moyer (1993) have proposed a decision-making model for selecting the optimal treatment procedure. They recommend first determining whether an significant performance discrepancy exists between actual and expected performance and the importance of this discrepancy has to be weighed. Performance discrepancies can be assessed in part by comparing the person's performance with the performance of someone judged to be competent at the task. Next they recommend conducting a structural and functional analysis. This is followed by a historical analysis of the person, behavior and procedure. This analysis is performed by examining the scientific literature and the clients records, interviewing people close to the case, and interacting with the client. Once these three steps have been completed it should be possible to make predictions about the likely effects and side effects of the treatment, and the risks that would be entailed by the client and the program implementors.

Once these three steps have been completed Axelrod et al. (1993) recommend choosing the least restrictive *effective* treatment. To the greatest extent possible one must eschew ineffective treatments that a functional analysis indicate would be ineffective. They state that "in the case of dangerous behaviors, people are entitled to the least restrictive effective treatment from the outset" (Axelrod et al., 1993, p 189). Choosing the least restrictive treatment involves weighing many factors (Van Houten et al., 1988). The overall level of restrictiveness of a procedure "is a combined function of its absolute level of restrictiveness, the amount of time required to produce a clinically acceptable outcome, and the consequences associated with delayed intervention" (Van Houten et al., 1988, pp. 383-384). This analysis is made more complicated by the differing histories of the client. For example, determining the overall level of restrictiveness of a procedure may seem relatively straight forward. However, they are no more straight forward in the practice of behavior analysis than they are in the practice of dentistry or medicine. For example, having a shallow cavity filled without freezing may be very intrusive for some people but for others less intrusive than having it frozen. Similarly some people would find surgery under local anesthetic more intrusive that the same surgery under general anesthetic, the converse will also be true for other people. This is the main problem with developing actuarial hierarchies of restrictiveness based on surveys. However, it is possible to objectively answer some questions such as: How rapidly the treatment should work; The risks involved if no treatment is implemented or if a slower acting treatment is implemented; The likely side effects of the treatment and risk of harm to the client or program providers; The amount of discomfort or embarrassment the procedure may produce; and, The degree to which the procedure would remove the person from other programs.

Programs that entail exposing the person to risk should also be reviewed by a peer review committee made up of other behavior analysts. The job of the peer review committee is to determine whether the treatment is clinically appropriate in relationship to the scientific literature, and whether it represents a sound application of behavioral principles. A procedure may also need the approval of a human rights committee. The separate mandate of the human rights committee would be examining issues surrounding consent, and whether the benefits of the treatment more than offset the social costs. Because a human rights committee is typically made up of lay people, they should not make treatment decisions. It is interesting to speculate why a human rights committee might wish to specify treatment in the case of behavioral engineering but would not wish to do so in the case of building a bridge.

One reason might be most lay persons lack of experience in building bridges, compared with their wealth of experience being involved with other people's behavior. Another reason may be related to the relative infancy of our technology. We have only been developing this technology over the past 30 years, and we do not yet have sufficiently numerous and diverse successes necessary to command that degree of respect. Further the connection between basic and applied research is often rather tenuous (Johnston, 1993). Johnston (1993) in an attempt to distinguish behavioral technology from common sense, and folklore, offered the following definition. "Behavioral technology refers to behavior change procedures the nature of whose influence has been established by experimental analysis in the terms of the natural science of behavior and for which applied empirical evaluation has established reliable and general effects" (p. 324). This definition implies that the technology is consistent with a model or theory of behavior and that the way that it works has been established through experiment. Technology is not built upon untested convictions presented in accord with prevailing popular opinions but upon research. The basic science underlying the technology should be understood and ideally each of the components should have been tested so that only necessary components are included. Finally it should produce reliable and general effects in the hands of a well trained behavior analyst. We expect that bridges will support traffic almost all of the time. Behavior analysis would be better respected by the public of our technology worked 80 percent as well. In some areas we have succeeded in producing reliable and theoretically understood technology. We have a technology for rapidly and reliably toilet training children (Azrin & Foxx, 1974), for treating rumination (Rast, Johnston, & Drum, 1984), for teaching elementary subjects (Gersten, Carnine, & White, 1984), and for using performance feedback in the classroom (Van Houten, 1980), to name a few. However, even these effective technologies do not meet all of the requirements of Jim Johnston's definition. It is clear that we will need to devote more effort to developing technology that meets this definition.

Even if we develop technology that is effective and reliable (much of the techniques we have developed to date are already better than those developed by those we are competing with) we will still have to work hard to get people to accept it because many people in the community may not be convinced that it is appropriate to have a science of behavior. They are more concerned with philosophical issues than empirical ones. One prominent behavior analyst told me that a "scientific" member of the non-aversives' camp criticized him for being "too objective."

Linscheid (1993) reported that The American Association on Mental Retardation refused to sell its mailing list to an organization sponsoring a conference because one of the speakers would be presenting data on SIBIS. This type of censorship illustrates what can happen when people have stronger allegiances to a treatment philosophy than they do to data. It is clear to see how this type of behavior could lead to infringements on people's right to effective treatment.

Don Baer (1993) said that for behavior analysts, good outcome defines good process. This is very consistent with our selectionist background. However, he also said that many of our critics behave as if good process defines good outcome. Their behavior appears to be under less control of a particular important form of consequence, data. How can we get the behavior of the general population under the control of data? If we are successful in developing such stimulus control, they will be more likely to respond to claims with "let me see your data" rather than "let me see your philosophy."

Summary

The client's right to effective behavioral treatment is to a large extent the right to treatment that: has been validated by careful behavioral analysis; addresses the environmental causes of behavior; and is evaluated and monitored on an ongoing basis. Although behavior analysts apply the theory of behavior developed by B. F. Skinner, they are under close stimulus control of the data, because this theory is an evolving natural science model of behavior.

Specifically, behavior analysts agree that clients have a right to a therapeutic living environment that is functional. Such an environment should be designed to shape appropriate behavior and to provide the establishing operations or setting events necessary to facilitate the acquisition of new functional behavior. In so doing this environment should also lead to greater freedom of movement while maximizing access to reinforcement. Behavior analysts also agree that the client has the right to behavioral assessment and ongoing evaluation. Behavioral assessment increasingly often includes a functional analysis of current behavior prior to developing a treatment plan. Such an analysis identifies relevant reinforcers, discriminative stimuli and setting events related to the behaviors of concern. The client also has the right to treatment decisions based on data, and further analysis if the treatment does not achieve its aims.

Behavior analysts also support teaching functional skills because they know that many problems are the result of behavioral deficits as well as excesses. Functional skills are viewed as behaviors that increase positive and negative reinforcement in ways that do not lead to punishment or placement in a more restrictive setting. To teach functional skills one has to first determine the function of current behavior and determine alternative behaviors that will be more efficient in producing those reinforcers.

Finally, behavior analysts believe that the client has the right to the most effective behavioral treatment available. Following a proper behavioral assessment, it should be clear what treatments will likely work and what treatments will surely fail. It is important that the treatment plan is determined by performing a functional analysis and an analysis of the treatment literature. It is not justifiable to apply treatments that the results of such an analysis indicate will be ineffective. Treatment hierarchies should only be used to select from among options that the analysis determines will likely be effective.

Behavior analysts frequently have to compete with fads that do not develop from an empirical model. Many of us can think of several treatments that are not based on any data at all. These models often do well for a while because they dovetail with a current popular view. Most people feel somewhat expert about behavior and they do not demand the same degree of evidence or credentials in support of a new treatment as they do in other areas that are viewed as more technical. It is important that we educate the public about the importance of a scientific account of behavior that is based on empirical data. Unless we can do so our clients will remain at the mercy of well intentioned people who are more committed to treatment philosophy than to appreciable results.

References

Axelrod, S., Spreat, S., Berry, B., & Moyer, L. (1993). A decision-making model for selecting the optimal treatment procedure. In R. Van Houten & S. Axelrod (Eds.), *Behavior analysis and treatment* (pp. 183-202). New York: Plenum Press.

Azrin, N. H., & Foxx, R. M. (1974). *Toilet training in less than a day.* New York: Simon & Schuster.

Baer, D. (1993). *Behavior analysis and education.* Paper presented to the conference, Behavior Analysis and Education: Focus on Measurable, Superior Instruction, Columbus, OH.

Bijou, S. W., & Baer, D. M. (1961). *Child development I: A systematic and empirical theory.* Englewood Cliffs, N.J.: Prentice-Hall.

Carr, E. G., & Durand, V. M. (1985). Reducing behavior problems through functional communication training. *Journal of Applied Behavior Analysis, 18,* 111-126.

Carr, E. G., McConnachie, G., Levin, L., & Kemp, D. C. (1993). Communication-based treatment of severe behavior problems. In R. Van Houten & S. Axelrod (Eds.), *Behavior analysis and treatment* (pp 231-267). New York: Plenum Press.

Day, M., & Horner, R. D. (1990, March). *Response efficiency and deceleration of problem behaviors via functional equivalence training.* Paper presented at the meeting of the Northern California Association for Behavior Analysis, San Francisco, CA.

Favell, J. E., & McGimsey, J. F. (1993). Defining an acceptable treatment environment. In R. Van Houten & S. Axelrod (Eds.), *Behavior analysis and treatment* (pp. 25-45). New York: Plenum Press.

Gersten, R., Carnine, D., & White, W. A. T. (1984). The pursuit of clarity: Direct instruction and applied behavior analysis. In W. L. Heward, T. E. Heron, D. S. Hill, & J. Trap-Porter (Eds.), *Focus on behavior analysis in education* (pp. 38-57). Columbus, OH: Charles E. Merrill.

Horner, R. D. (1980). The effects of an environmental "enrichment" program on the behavior of institutionalized profoundly retarded children. *Journal of Applied Behavior Analysis, 13,* 473-491.

Horner, R. D., & Billingsley, F. F. (1988). The effect of competing behavior on the generalization and maintenance of adaptive behavior in applied settings. In R. H. Horner, R. L. Koegel, & G. Dunlap (Eds.), *Generalization and maintenance: Lifestyle changes in applied settings* (pp. 197-220). Baltimore: Paul H. Brookes.

Iwata, B. A., Vollmer, T. R., Zarcone, J. R., & Rodgers, T. A. (1993). Treatment classification and selection based on behavioral function. In R. Van Houten & S. Axelrod (Eds.), *Behavior analysis and treatment* (pp. 101-125). New York: Plenum Press.

Johnson, J. (1993). A model for developing and evaluating behavioral technology. In R. Van Houten & S. Axelrod (Eds.), *Behavior analysis and treatment* (pp. 323-343). New York: Plenum Press.

Koegel, R. L., & Frea, W. D. (1993). Treatment of social behavior in autism through the modification of pivotal social skills. *Journal of Applied Behavior Analysis, 26,* 369- 377.

Kantor, J. R. (1959). *Interbehavioral psychology.* Granville, OH: Principia.

Kennedy, C. H. & Itkonen, T. (1993). Effects of setting events on the problem behavior of students with severe disabilities. *Journal of Applied Behavior Analysis, 26,* 321-327.

Lerman, D. C., & Iwata, B. A. (1993). Descriptive and experimental analyses of variables maintaining self-injurious behavior. *Journal of Applied Behavior Analysis, 26,* 293- 319.

Linscheild, T. R. (1993). The development and evaluation of the self-injurous behavior inhibiting system: A personal perspective. In R. Van Houten & S. Axelrod (Eds.), *Behavior analysis and treatment* (pp. 345-365). New York: Plenum Press.

Michael, J. (1982). Distinguishing between discriminative and motivational functions of stimuli. *Journal of the Experimental Analysis of Behavior, 37,* 149-155.

Rast, J., Johnston, J. M., & Drum, C. (1984). A parametric analysis of the relation between food quantity and rumination behavior. *Journal of Experimental Analysis of Behavior, 41,* 125-135.

Rolider, A., & Van Houten, R. (1993). The interpersonal treatment model: Teaching appropriate social inhibitions through the development of personal stimulus control by the systematic introduction of antecedent stimuli. In R. Van Houten & S. Axelrod (Eds.), *Behavior analysis and treatment* (127-168). New York: Plenum Press.

Skinner, B. F. (1953). *Science and human behavior.* New York: MacMillan Company.

Van Houten, R. (1980). *Learning through feedback.* New York: Human Sciences Press.

Van Houten, R. Axelrod, S., Bailey, J. S., Favell, J. E., Foxx, R. M., Iwata, B. A., & Lovaas, I. (1988). The right to effective behavioral treatment. *Journal of Applied Behavior Analysis, 21,* 381-384.

Wacker, D. P., & Steege, M. W. (1993). Providing outclinic services: Evaluating treatment and social validity. In R. Van Houten & S. Axelrod (Eds.), *Behavior analysis and treatment* (297-319). New York: Plenum Press.

Zarcone, J. R., Rodgers, T. A., Iwata, B. A., Rourke, D. A., & Dorsey, M. F. (1991). Reliability analysis of the motivational assessment scale: A failure to replicate. *Research in Developmental Disabilities, 12,* 349-360.

Discussion of Van Houten

How Far is Too Far?

Ramona Houmanfar
University of Nevada

Van Houten has provided some specific techniques and procedures for the provision of effective treatment to insure clients' rights. His analysis focuses on four primary rights, which are: The right to a therapeutic living environment; the right to behavioral assessment and ongoing evaluation; the right to a behavioral curriculum that teaches functional skills; and the right to the most effective behavioral treatment procedures available.

Van Houten's main concern is with the last of these rights and is phrased in the form of a question, "How can we get the behavior of the general population under the control of data?" He asserts that without informative and thorough data to support it, a treatment is not known to be effective. The purpose of this paper is to elaborate on this issue within the context of a behavior analytic/pragmatic perspective. Accordingly, some points and suggestions will be made with respect to the issue of control and the role of behavior analysts as it is portrayed by our culture.

The Right to the Most Effective Behavioral Treatment

According to Van Houten, in order to promote a reliable and effective technology, behavior analysts have to take the extra step of convincing the public to accept our science of behavior in addition to applying it in an appropriate manner. Tough, Van Houten does not state it explicitly, it seems apparent that the main problem for the public in accepting a science of behavior may be summarized in the word "control." Is it not the word "control" and its implications which have historically kept us from rapidly succeeding with the application of our science? Simply said, the public does not necessarily want to be controlled. A different understanding of the role of behavior analysts as promoters of the science of behavior may be useful.

The Role of the Behavior Analyst

In *A Case History in Scientific Method* (Skinner, 1956), Skinner discusses the formation of scientific principles and practices which according to him would not ordinarily be recognized by scientific methodologists. Among these scientific achievements were the development of the cumulative record and the principles of extinction and intermittent reinforcement. These were the products of equipment failure, the experimenter being tired of carrying the rat back to the experimental chamber, or running out of reinforcers. This is all to illustrate the willingness of the scientist to accept that the manipulation of environmental conditions alone could bring about a wholly unexpected practical control which also includes the shaping of his or her behavior by those environmental contingencies. Simply stated, in order for us behavior analysts to be successful and effective, we must admit that we are affected by the environmental contingencies which we set up for others. There are rules which we set up ourselves or we follow in order to be successful behavior analysts. While the control exerted over our own behavior as scientists may not be able to be as complete or as successfully arranged as that exerted over other subjects, it is useful to recognize this control and how it comes about.

When taking a pragmatic approach, we find that questions generate other questions and sometimes such a process leads to a desired though not planned outcome. Some such outcomes are seen in experimenter's or teachers' or consultants' behavior as well as in the behaviors of subjects or students or staff.

The role of the behavior analyst is an important component in any effective treatment implemented at any of the four levels of rights to effective treatment described by Van Houten. This is not to say that the scientist's role is overlooked in Van Houten's analysis but rather that it is not fully incorporated into the context of promoting a behavior analytic perspective at the cultural level.

The question of how far is too far with respect to attainment of control on the part of behavior analysts is a question which could be answered and responded to in different ways given the contexts within which it is asked. Within the context of the right to effective treatment, however, the role of the behavior analyst needs to be an interactive component, understood as controlling as much as it is being controlled by other setting factors. We have gone too far when we, as behavior analysts, expect the culture to accept control over their behavior without an explicit acknowledgment of reciprocation.

References

Skinner, B. F. (1956). A case history in scientific method. *American Psychologist, 11*, 221-233.

Chapter 7

Ethical Advocacy in Developmental Disabilities: A Performance Engineering Perspective

David Luke
Sierra Regional Center
Jacqueline E. Collins
University of Nevada

It is a difficult task to understand how the behavioral sciences deal with the issues of ethics and advocacy for persons with developmental disabilities. It is apparent that these global concepts are inherently in conflict. For example, words such as "good," "right," "understanding," and "sensitive" are used in the description of ethics and advocacy. In contrast, the behavioral sciences are aligned with such words as "objectivity," "observation," and "data." Fundamentally, the conflict is this: In order to observe or take data on "good" and "right," we must first determine what characteristics in the environment are considered good and right. If that route is taken and the behavioral sciences are able to quantitatively evaluate ethical and advocacy conditions, what could be more "ethical" than an exact indication of the amount of ethical behavior occurring? How precise can the analysis of ethical behavior be if it has no accurate definitional character? What is required is groundwork upon which the behavioral sciences can then build successful inquiries.

The focus of this chapter will thus be to build a framework upon which behavior analysis can draw in dealing with issues of ethics and advocacy. The first step is the definition of these terms; the second step a conceptualization of a behavioral or performance engineering perspective.

Defining ethics and morals

The term ethics is derived from the Latin word *ethicus* originally derived from Greek terms meaning custom or habit. A pragmatic sense of the notion of ongoing practice or convention is implied in its origin. Webster's Encyclopedic Dictionary (Thatcher, 1971) defines ethical as *"Relating to morals,"* and *"The science which treats of the nature and grounds of moral obligation...the science of duty."* Ethics can thus be construed as relating to the ongoing practice, customs or duty as applied to moral behavior.

This definition underlines the fact that ethics is intimately related to the concept of morals or morality. Webster's (Thatcher, 1971) defines moral as *"Relating to right and wrong as determined by duty, governed by the laws of right and wrong...capable of distinguishing between right and wrong..."* Given that morality describes practices related to right and wrong, ethics can be seen as the study of factors of right and wrong in everyday circumstances.

"Advocate" is derived from the Latin word *advocatus*, meaning to summon one to aid; its component parts mean "to call or summon as in voice, or vocal". Advocate is further defined as (Thatcher, 1971) *"One who pleads the cause of another in a court of law; one who defends, vindicates or espouses a cause by argument...a defender..."* An advocate for persons with developmental disabilities then is someone who defends persons with developmental disabilities. Ethical action then implies a range of behavior guided by rightness or goodness. This behavior is ethical advocacy for persons with disabilities if it achieves rightness in conduct, services, social practices and outcomes towards persons with disabilities. This is a broader formulation than the more common use of advocacy which is the support for services provided for persons with developmental disabilities.

Accreditation Council Definitions

Advocacy has been classified still further by professionals in the field of developmental disabilities. The organization that specializes in evaluating services, The Accreditation Council on Services for Persons with Disabilities (ACD) has specifically defined and classified advocacy as it pertains to persons with disabilities (1993). According to the ACD, advocacy is action to promote the well being of persons with developmental disabilities principally where rights are concerned. The council specifies four kinds of advocacy and are defined in Table 1.

Advocacy is then speaking, putting forth argument or otherwise holding forth for the cause of persons with developmental disabilities. For example, advocacy is ethical in so far as it promotes the rightness of action by service providers toward persons with developmental disabilities in everyday life. Advocacy can also be seen in a larger sense as a manifestation of social justice.

In some cases the consideration of advocacy issues would prove quite useful in empirical investigations. It seems to be the case in many empirical studies concerning persons with developmental disabilities that outcomes are based on information assumed by the investigators. These outcomes usually presuppose that the interventions used are beneficial to consumers without any information from the consumers themselves. One study by Lazano (1993) concluded that the amount of independent living skill services provided for consumers with developmental disabilities did not have a significant effect on the level of skills maintained by consumers living independently. However, the consumers surveyed in this study were never asked what services they wanted or what skills they considered important for living independently. It is reasonable to assume that if a person deems a skill to be important, training in that skill would be more effective.

Table 1

Levels of Advocacy Defined by Accreditation Council

Advocacy

Refers to speaking for, or on behalf of, a position, cause, or individual, especially when rights or interests are at risk or have been violated.

Self-Advocacy

Refers to speaking on behalf of oneself in terms of one's wants, needs, and desires.

Class Advocacy

Refers to the actions needed to promote the interests of a group of people with common needs or characteristics, such as individuals with developmental disabilities.

Systems Advocacy

Refers to concerted action to change the policies or mode of operations of a system of services such as the school system or the transportation system. System advocacy also includes legislative advocacy.

The next section provides a comprehensive approach to integrating scientific and ethical views regarding advocacy for persons with developmental disabilities.

Gilbert's Engineering Performance Model

In *Human Competence: Engineering Worthy Performance* (1978), Thomas F. Gilbert proposed what he called a teleonomic science. This conceptualization is an engineering approach to worthy performance. Gilbert distinguishes it from a strictly behavioral perspective in that teleonomics or performance engineering deals with attaining accomplishments in applied settings, and within the context of a continually changing world. While his method includes the application of behavioral principles, it also addresses subject matter on levels which are not necessarily dealt with at the individual behavioral level. For example, his system embraces such wide ranging topics such as philosophies, logistics and tools.

Gilbert (1978) discusses what he calls worthy performance. Worthy performance is defined through identifying accomplishments or outcomes that are of value. An accomplishment is the final product that has positive value. The cost of an accomplishment is also a consideration. An engineer is willing to draw on all available tools to attain an accomplishment so far as the methods are legal and ethical. The various methods to the accomplishment can be evaluated based on their respective costs. The predominant cost to attain an accomplishment is usually the cost of behavior, although materials or other costs may be involved. This engineering process then identifies the less costly effective method as the most worthy approach. Behavioral interventions are seen as important in so far as they are the most cost effective route to the accomplishment.

From an advocate's perspective, Gilbert's performance engineering model suggests ways to achieve the greatest benefit within the range of available resources. When available resources are best used to achieve good ends for the greatest number of persons, then an ethical approach is achieved. Such a rational and systematic approach can be seen as a moral imperative, because to do otherwise would be seen as denying the best outcome to some individuals. In that light, this chapter is an advocacy effort in that it applies this efficient system to achieving moral ends for persons with developmental disabilities.

Gilbert's Vantage Points

Gilbert provides an orderly approach to describing philosophies and their application such that engineering solutions to real life problems are possible. He identifies a hierarchy of six *vantage points* or levels. The levels in descending order are philosophical, cultural, policy, strategic, tactical, and logistic. Successively lower levels define accomplishments consistent with higher levels of vantage in a particular system. Therefore, a level can be judged for its effectiveness in terms of the next higher level. Specific levels are also analyzed for efficiency or cost effectiveness within themselves. Gilbert describes techniques to measure cost worthiness or cost effectiveness and he identifies ways to improve cost effectiveness. When a system is in obvious need of change it is the management at higher levels which hold the greatest potential for changing the system and achieving greater accomplishments. Therefore, when engineering changes within an organization, it is important first to analyze these higher levels, secondly to interpret them into objectives for progressively lower levels.

Philosophical level: Ideals

At the highest level are philosophical beliefs which are expressed as ideals. Ideals are the accomplishment at the philosophical level. For example, one philosophy holds that each and every person is naturally endowed with value. This and related humanitarian philosophies underlie the United States and other Western societies.

These philosophies have direct relevance to establishing the values and ethics of persons with disabilities. In accordance with this philosophy it is possible to judge behavior for its ethical rightness or wrongness. The American ideal is that there should be equality of opportunity for all persons. Accordingly, this philosophical ideal should apply to all persons including those with disabilities. To the extent that persons with disabilities are denied equal opportunities or rights, their treatment is unethical. At this level, advocacy is philosophical and might involve articulating ever better statements of the philosophy and related ideals.

Cultural Level: Goals

Philosophical ideals feed into the next lower level, which Gilbert calls the cultural level. The context of the cultural level is governmental or cultural groups. At the cultural level an accomplishment is achieved when cultural goals are defined as they grow out of the philosophical ideals. The more consistent and aligned these goals are with the philosophical level the more right, moral or ethical they become. The philosophical ideals of natural and inalienable human rights became accomplishments at the cultural level when these themes were adopted in the Constitution, Bill of Rights and assorted federal laws. The federal Developmental Disabilities Assistance and Bill of Rights Act originally passed in 1975, defined rights and other goals for persons with developmental disabilities. These goals include independence, integration and productivity. Federal funding mandates, such as Medicaid, provide governmental resources to achieve the goals.

At this level it is possible to begin to evaluate whether or not goals are being met. Questions have been raised as to whether the funding mechanisms and resulting incentives have led to achievement of the goals. It is now widely believed that the incentives created by Medicaid have led states to an improper emphasis on institutionalization of persons with developmental disabilities. National research is beginning to assess how well the cultural goals are being met within our society. In 1987, Congress required that each state conduct surveys of consumers to determine how much they valued the goals of integration, productivity and independence. They were also asked how much they felt those goals were being realized. While strongly subscribing to the goals, the consumers reported that they were largely unrealized in their daily lives. (Larson & Lakin, 1989).

The most recent expression of these national goals is seen in the Amendments to the Developmental Disabilities Assistance and Bill of Rights Act, passed in August of 1993. This law expresses and clarifies national goals and values for persons with developmental disabilities. The nation's goals include:

> ...providing individuals with developmental disabilities with the opportunities and support to: make informed choices and decisions; live in homes and communities in which such individuals can exercise their full rights and responsibilities as citizens; pursue meaningful and productive lives; contribute to the life of their family, community, state and nation; have interdependent friendships and relationships with others; and achieve full integration and inclusion in society. (Bacon, 1993, p. 1)

This act clearly aligns with the overarching cultural philosophy. An engineering approach might extend the evaluation of these accomplishments and goals by linking associated costs in a concrete and specific way.

It is easy to see the relationship between advocacy for persons with disabilities and a fuller achievement of social values for each individual in our society. Although the rights to vote, marry, and enter into contracts are not limited in the Constitution, the reality is that these rights have been denied to persons with developmental disabilities. To date, while the nation has fallen short of full achievement, it nevertheless has made dramatic gains over recent decades.

The nation, with its legislative and executive powers to encourage and discourage, can promote cultural goals. This often occurs in spite of resistance such as was seen in the various civil rights issues of recent years. It is therefore not surprising to find advocates for persons with developmental disabilities targeting changes in federal laws. Moreover, the philosophical ideals are often clarified through the judicial system. Here advocates have aggressively pursued philosophical ideals by appealing to state and local legal systems.

Policy Level: Missions

Below the cultural level is the policy vantage level. The policy level occurs in the context of agencies such as governmental or private service agencies. These agencies exist for purposes of achieving cultural goals. An accomplishment at the policy level is a mission. A mission defines the basic purposes of the institution and guides a program of action.

Some agencies may have written mission statements. In other cases, it may be that missions are unarticulated or may not be fully accepted within an organization. In these cases, organizations may take on alternate goals of their own. These practices can become incompatible with current values and goals.

An example of this is large public facilities for persons with developmental disabilities. Most of the states are moving to downsize or close these facilities, usually in the face of advocate lawsuits. These lawsuits have documented that rights denials stemming from the practice of warehousing persons in large facilities are common in these settings. It is an increasingly common belief among professionals that institutional practices inevitably restrict persons, deny their rights, and consequently are unable to achieve cultural goals for individuals. Although some contend that institutions will always be necessary, this assumption is being tested by several states that are now operating without large facilities. Empirical work will further determine how well these changes achieve cultural goals.

If professionals are to act ethically they must understand the larger social goals and policies and agency missions. Behaviorally trained professionals are uniquely qualified to assist in operationally defining significant accomplishments. For example, in order to be independent a person must be able to act functionally within his/her environment. Left undefined and unmeasured, the status of progress is subject to only crude evaluation. By operationally defining and empirically measuring these concepts, the effectiveness of missions can be enhanced.

Many agencies whose mission is clearly articulated may still fail to be consistent with cultural goals and values. This alignment with the cultural goals and philosophical ideals is a prerequisite for ethically directed contributions by the agency. Increased behavioral understanding of missions, values, and their controlling functions in organizations is needed. The understanding of missions as rules that govern behavior could contribute to applied organizational practices. Until the mission statements can be translated into effective plans of action, progress is dependent on random acts of good will rather than worthy performance. It is this issue that is addressed at the next level.

Strategic Level: Responsibilities

This strategic level represents the development of a program to achieve the mission. The strategy specifies the roles and jobs that need to be undertaken by persons for an agency to achieve its mission. Strategic planning is increasingly discussed in management books. Some understanding of the agency's strategy can be seen in written plans, organizational structure, resource allocation, and staff training. This planning must be translated into employee performance. Employees' inability to recognize their role in the big picture, including values and goals, undoubtedly hampers accomplishments. As such, their behavior may often be governed by incorrect rules or values. Effective work at the strategic level might include staff training and the gaining of a better understanding of how employees adapt to rapid change. Effective use of personnel resources may have a powerful advocacy potential for persons with developmental disabilities.

In 1990, Amado, Lakin, and Menke reported on the relative effects of community versus institutional care on the skills and behavior of individuals with developmental disabilities. They found that in many of the studies conducted there was a statistically significant improvement in adaptive skills when consumers received community rather than institutional care. They also reported that there generally was no change in maladaptive behavior across settings. A report such as this can guide agencies in strategic planning leading to changes in the direction of programming for persons who are about to move into a community. This, literally, may require entirely different roles for employees.

Currently, the authors of this chapter are conducting a project to examine the level at which the Nevada State Division of Mental Health upholds its missions and values. This division's mission statement is to aid persons with mental retardation and their families to live as normal a life as possible by providing residential placement, training, support and therapeutic assistance.

The Division for Developmental Disabilities in Denver, Colorado has designed an assessment tool called the Colorado Progress Assessment Review or COPAR (Division for Developmental Disabilities, 1992a). It was designed to analyze how effectively the mission statement of that division was being met. The mission of that division is to offer the necessary supports all people with developmental disabilities to have an opportunity to: 1) be included in Colorado community life; 2) make increasingly responsible choices; 3) exert greater control over their life circumstances; 4) establish and maintain relationships and a sense of belonging; 5) develop and exercise their competencies and talents; and, 6) experience personal security and self-respect. This assessment and review instrument can be used to indicate whether an agency is following through on outcomes which are in line with these values and missions. The mission of that agency was in line with the mission of the Nevada State Division of Mental Health such that the COPAR could be used to evaluate this system as well.

One value that underlies the mission of this agency is decision making. This value is accomplished when choices are made by consumers that affect their lives. These decisions are related to residence, employment, and the types of programs and services consumers receive.

The COPAR addresses these issues in a section on consumer decision making. Several questions are asked of a consumer, or a staff person if the consumer is unable or unwilling to respond to the questions. Many of the issues discussed before are directly addressed in this section. Questions such as who chooses your friends, where you live, who you live with, what time you go to bed, who your doctor is, and if you have a key to your home are included.

The issue of consumer decision making was analyzed at an organizational level. The level of decision making by consumers was surveyed across different residential settings by Northern Nevada's Sierra Regional Center. Figure 1 represents the average level of decision making within various home types, using the COPAR instrument.

The purpose in gathering these data was to look at which types of housing—intermediate care facilities, natural homes, group homes, or supported living arrangements—maintain the value of consumer decision making for people with developmental disabilities. Several people from each environment were sampled.

It is evident that supported living arrangements and group home settings offer an overall higher level of decision making on the part of the consumer than do intermediate care facilities or natural homes. One explanation of this difference could be a function of the level of consumer disability in each of the home types. However, analysis by the Colorado Division in that state found that, when adjusted for disability, supported living arrangements still provided for greater consumer decision making (Division for Developmental Disabilities, 1992b).

Questions in this section of the COPAR were separated into two areas. One area concerned items regarding decisions about personal matters. Personal matter questions included: who chooses your friends, what time to go to bed, how you spend your personal time, and so on. Figure 2 demonstrates the average level of decision making in personal matters. The second area included items concerning decisions made in home or work settings. These items looked at who chooses where you work, where you live, who lives with you, and the staff in your home. Figure 3 represents an average of these items across home types. Taken together, these data show that group home and supportive living arrangement settings afford more consumer decision making than do intermediate care facility and natural home settings.

It is further apparent from these data that a reevaluation of the jobs and roles within the agency should be considered. Roles at several different levels can be adjusted through the information obtained with these data. At administrative levels money can be allocated to foster the settings that promote greater individual choice. At a consultation level, programs can be written that will foster decision making. Finally, direct care staff can be trained to implement programs that allow greater independent decision making.

Tactical level: Duties

Once roles have been defined at the strategic level, they must be sharpened by defining duties. Gilbert (1978) refers to this as the tactical level. Duties are specific tasks which contribute to fulfilling the responsibilities of a job that has been identified at the strategic level. Duties for employees who work with persons with developmental disabilities may include activities such as developing training, behavior management and individual education plans, which indicate distinctive tasks to be applied.

One difficulty faced at this level is that these programs are not usually examined for their alignment with higher level values and goals. For example, many times behavior analysts have been called upon to eliminate problem behaviors which historically have required the use of controversial aversive or restrictive procedures.

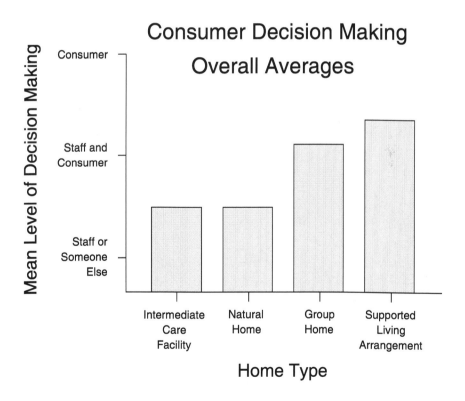

Figure 1. Average level of decision making shown by COPAR.

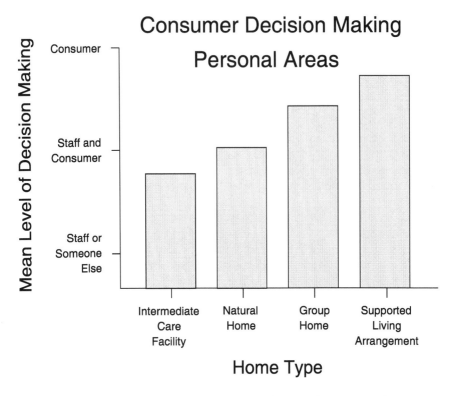

Figure 2. Average level of decision making shown by COPAR in personal matters.

Although understandable in the context of the times, these procedures are becoming less acceptable and are increasingly seen as inconsistent with individual rights. The fact that some states are making aversive procedures illegal is a case in point. It is important when designing the duties of a job that programmers structure duties within the value system defined by the agency.

Logistic level: Supplies

Gilbert's final level is called logistical. Logistics are the specifics of mobilizing resources at the right place and time for purposes of carrying out tasks. In order to carry out duties, time, place and resources must be scheduled. Advocacy demands that logistical support be directed toward the mission. The best use of logistical support is when it advances the essentials of the mission.

Summary

This interpretation has identified contemporary goals, values, and policies as seen from a perspective of advocacy for persons with developmental disabilities. This illustration of ethics, advocacy, and behavioral sciences is admittedly a cursory look. In spite of this, a framework is provided to evaluate projects and opportunities in a larger ethical context. This interpretation also provides a form to classify the level at which values or assumptions are being made.

The scientific community cannot ignore existing cultural values without consequence. For example, the federal government has recently admitted to radiation testing on unwitting persons, some of whom had mental retardation. Clearly, such a scientific and political endeavor is in conflict with cultural values. When science is not aligned with cultural values, its activities can easily become unethical. On the other hand, science, when aligned with cultural values, offers a powerful method to promote ethical outcomes and, as such, can be an integral element of advocacy.

The way is open for behavior analysts to thrust themselves into the forefront of applying scientific approaches towards the enhancement and expansion of progressive cultural values. Choice, inclusion, and productivity are behaviors of current interest because they are the component skills of greater independence for persons with developmental disabilities. As a science, behavior analysis brings unique approaches and skills to these challenges. A performance engineering perspective

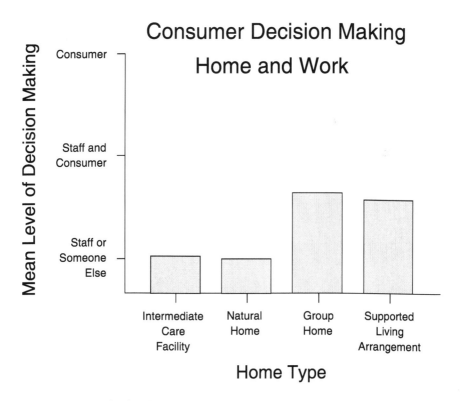

Figure 3. Average level of decision making shown by COPAR in home and work settings.

can help guide our behavior by making it consistent with ethical values. By embracing these values we increase the probability of socially meaningful contributions.

References

Accreditation Council on Services for People with Developmental Disabilities. (1990). *Standards and interpretation guidelines for services for people with developmental disabilities*. Landover, MD: Author.

Amado, A. N., Lakin, K. C., & Menke, J. M. (1990). *1990 Chartbook on services for people with developmental disabilities*. Minneapolis: University of Minnesota, Center for Residential and Community Services.

Bacon, A. (1993). DD Act amendments pass senate. *American Association on Mental Retardation: News & notes, 6* (5), 1.

Division for Developmental Disabilities. (1992a). *Colorado progress assessment review: COPAR, abbreviated version*. Denver: Author.

Division for Developmental Disabilities. (1992b). *Director's Report*. Denver: Author.

Gilbert, T. F. (1978). *Human competence: Engineering worthy performance*. New York: McGraw-Hill.

Lazano, B. (1993). Independent living: relation among training, skills, and success. *American Journal on Mental Retardation, 98*, 249-262.

Larson, S. A., & Lakin, K. C. (1989). Deinstitutionalization of persons with mental retardation: The impact on daily living skills. *Journal of the Association for Persons with Severe Handicaps, 14*, 324-332.

Thatcher, V. S. (Ed.). (1971). *The new Webster's encyclopedic dictionary of the English language*. Chicago: Consolidated Book Publishers.

Discussion of Luke and Collins

A Performance Engineering Model

Cynthia A. Reinbold
University of Nevada

Luke and Collins address the issue of advocacy, particularly from the role of an institute, in working with the developmentally disabled. Through the use of Webster's Encyclopedic Dictionary the authors defined advocacy; this allowed Luke and Collins to focus their paper which would have otherwise been extremely vague due to the topic's enormity. An advocate is defined as "One who pleads the cause of another in a court of law; one who defends, vindicates or espouses a cause by argument...a defender..." (Thatcher, 1971).

An institutional interpretation of advocacy is complex in that it must encompass different roles for varying levels of care or interactions. Thomas F. Gilbert's performance engineering model (1978) allows a behavioral objective to be defined and clarified at several different organizational levels. Gilbert is able to examine a goal from many distinct levels; philosophical, cultural, and strategic, to name a few. This type of multilayer analysis is very convenient for an organization such as an institute. The authors' chose their assessment device well.

By placing advocacy into a performance engineering model (Gilbert, 1978), investigators are able to identify behavioral roles or actions which each level of an organization could carry out in order to fulfill its agency mission statement. In particular, the authors' describe measuring advocacy at the consumer level. Through the use of the Colorado Progress Assessment Review (Division for Developmental Disabilities, 1992), COPAR, administrators are attempting to measure advocacy at the direct care level. The COPAR is a questionnaire that provides numerical scores as evaluations of various types of independent living skills and activities for a person. The concept of a numerical system is beneficial to furnishing objective scores as assessments of a person's satisfaction in an area, such as advocacy, which has not been widely studied.

However, problems concerning biased answers arise when comparing scores or verifying the reliability of COPAR scores. Recall that at times staff members are requested to assist or provide information in completing the COPAR (1992). The information they provide may be misleading. Concerning this problem two suggestions were offered by persons attending the Nevada Conference on Ethics and Developmental Disabilities: 1) complete two or more COPARs for any client requiring staff assistance; 2) different staff persons should be used in an effort to attain more reliable measures; and, 3) create a more reliable assessment device for use in this type of evaluation.

A problem briefly discussed by Luke and Collins concerned how an organization would actually attain the goal of consumer oriented advocacy. While a solution was not identified, this question brought forth an important issue. Appropriate behavior can be identified through the use of Gilbert's (1978) behavior engineering model. Yet, how to achieve this type of complex, organizational goal is not addressed. Rules would be the quickest manner in which to communicate a change in agency objectives. However, what consequences could be constructed in an institute to enforce rule compliance of a new policy at all organizational levels? This question remains unanswered by Luke and Collins.

The application of behavior analytic techniques to a traditionally intangible area is exciting. Behavior analytic philosophy, to a small degree, has described the area of advocacy. Luke and Collins proceed a step further in conducting outcome based evaluations of an advocacy mission statement in an institute for the developmentally disabled. Through measurement and description, the area of behavior analysis is equipped to evaluate the progression toward, or attainment of, an organizational goal. This expansion in the application of behavior analysis to more complex and elusive areas is significant and of great interest to those practicing in this field.

In the area of ethics and the developmentally disabled, psychology, in particular the field of behavior analysis, has a great deal to offer. This role should not be simplified or overlooked. Providing performance based assessments is of great value in evaluating a person's or an institute's objective to advocate for the ethical treatment of the developmentally disabled.

References

Division for Developmental Disabilities. (1992). *Colorado progress assessment review: COPAR, abbreviated version.* Denver: Author.

Gilbert, T. F. (1978). *Human competence: Engineering worthy performance.* New York: McGraw-Hill.

Thatcher, V. S. (Ed.). (1971). *The new Webster's encyclopedic dictionary of the English language.* Chicago: Consolidated Book Publishers.

Chapter 8

Adult Services: Opportunities to Demonstrate Competence

Stephen C. Moore
Nevada University Affiliated Program in Developmental Disabilities

Not long ago a young lady with Down syndrome, Cathy, came to my office to discuss an agenda she believed was important for people with developmental disabilities. The agenda was impressive; part altruistic (e.g., helping people in the hospital who had no family close by), part philosophical (her boy friend should be allowed to visit her whenever she wanted, not every other weekend as the home trainer had mandated), but all of it centered around the idea that we needed to provide better services for adults with developmental disabilities. Indeed, one of her agenda items was to find ways to make a video of the three major sheltered workshops in the Reno area. Then the video could be shown to workshop administrators and clients, so that other workshops could utilize the best features demonstrated by their counterparts. People with disabilities could use the video to make decisions about where they might want to work.

While her agenda was impressive in its own right, I was more impressed with the idea that this lady was currently working in a sheltered workshop and living in a supervised apartment, but had managed to find me without ever getting help from professionals in the field. Despite the belief by professionals that she needed close supervision in her work and living arrangements, she had managed to find the correct bus to the university, find the College of Education, find my office within the College of Education, and present me with her ideas about what needed to be done to provide better services. The point is, I think, that when Cathy had the opportunity to demonstrate competence, she did so.

My friend Brett, who happens to have autism and is nonverbal, was working in a work activity center where he was responsible for placing five golf tees in a plastic bag. Then he would pass the bag to the next person in the assembly line. That person would then dump the tees out of the bag so that the next person in line could fill the bag with five more tees. Brett was urinating in his pants as often as 14 times per day and physically assaulting co-workers 2-3 times per week. When he started assaulting staff, the decision was made to send him back to the state training school (institution), and a 45-day Intent to Dismiss from Services was initiated.

Brett did not go to the institution, and he has held a regular job in the community for over two years. The job was one of his choosing, not one we chose for him. His employer is extremely pleased with his work and co-workers say "...he's a nice guy, he just can't talk." He has not urinated in his pants, nor has he demonstrated the aggressive behavior that had been of some much concern. Again, the point is that when we gave him an opportunity to perform, he demonstrated clearly that he was capable of functioning competently in a community-based environment.

Joannie is a young woman with a variety of congenital disabilities, including mental retardation. She has recently been assigned to a supported employment program. The program is not one of her choosing. As a result, she has embarked on a campaign of letter writing in order to get the referral changed to an agency of her choosing, and to an agency to which she is assigned. Her most recent letter has been to demand a new case manager; one who will not make arbitrary decisions about Joannie's life.

Finally, Vicki is a young woman with Rubenstein-Taybi syndrome. She has worked in a sheltered workshop for most of her adult life. She works on a contract which calls for her to cut and bundle tent strings for the Army. She is very slow. Her production is listed at approximately 10% of the norm, and frequently she displays the tic movements characteristic of Rubenstein-Taybi syndrome. When Vicki was given the opportunity to select a job in the community, she picked the deli at K-Mart where she was responsible for constructing submarine sandwiches. The task analysis called for a fairly complex 10-step process in order to correctly make the sandwiches. Vicki learned the steps within the first week she was employed, with the exception that she put on more onions than was usual. Despite this, K-Mart personnel were very pleased with her work because she was meeting the production norms and because a cadre of customers specifically bought Vicki's sandwiches with the extra onions. Vicki was demonstrating competence far beyond what we, as professionals, would have anticipated.

It seems to me that any conversation concerning the ethics of providing services for adults with developmental disabilities starts with effective interventions. I believe that Cathy, Brett, Joannie and Vicki are not exceptions; rather, they are fairly typical of all people. I believe we have not done an adequate job of providing effective interventions for those individuals who make up our constituents. I believe that by failing to do so, we, as professionals, have behaved unethically.

A major impetus of services for people with developmental disabilities in recent years has been to discuss providing opportunities to demonstrate competence and make choices for people with disabilities (e.g., Wehmeyer, 1992). However, many environments specified for people with developmental disabilities are designed to control behavior, rather than foster independent performance. As Lipsky and Gardner (1989) suggest, current models of intervention specifically fostered the idea that people with disabilities are unable to make decisions because individuals with disabilities are denied the opportunity to demonstrate competence. Consequently, people with developmental disabilities receive intervention that is based on restricting independent performance.

Since the medical or clinical model that is widely used in service deliver fails to acknowledge the potential capabilities of individuals with disabilities, it is clear that interventions do not provide opportunities to build independence (Guess, Benson, & Siegal-Causey, 1985; Kishi, Teelucksingh, Zollers, Park-Lee, & Meyer, 1988). The feature of exclusion from opportunities to demonstrate competence displayed in current intervention models stretches across age groups and environments (Moore & Ellerd, 1993; Murtaugh & Zettin, 1990).

Ineffective Dimensions of Service Delivery

Systems Dimension

The lack of effective interventions for adults exist on at least two dimensions. These dimensions include a systems dimension and an individual dimension. First, the systems dimension. Our service systems are not designed to ensure quality treatment (Lipsky & Gardner, 1989). Service systems are designed to maintain the system first and provide services second. When we analyze how decisions concerning individuals with developmental disabilities are made, we see a fairly stable pattern. That is, when we identify the incentives and disincentives for agencies as opposed to the incentives and disincentives for individuals, we almost always find a mirror image; incentives for the agency are mirrored by disincentives for the individual, and vice versa.

It is important to note that this pattern occurs at every level of systems. For example, lack of funds always is a limiting factor in adult services. While funding is clearly a critical issue for state developmental disabilities divisions and for state vocational rehabilitation agencies, agencies which are mandated to provide services for people with disabilities, the bottomline is that people with developmental disabilities are not receiving effective interventions because, in many cases, interventions are not being provided at all. Indeed, in virtually every state in the country there are waiting lists for individuals leaving the special education system and trying to enter adult service systems. In Montana, for example, a state with less than 900,000 people, the waiting list contains the names of approximately 1,200 individuals and the average wait is between 6-7 years. The individuals on the list are waiting for someone already receiving services to die or move out of the state, because that is the only way to get off the list and into the service delivery system.

We can follow the same pattern with agencies and organizations which provide services for adults with developmental disabilities. For example, sheltered workshops were designed to provide generic vocational training for people with severe disabilities. Unfortunately, this generic approach has been less than stellar. Here are a few things that we know about sheltered workshops (Whitehead, 1989): 1) An individual with a disability will never leave the workshop if he or she has been there for two years or more; 2) the most capable workers with disabilities at the sheltered workshop never leave; 3) time samples used to establish pay rates for individuals with disabilities in sheltered workshops provide financial incentives to the workshop; 4) the average pay received by an individual with disabilities in a sheltered workshop is between 12-15 cents per hour; and 5) sheltered workshops maintain a 10% "positive placement" rate.

In order to understand how sheltered workshops operate, it is important to understand the reinforcement that maintains workshop behavior. First, it is financially beneficial to maintain a full census in the shop. In most states, sheltered workshops are funded by state agencies for the number of people with disabilities who are engaged in in-house training activities. Consequently, there is virtually no financial incentive for placing individuals with disabilities into environments from which competence can be demonstrated. Placement opportunities are not made available because it is financially impractical to do so. As a result, only cursory efforts are made to place people with disabilities into community environments.

Next, sheltered workshops make additional money from subcontracts with local businesses. With these subcontracts, the workshop agrees to produce a product for the business using people with disabilities as the primary labor force. The automatic assumption is that people with disabilities cannot produce at normal rates, so a Department of Labor certificate is obtained in order to pay sub-minimum wages. The degree at which sub-minimum wages can be paid is based on a time sample used to determine the number of widgets a "normal" worker can produce. The time sample is conducted by having a non-disabled worker perform the task over three 2-minute intervals; once in the morning, once just before or just after lunch, and once just before quitting time. Then the total number of widgets produced are computed and multiplied by 10 in order to get an hourly production rate. Then, the pay of the workers with disabilities is computed based on a comparison with the production rate of the "normal" worker.

The problem with a time sample is that there are no "normal" workers in a sheltered workshop. Rather, there are supervisors who are not physically engaged in the activity over the entire day. When the supervisors participate in the time sample, they produce as fast as they can for each 2-minute interval, and then go back to their normal activities, supervising the workers with disabilities. A worker, with or without disabilities, cannot hope to produce at the established rate over long periods of time. As a result, the established hourly pay scale is heavily skewed toward low worker wages. Since the subcontracts have been established at a fixed rate, any funds generated by the difference between an exploitive time sample and the fixed labor rate established by the subcontract can be banked by the sheltered workshop.

While there is a clear financial incentive for keeping wages low, there is also an incentive for completing the subcontracts in a timely manner. For example, a subcontract is often established with specific timelines in which the work must be completed. Should the workshop fail to meet the established timelines, penalties are withheld from the contracted price for completing the contract. Consequently, the workshop is seldom anxious to place the best workers into community employment. The best workers are needed to insure the subcontracts are completed on time. Rather, those workers with less obvious skills are placed into jobs in the community, and the best workers are maintained in the workshop to help complete the subcontracts. This procedure helps the workshop maintain the 10% positive placement rate.

The 10% positive placement rate is an interesting issue: It has nothing to do with successful placements into community employment. Consider this scenario. A worker with disabilities is placed as a dishwasher in a local restaurant. That is a positive placement. The worker does not want to be a dishwasher, and after several weeks he quits his job. Since the worker still has a developmental disability, the workshop takes him back. By returning the worker to the workshop, a second positive placement has been achieved. Some sheltered workshops maintain their positive placement rate every year with just one individual with disabilities. As with my friend Joannie, jobs are assigned. As a result, job placements fail because they are jobs that are 1) not wanted by the individual with disabilities, 2) not systematically trained, or 3) both.

State vocational rehabilitation (VR) agencies are not immune to systematically excluding people with developmental disabilities from effective interventions. VR agencies use a series of double digit status codes to track individuals through the system. For example, status 00 is simply a referral status; an individual is applying for access to the VR system. Status 10 indicates that, after extensive evaluation, the individual has a confirmed disability which creates a handicap to employment and that he or she can profit from rehabilitation services. Status 26 means that the individual has been successfully rehabilitated, defined by continuous employment for 60 successive days. Of all the status codes, perhaps the most interesting is status 08. Status 08 is used extensively to wash people out of the system even after they have been previously admitted. Frequently, status 08 is used when all available rehabilitation funds have been expended. Since money is unavailable to pay for services, status 08 is the mechanism that dumps people out of the system. Unfortunately, these individuals must then reapply and go through the evaluation process once again.

Clearly, financial considerations have an impact on how status 08 is used within VR services. However, the system is designed to be flexible enough to identify other reasons for using the status 08 code. For example, individuals are washed out of the system using status 08 because they have been determined to be unmotivated toward rehabilitation. Some individuals with disabilities have been determined to be unmotivated toward rehabilitation because he or she missed one appointment with a rehabilitation counselor. Status 08 is used also to wash out individuals, after they have been admitted to the system, because they are "unable to benefit from rehabilitation." It is important to note that these decisions are made almost exclusively by individual VR counselors. Since VR counselors frequently control their own pot of money, those same counselors are making decisions about who can benefit from rehabilitation. Preliminary research (Rose, 1991) also suggests that many counselors have preconceived notions as to the rehabilitation potential of some types of disabilities, including developmental disabilities. That is, some counselors believe that people with mental retardation are unable to benefit from rehabilitation, while others believe that people with a mental illness cannot benefit from rehabilitation. Consequently, people with developmental disabilities are subjected to the luck of the draw in terms of the counselor to whom they are assigned. If they are assigned a counselor who believes that people with developmental disabilities cannot benefit from rehabilitation, there is a good chance that they will be washed out of the system via status 08.

While developmental disabilities division and vocational rehabilitation services are the ones discussed here, it is important to note that at every level, systems gear their services in such a way that the organization or agency receives the reinforcement at the expense of the individual with disabilities. One must wonder then how ethical our systems are when it comes to providing services to the people we say we serve.

Individual Dimension

The second dimension of ineffective treatment is the individual dimension. Salzberg and his colleagues (Salzberg, Martella, Marchand-Martella, Morgan, Christensen, & Moore, 1992) summed up the individual dimension very succinctly when they said that excellent staff are essential for excellent programs. There are very few excellent adult programs. This view was mirrored by Mithaug, Horiuchi, and Fanning (1985) when they suggested that the reason many adults with disabilities fail to make a successful transition to adult life is because service providers stop teaching critical skills after individuals with disabilities leave the school system.

Unfortunately, teaching is not viewed as a critical component of adult training programs. For example, some of my research looked at the qualifications of sheltered workshop floor supervisors (Moore, McCuller, & Salzberg, 1988). Only 40% of these individuals had college degrees, and of that number, few (23.4%) of those with college degrees had degrees directly related to disabilities (e.g., special education, psychology, or rehabilitation). Clearly, a college degree does not insure that staff have received quality training. However, all of us that work at universities assume that the training we provide our students transfers to direct service. If not, then best practices as we know them are probably not occurring in the direct service settings.

Since college degrees are not a major requirement for sheltered workshop supervisory staff, then clearly in-house training must pick up the slack. This is not the case. Moore et al. (1988) found that in-house training was not provided at all by more than 23% of the sheltered workshops. Indeed, of those workshops that did provide in-house training, approximately 75% of the training dealt with filling out agency paperwork, rather than on methodology for training appropriate vocational skills to those individuals being served. Fostering independent performance is clearly not a priority for many of these community-based institutions.

The criteria used by the sheltered workshops to hire individuals as floor supervisors was also varied in the Moore et al. study (1988). Experience with people with disabilities (34%) was valued more than an education (26%). There was no indication that good experience was valued any more highly than experience which was less than exemplary. For example, some of the workshops considered living with a family member with a disability as highly as actual working with individuals in vocational settings.

Not surprisingly, turnover rates are quite high for adult vocational training program staff (Moore, Godbolt, Schwarz, Moriber, & Salzberg, 1991). That may have something to do with how they are reinforced. If, for example, we consider pay as acceptable reinforcement for the work performed, then staff in sheltered workshops are not being sufficiently reinforced. For example, Salzberg, et al. (1992) found that special education teachers were paid, on an average, 22% more than sheltered workshop supervisors, positions with approximately the same responsibilities. It logically follows that the more capable and competent staff will be more inclined to go to the public school system rather than to the adult rehabilitation network. Individuals who have skills to compete for higher paying jobs rarely accept employment in lower paying jobs. Additionally, when more attractive paying jobs become available, individuals tend to leave lower paying jobs. Consequently, my friends Cathy, Brett, Joannie and Vicki will receive less quality in their training programs.

Ethical Solutions

Fortunately, there are solutions to these ethical issues. These solutions hinge on the idea that we do not know what deficits are in place until we give people the opportunity to demonstrate their level of competence, just as was done with Cathy, Brett, Joannie, and Vicki. Before this can happen, we need to make some adjustments in how we provide services, both on a systems level and on an individual level.

Systems Level

In order for major systems (e.g., vocational rehabilitation, developmental disabilities divisions) to change, they must rearrange the consequences they provide to organizations and agencies which provide the direct services. Rather than paying to maintain the agency, major systems must pay agencies to provide effective services. These services must be functional and must be specific to the individual. In other words, major systems must stop paying for generic job skills training established to ease the service delivery by agency staff. Rather, skills taught must be data-based and must concentrate on the needs of specific individuals with disabilities. Additionally, these services must be provided only after the specific individual with disabilities has been given the opportunity to perform the skills in the environment in which they are to be used.

When we provide these opportunities, we are often surprised at the skills and abilities in the repertoires of individuals with disabilities. For example, in a case study conducted by Stevens, Moore, Register, and Salzberg (1993), four women with moderate to severe mental retardation improved their dress and hygiene to meet worksite criteria simply by allowing them to participate in community employment environments. There was absolutely no dress or hygiene training provided.

From a social perspective, it seems to be ethically necessary to be accountable for how monies in systems are spent. Yet we know that in states like Nevada, the cost of successfully providing services based on individual needs and desires is approximately half of the cost of providing institutional services, including services provided by sheltered workshops and group homes (Mansmith, personal communication, February, 1993). From an ethical perspective, major systems must stop reinforcing direct service agencies for ineffective, high cost programs. When this reinforcement stops and major systems reinforce agencies based on the most effective services, direct service systems will begin to provide appropriate services.

Individual Dimension

When direct service agencies are no longer being reinforced for ineffective services, major changes in the skills and abilities of direct service staff will be required. High on the list of priorities for change will be the training requirements of agency staff. For example, staff will need to be trained in behavior analysis technology, to include the identification and delivery of appropriate consequences, and the assessment of behavior in functional environments. It will be critical that agency staff have a firm empirical orientation in order to avoid the reliance on unfounded methodologies, as exemplified by the recent silliness surrounding facilitated communication.

In addition to training, direct service agency staff will require adequate pay. It is wonderful when staff tell us they work in the adult services field because they love the work, but good staff tend to be good staff in areas other than adult service areas, too. When other areas are willing to pay for staff services, good staff tend to leave the field.

Both training and remuneration have implications for those of us who work for universities. We must be training behavior analytic procedures in natural environments as well as in laboratory settings. In this way, preservice adult service staff can make an appropriate transition from the relative restrictiveness of the laboratory environment to the functional applied setting with much greater ease. When we graduate preservice students from our programs with skills firmly in place, these students will command higher pay than individuals without similar training. The more of these well-trained preservice students we graduate, the more pressure will be placed on direct service agencies to hire trained personnel.

Conclusions

We must continue to explore the limitations of our own assumptions about the boundaries placed on individuals with disabilities. Clearly, we have taken service delivery out of the realm of providing the best possible services for individuals with developmental disabilities and placed service delivery into the realm of providing the best services we can provide provided those services do not interfere with the organization of our systems. Further, we have helped maintain the limits imposed by systems by hiring staff who have been undertrained and under-paid. These are unethical procedures inconsistent with the need to increase the autonomy and independence of people with developmental disabilities.

Despite the fact that adult service provision continues to operate from what I view as an unethical perspective, there is hope that ethical practices can be established and maintained. When individuals with developmental disabilities, like my friends Cathy, Brett, Joannie, and Vicki, are given the opportunity to demonstrate competence, they often surprise us with their established skills and abilities. Indeed, ethical procedures would seem to depend on the needs individuals with developmental disabilities express rather than on the procedures we want to provide. As we realize the difference between these two perspectives, more of our services to adults with developmental disabilities will become truly ethical services.

References

Guess, D., Benson, H. A., & Siegal-Causey, E. (1985). Concepts and issues related to choice-making and autonomy among persons with severe disabilities. *Journal of the Association for Persons with Severe Handicaps, 10,* 79-86.

Kishi, G., Teelucksingh, B., Zollers, N., Park-Lee, S., & Meyer, L. (1988). Daily decision-making in community residences: A social comparison of adults with and without mental retardation. *American Journal on Mental Retardation, 92,* 430-435.

Lipsky, D. K., & Gardner, A. (1989). Building for the future. In D. K. Lipsky & A. Gardner (Eds.), *Beyond separate education: Quality education for all.* Baltimore: Paul H. Brookes.

Mithaug, D. E., Horiuchi, C. N., & Fanning, P. N. (1985). A report on the Colorado statewide follow-up survey of special education students. *Exceptional Children, 51,* 397-404.

Moore, S. C., & Ellerd, D. A. (1993). Job retention of persons with disabilities placed in rural individualized supported employment: A model program. Manuscript submitted for publication.

Moore, S. C., McCuller, G. L., & Salzberg, C. L. (1988). Professional skill levels of sheltered workshop staff: Selection criteria and post-employment training. *Journal of Rehabilitation, 12,* 5-9.

Moore, S. C., Godbolt, F., Schwarz, M., Moriber, L., & Salzberg, C. L. (1991). Factors contributing to the attrition of supported employment job coaches. *Journal of Rehabilitation, 57,* 47-50.

Murtaugh, M., & Zettin, A. G. (1990). The development of autonomy among learning handicapped and nonhandicapped adolescents: A longitudinal perspective. *Journal of Youth and Adolescence, 19,* 245-255.

Rose, P. (1991). *Montana vocational rehabilitation counselors use of status codes.* Unpublished master's thesis. Eastern Montana College, Billings, MT.

Salzberg, C. L., Martella, R. C., Marchand-Martella, N., E., Morgan, R. L., Christensen, A. M., & Moore, S. C. (1992). Quality of vocational outcomes for adults with disabilities: One fundamental impediment. *Journal of Vocational Rehabilitation, 2,* 46-52.

Stevens, M. L., Moore, S. C., Register, S., & Salzberg, C. L. (1993). Collateral benefits of community participation for persons with severe disabilities entering supported employment. Manuscript submitted for publication.

Wehmeyer, M. L. (1992). Self-determination and the education of students with mental retardation. *Education and Training in Mental Retardation, 27,* 302-314.

Whitehead, C. (1989). *Final report: National study of rehabilitation facilities and their involvement in the integrated employment initiatives.* Washington, D. C.: Author.

Discussion of Moore

Being Guided by the Data

MaryAnn Demchak
University of Nevada

In his discussion of adult services and the opportunity for people with developmental disabilities to demonstrate competence, Moore makes the point that we do not allow these individuals to demonstrate competence because of lack of interventions on two levels: the systems dimension and the individual dimension. He then goes on to propose solutions for each dimension that would begin to allow individuals with disabilities to demonstrate competence.

Moore summarizes the individual dimension by stating that excellent staff equals excellent programs and proposes that we hire well-trained staff. However, it is insufficient that we simply hire well-trained staff. Rather, we must ensure that staff continue to receive training in order that they remain up-to-date with current effective practices. Thus, agencies must provide for ongoing training in areas other than filling out agency or state forms, first aid procedures, and so forth. Additionally, staff should receive training that provides a balanced picture; that is, information should be provided from psychological, behavioral, and special education research. Each of these areas has valid and reliable research that has implications for practice in the delivery of services to adults with developmental disabilities. Finally, we must develop a means of ensuring that staff continue to be competent after they complete training programs. Additionally, we must have means of ensuring that staff continue to display the competencies that they acquired in their training programs. Finally, we must be willing to accept that individuals with disabilities may choose to discontinue working with particular service providers when those service providers are performing inadequately. That is, we must recognize that it is within the rights of individuals with disabilities to terminate the services of case managers, job coaches, or other service providers.

The systems dimension is more complex than is the individual dimension. Moore discusses the importance of giving individuals with developmental disabilities the opportunity to demonstrate competence. When we provide these individuals with such opportunities, we are frequently surprised at the skills and abilities they demonstrate. Often, in adult services as well as in schools, we do not provide these opportunities. Instead, we provide services that benefit the system rather than benefit the individual with disabilities. To change the system dimension is much more ambitious and difficult than is changing the individual dimension. Moore proposes that we rearrange the consequences (i.e., funding provided) to organizations and agencies. However, in order to bring about this type of change many other changes need to occur. First, we must educate professionals and the public regarding the benefits of current effective practices. For example, there are many professionals who continue to be unaware of the benefits of inclusive programs in both education and employment. Data exist that show inclusive programs in the schools are beneficial for both students with disabilities as well as those without disabilities. Benefits for students with disabilities include a) decreased rates of inappropriate behavior, b) increased social initiations and interactions, c) enhanced skill acquisition and generalization, particularly in the areas of communication, play skills, and social skills, and d) increased proportion of IEP objectives achieved (Halvorsen & Sailor, 1990). Perhaps, most important there are data that demonstrate that parental expectations for children's futures improve and there is increased inclusion in future environments (Halvorsen & Sailor, 1990). More difficult to subject to empirical validation are quality of life issues such as development of friendships, invitations to birthday parties, and simply encountering acquaintances in community settings.

As students with developmental disabilities progress through school in inclusive programs, both these students, as well as their parents, will not accept the status quo in adult services. These individuals are already beginning to demand inclusive adult community programs to a greater degree than are currently available. Similar to inclusive education programs, data demonstrate that community employment is beneficial for individuals with disabilities in that it results in a) greater community participation, b) increased wages and self-sufficiency, c) development of new skills, and d) increased relationships and interactions with people without disabilities (Rusch, Chadsey-Rusch, & Johnson, 1991). Once again many of the professionals who are involved with delivery of services to adults with developmental disabilities must be educated regarding community programs, their benefits, and how to implement services that reflect current effective practices.

Not only do the data exist that tell us that inclusive community programs work, we also have information that tells us how to implement inclusive programs for both children and adults (e.g., Nisbet, 1992; Snell, 1993; Sowers & Powers, 1991). However, even if these data and information were not available, we would need to advocate strongly for inclusive programs for individuals with disabilities as a civil rights issue. In the 1960s and 1970s there was extensive litigation and legislation involving individuals with disabilities and basic rights such as the right to humane treatment, the right to education regardless of severity or type of disability, and the right to nondiscriminatory evaluation. (See Turnbull, 1993, for a review.) Even though many of these issues were resolved satisfactorily, there continues to be other basic rights issues that are currently being examined in the courts. For example, court cases in New Jersey (Oberti v. Board of Education of the Borough of Clementon School District, 1993) and in California (Board of Education, Sacramento City Unified School District v. Holland, 1992) have dealt with placement in the least restrictive environment (i.e., in the general education classroom with nondisabled peers) and have supported the right of students with disabilities to be educated in inclusive settings. Additionally, the rulings in each of these cases has supported the necessity of reexamining the manner in which we view the supports that can be provided in general education settings. Similarly, there is a new paradigm emerging in community services for adults with disabilities (Smull & Bellamy, 1991). For inclusive school and adult programs, the new paradigm emphasizes changing the way that we view individuals with disabilities and altering the manner that we provide services. We are moving from a system of formal, segregated supports to a system of informal, integrated supports.

Although we know the benefits of inclusive programs, there is much work that is still needed. For example, attitudes of professionals as well as families need to change; that is, we must view individuals with disabilities as competent, contributing individuals with the same rights as individuals without disabilities. Professionals must be educated regarding how to provide supports in inclusive settings. Finally, we must advocate for changes to current legislation and funding strategies that perpetuate outdated, segregated practices. Rather than continuing to discuss the "why" of inclusive practices we must begin to plan the "how" of inclusive programs. It is time to hold a "working conference" that results in developing specific strategies that will facilitate the paradigm shift that is already occurring in the delivery of services to children and adults with disabilities.

References

Board of Education, Sacramento City Unified School District v. Holland, 786 F.Supp. 874, 73 Ed. Law Rep. 969 (E.D.Cal., 1992).

Halvorsen, A. M., & Sailor, W. (1990). Integration of students with severe and profound disabilities: A review of research. In R. Gaylord-Ross (Ed.), *Issues and research in special education* (pp. 110-172). New York: Teachers College Press.

Nisbet, J. (1992). *Natural supports in school, at work, and in the community for people with severe disabilities*. Baltimore: Brookes Publishing.

Oberti v. Board of Education of Borough of Clementon School District, 995 F.2d 1204, 83 Ed. Law Rep. 1009 (3rd Cir. N.J. 1993).

Rusch, F. R., Chadsey-Rusch, J., & Johnson, J. R. (1991). Supported employment: Emerging opportunities for employment integration. In L. H. Meyer, C. A. Peck, & L. Brown (Eds.), *Critical issues in the lives of people with severe disabilities* (pp. 145-169). Baltimore: Brookes Publishing.

Smull, M. W., & Bellamy, G. T. (1991). Community services for adults with disabilities: Policy changes in the emerging support paradigm. In L. H. Meyer, C. A. Peck, & L. Brown (Eds.), *Critical issues in the lives of people with severe disabilities* (pp. 527-536). Baltimore: Brookes Publishing.

Snell, M. E. (1993). *Instruction of students with severe disabilities* (3rd ed.). New York: Merrill.

Sowers, J., & Powers, L. (1991). *Vocational preparation and employment of students with physical and multiple disabilities*. Baltimore: Brookes Publishing.

Turnbull, H. R., III. (1993). *Free appropriate public education: The law and children with disabilities* (4th ed.). Denver: Love Publishing.

Chapter 9

Pharmacological Treatment of Behavioral Problems in People with Mental Retardation: Some Ethical Considerations

Alan Poling
Western Michigan University

Mental retardation is a common developmental disability, and pharmaco-therapy is a common treatment for behavior disorders exhibited by people with mental retardation. The use of psychotropic drugs with this population has been a controversial topic for many years. In 1958, Thomas Greiner predicted that, "in the years to come, the retarded may claim an all-time record, of having the greatest variety and largest tonnage of chemical agents shoveled into them" (p. 347).

Unfortunately, this prophecy proved true. Several surveys, reviewed elsewhere (Aman & Singh, 1988a; Gadow & Poling, 1988), indicate that roughly 30 to 50% of mentally retarded adults living in institutions and 25 to 35% living in community settings receive psychotropic medications. The drugs most often used with these individuals are neuroleptics, such as thioradazine (Mellaril), mesoridazine (Serentil), haloperidol (Haldol), and chlorpromazine (Thorazine). Fewer data are available concerning prevalence rates for children with mental retardation. They appear to be lower (perhaps 3 to 8%), but still significant. Stimulants, especially methylpheni-date (Ritalin), and neuroleptics appear to be the psychotropic drugs most used with mentally retarded children.

Greiner also emphasized the need for high-quality research concerning drug effects in people with mental retardation. He admonished scientists who conducted shoddy research, warning that, "If your aim is to helping the retarded, I urge you to avoid the casual clinical trial of drugs. Make them good trials, or don't make them at all" (1958, p. 347).

Unfortunately, this advice passed largely unheeded. As others have emphasized (e.g., Aman & Singh, 1980, 1983; Lipman, DiMascio, Reatig, & Kirson, 1978; Sprague & Werry, 1971), many of the early studies of drug effects in people with mental retardation lacked methodological rigor and, therefore, are difficult to interpret with confidence.

In addition to cautioning against overprescribing medications and conducting methodologically-flawed research, Greiner emphasized that people with mental retardation require special protection from drugs that might produce deleterious, but subtle, effects:

> Sensible adult patients will usually balk when a drug is causing symptoms, but the very young and the very old are forced to take drugs, can't complain or stop toxic symptoms, may not even connect them with the drug. The mentally deficient of any size or age cannot protect themselves either, and they also merit special care to avoid toxic doses. (p. 349)

Unfortunately, such special care is not easy to define, or to provide.

Fortunately, although the problems that Greiner anticipated have not totally disappeared, real progress has been made. Research examining psychotropic drug effects in mentally retarded people has increased in quantity and quality (Aman, 1987; Singh & Beale, 1986), and much of the recent work has emphasized possible untoward drug effects (Aman & Singh, 1991). A substantial, and clinically useful, data base relevant to psychopharmacology and mental retardation now exists (e.g., Aman & Singh, 1988b; Gadow & Poling, 1988).

Moreover, a series of court cases, beginning with the benchmark *Wyatt v. Stickney* case of the early 1970s, called national attention to the fact that institutionalized people with mental retardation too often received neuroleptic drugs at high doses for long periods, without good reason. These cases, considered elsewhere (Beyer, 1988; Sprague, 1982, 1988), provided impetus for major social and legal changes which powerfully influenced how psychotropic medications are used with mentally retarded people, regardless of whether they reside in institutions. Largely as a result of legal decisions, standards for using drugs in institutions and community placements have been promulgated, and useful procedures for monitoring drug effects have been developed (e.g., Kalachnik, 1988).

Despite these advances, the prescribing of psychotropic drugs for the control of behavioral problems in people with mental retardation continues to generate legitimate controversy (Gadow & Poling, 1988). The controversy involves two main issues. One is whether the right people are being treated. The other is whether treatment regimens are managed appropriately.

The first issue reflects, in part, a diagnostic problem that stems from the fact that caregiver opinions about the nature and severity of the patient's behavioral problems are often the basis for deciding whether to medicate the patient. In many cases, drugs are used with mentally retarded people to suppress relatively nonspecific target behaviors (Aman & Field, 1985; Sovner & Hurley, 1984; Werry, 1988), and there are significant concerns as to whether such practices provide a rational match of patients and interventions. Moreover, the recognized adverse side effects of psychotropic medications raise questions about the use of such agents to manage behavioral problems that are not especially severe, or those that may respond to nonpharmacological interventions. Finally, when a decision to medicate is made, questions inevitably arise concerning how to monitor outcomes and manipulate treatment parameters so as to maximize quality of life for the patient.

Many of these questions can be construed as ethical issues, in that they involve deciding whether particular treatment decisions are good or bad, right or wrong. The present chapter offers practical suggestions for the ethical use of psychotropic drugs with mentally retarded people. These suggestions are based on the author's knowledge of the literature concerning psychopharmacology with mentally retarded people, and his experiences in dealing with mentally retarded people and those who provide services for them. They rest on three fundamental assumptions. The first is that "good" treatment first and foremost improves the quality of life of the treated individual. The second is that the ethical considerations relevant to pharmaco-therapy are not fundamentally different from the ethical considerations relevant to the use of other kinds of interventions. The third is that "ethical" practices are those that are supported by a) legal decisions, and b) the majority of people with a legitimate interest in those practices.

Myths, Misinformation, and Medication

In the vast majority of cases, people with mental retardation do not decide whether or not to take a particular psychotropic medication. Instead, the decision is made for them by one or more caregivers. In far too many cases, those making decisions concerning medication are far from expert in the psychopharmacology of mental retardation. As Ken Gadow and I related five years ago, "Based on our professional experiences and research activities, we believe the greatest single problem concerning the use of psychoactive drugs with mentally retarded people is that care providers lack adequate information about and training in this area" (Gadow & Poling, 1988, p. xv).

Empirical support for the contention that many caregivers are poorly informed concerning the effects of psychotropic drugs comes from a study by Aman, Singh, and White (1987). They surveyed direct caregivers (called "psychopaedic nurses") in two New Zealand public residential facilities serving persons with mental retardation. One question asked the nurses to evaluate their level of preregistration and in-service training concerning psychotropic drugs. Three answers were possible: too little, just right, and too much. With respect to preregistration training, 81% of the respondent regarded the amount of training as too little. Even more (89%) reported that they had received too little in-service training. When the nurses were asked to specify drug-related topics about which they would like to learn more, the topics listed most often were side effects (53%) and clinical indications for the use of various drugs (30%). These data and others collected by Aman et al. (1987) led the authors to conclude that there is "a need for more education on a variety of social, pharmacological, and behavioral issues as they relate to medication use" (p. 449). That need, it appears, is not limited to New Zealand, or to nurses.

Poorly informed care providers are apt to form opinions concerning drug usage on the basis of limited and idiosyncratic personal experience. Their opinions too often are influenced by, and reflect, what Sovner (1988) termed "a set of myths." He lamented that:

It has been disturbing to watch the practice of psychopharmacology with developmentally disabled persons be shaped by a set of myths about the effects of psychotropic agents. Psychotropic drug therapy, per se, is neither intrinsically good nor bad. It is the quality of implementation that determines whether it will be of value. The use of psychotropic drug therapy to treat emotional and behavioral problems in developmentally disabled persons is a distinct clinical discipline (Sovner, 1987). It requires an understanding of the ways in which mental retardation influences the diagnostic process, an understanding of normal emotional and behavioral responses in the developmentally disabled, and the impact of drug therapy upon the habilitation process. Finally, it requires a sound empirical database for diagnosing drug-responsive disorders and selecting the most appropriate psychotropic agent. (p. xi)

Sovner (1988) discussed five specific myths, summarized in Table 1. Those myths are consistent with the negative opinions about drug therapy held by many caregivers (Plotkin & Gill, 1979) and, as Sovner (1988) noted,

[These myths] have influenced the thinking and actions of not only service providers, but also advocates and administrators. In many states, they have become the basis for psychotropic drug regulations that have had a detrimental effect on the delivery of mental health services to duly diagnosed persons. Some patients have been denied drug therapy solely on the basis of misinformation about the effects of medication. (p. vii)

It is sadly ironic in the context of discussing the ethics of drug treatment that antidrug sentiment appears to have gained support from studies fabricated by Stephen E. Breuning. According to the Panel of Senior Scientists convened by the National Institute of Mental Health (NIMH) to investigate his work, "[Breuning] engaged in a lengthy and premeditated course of scientific misconduct with the intent of misleading the scientific community and the federal granting agency" (National Institute of Mental Health, 1987, p. 39).

From 1979 through 1984, Breuning "produced one-third of the literature in the psychopharmacology of the mentally retarded (R. L. Sprague, quoted in *Time*, June 1, 1987, p. 59). His reported studies characteristically employed elegant designs and reported compelling results, many of which conflict with or are unsupported by the of other researchers (Aman & Singh, 1986). As Aman and Singh (1991) noted,

It is likely that Breuning's findings, which usually indicated strongly adverse effects due to the neuroleptics, confirmed the worse fears (and beliefs) of workers in the field (Aman & Singh, 1986). There is, perhaps, an important lesson here. There is no doubt that the use of drugs in mentally retarded people can be an emotive topic, especially given evidence of overusage of drugs in the past. However, it is important that workers maintain an open mind about the use of such therapeutic procedures, lest they otherwise inadvertently adopt extreme positions that are counter to the interests of those they wish to serve. (p. 350)

Table 1: Five Myths Concerning Psychotropic Drug Use

Myth 1. Psychotropic drug therapy directly affects behavior. In actuality, psychotropic drugs alter the physiological substrate underlying behavior, usually by modulating neurotransmitter activity. Therefore, the behavioral effects of a given drug are not invariant.

Myth 2. Psychotropic drug therapy is a second line intervention, one to be reserved for those clients for whom psychosocial interventions have failed, or there is a lack of resources to implement an effective psychosocial program. In some cases, behavioral problems exhibited by mentally retarded people reflect a drug-responsive psychiatric disorder. When this occurs, medication is likely to be only effective intervention, and should be primary.

Myth 3. The Food and Drug Administration approves the use of drugs for specific indications. Although pharmaceutical companies licensed by the Food and Drug Administration to market a given drug can only advertise that it is effective in those conditions for which it has documented efficacy (labelled indications), it can also be used legally for other conditions (unlabelled indications).

Myth 4. A drug withdrawal program should always be built in to any psychotropic drug therapy regimen. For some patients to derive maximal benefits, psychotropic drug therapy must be continued indefinitely. It is senseless to insist on repeated drug withdrawal trials for individuals who relapse when drug therapy is withdrawn.

Myth 5. Psychotropic drug therapy always decreases cognitive functioning and prosocial behavior. This is simply untrue.

Note: The five myths are repeated verbatim from Sovner (1988). The explanations following each are based on more detailed discussions by him.

Keeping an open mind, and cultivating an informed one, are prerequisites if caregivers wish to behave appropriately with respect to the drug treatment of people with mental retardation. Two relatively recent books (Aman & Singh, 1988b; Gadow & Poling, 1988) provide a good starting point for learning about drug effects in this population. The optimal strategy for keeping abreast of current developments is diligent monitoring of the scientific literature. A reasonable alternative for many caregivers is attending workshops offered by experts who not only monitor, but contribute to, that literature. People whom I can recommend as providers of up-to-date and unbiased information are Michael Aman, Kenneth Gadow, Stephen Schroeder, Nirbay Singh, and Travis Thompson, although there undoubtedly are others.

As an important aside, it is worth emphasizing that final authority for prescribing psychotropic drugs rests with members of the medical profession. Therefore, care providers who are not physicians often believe that there is no need for them to learn the psychopharmacology of mental retardation. This is erroneous, for two reasons. One is that physicians often solicit opinions from other people in making treatment decisions, and the best opinions are from well-informed individuals. The other is that it is neither safe nor reasonable to assume that a given physician is well trained in the psychopharmacology of mental retardation. As Sovner (1987) pointed out, this is a separate clinical field, and it is one often ignored in medical schools. Even psychiatrists who are otherwise exquisitely trained in the use of psychotropic drugs may have little or no familiarity with mental retardation. Consulting standard reference books about clinical psychopharmacology helps them but little; most never even mention the topic.

It could be argued, of course, that mental retardation does not influence treatment practices, therefore, there is no reason for physicians to be trained specifically in the psychopharmacology of mental retardation. On examination, such argument fails in three regards (Gadow & Poling, 1988). First, research findings suggest that mentally retarded people do not always react to psychotropic drugs in the same manner as other patients. Differential response to treatment appears to be most striking in severely to profoundly mentally retarded individuals, but there is some indication of differential reactivity in mild to moderately impaired patients. Second, just as drug effects cannot be generalized without qualification to this population, it is unclear to what extent conventional diagnostic constructs can be applied to the behavioral problems of mentally retarded people. Third, standard drug evaluation procedures and instruments are often of marginal value for mentally retarded patients.

In sum, to optimize patient benefits, physicians who prescribe drugs for mentally retarded people must be adequately trained in the psychopharmacology of mental retardation. Because most physicians are not, it is unwise for other caregivers to incautiously assume that a physician's decisions concerning drug use are sagacious, or to transfer all responsibility for appropriate drug use to the physician.

Steps in Drug Treatment

The general steps involved in a data-based approach to the pharmacological management of *any* behavioral disorder (Poling & Bradshaw, 1993) are depicted in Figure 1. These steps must be understood prior to meaningful discussion of what constitutes appropriate, and ethical, drug use in specific situations. Therefore, they are briefly reviewed here.

Although not indicated in Figure 1, the decision to medicate is made in response to a problem: Something that the patient is doing (or, less often, failing to do) is creating difficulties for that person, or for others with a legitimate interest in the patient. The problem might involve one or two discrete responses, as in nighttime bedwetting (enuresis) or self-injurious face-slapping, or it might involve

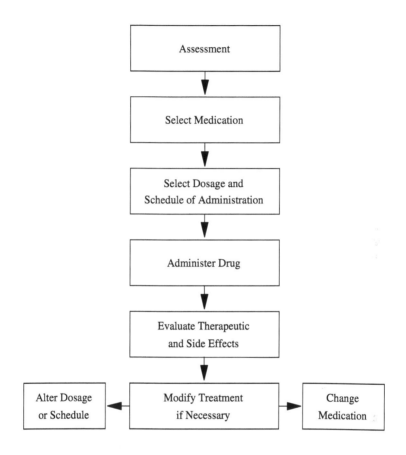

*Figure 1. Simplified sequence of the steps involved in the
pharmacological treatment of a behavior disorder*

a broad range of signs and symptoms, as in clinical depression. In an attempt to solve the problem, medical assistance is sought.

The first step in providing assistance is assessment. Assessment involves collecting information about a patient, and it serves two main functions. One is to guide caregivers in determining an individual's needs and developing interventions to meet these needs. The other is to ascertain whether the selected interventions are successful.

When much if not most of an individual's behavior is troublesome, it is common to consider the specific behavior problems as indications of a clinical disorder. Psychiatric diagnosis involves categorizing people according to the troublesome things that they say and do. It is on this basis that the various forms of mental illness are distinguished, frequently based on criteria described in the *Diagnostic and Statistical Manual of Mental Disorders, Third Edition, Revised (DSM-III-R)*, published by the American Psychiatric Association (1987). Appropriate psychiatric diagnosis is important, because the various classes of psychotherapeutic agents are fairly selective in their ability to modify the symptoms of mental illnesses (Baldessarini, 1990; Poling, Gadow, & Cleary, 1991).

After having completed initial assessment, a treatment is selected. The first question to be answered is whether the problems revealed through systematic assessment actually merit intervention. If they do, the second question concerns whether pharmacotherapy or an alternative, nonpharmacological intervention, is appropriate.

In recent years, formal decision-making strategies that can be employed for evaluating potential interventions have generated considerable interest. For example, Meinhold and Mulick (1990, 1993) proposed that a decision-making model developed by Lawless, Jones, and Jones (1986) is a useful aid for making decisions concerning "aversive" behavioral interventions relative to potential alternatives. Similar ethical and practical issues are relevant to the use of "aversive" behavioral interventions and psychotropic drugs, and the suggestions of Meinhold and Mulick (1990, 1993) concerning the rational, unbiased evaluation of "aversive" behavioral interventions are relevant to the use of psychotropic drugs. Although it will not be discussed in detail here, the model they propose for evaluating interventions is shown in Figure 2. If nothing else, such a model is of value in formalizing the decision-making process and making clear the dimensions to which caregivers are attending in making their choices.

Should a decision be made to initiate drug therapy, questions relating to the choice and administration of a specific agent must be addressed. In a general way, the manner in which drugs are classified reflects empirical findings concerning their range of efficacy. Data indicate, for example, that neuroleptics are the drugs most likely to be useful in managing schizophrenia and other psychoses, anxiolytics in dealing with anxiety, antidepressants in treating unipolar depression, lithium in controlling bipolar affective disorders and mania, and stimulants in dealing with attention deficit disorder in children (Poling et al., 1991). Once a person is assigned to a diagnostic category, the initial choice of a drug class characteristically is simple and straightforward. If, for instance, the client is diagnosed as schizophrenic, a neuroleptic is indicated.

There is growing interest in psychiatric disorders in people with mental retardation ("dual diagnosis") (e.g., Matson & Barrett, 1982). Surveys suggest that such persons exhibit the full range of psychiatric disorders evident in the population at large (Menolascino, Levitas, & Greiner, 1986; Sovner, 1986), and that the prevalence of psychiatric orders is elevated in people with mental retardation (Bruininks, Hill, & Morreau, 1988; Menolascino et al., 1986).

As Aman, Hammer, and Rojahn (1993) pointed out,

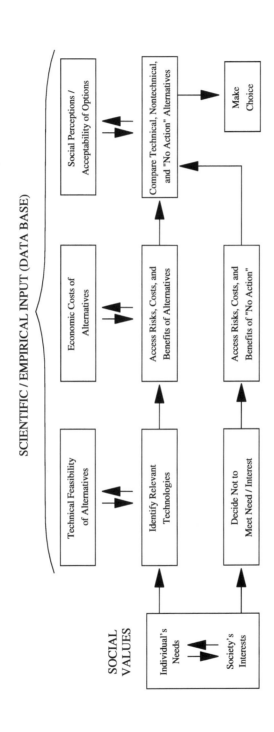

Figure 2. A model for the process of decision-making about alternative technologies. Note: Adapted from Lawless, E. W., Jones, M. V., & Jones, R. M. (1986). Methods for comparing the risks of technologies. In V. T. Covello, J. Menkes, and J. Mumpower (Eds.), Risk evaluation and management (pp. 157-182). New York: Plenum Press. Copyright 1986 by Plenum Press. Adapted by permission.

The most compelling and rational case to be made for psychotropic drugs in mental retardation is among those with true psychiatric conditions, or dual diagnosis. Unfortunately, however, there is only a small handful of studies in this field examining the major psychotropic drugs in well-established disorders, and many of these are poorly controlled (Aman, 1987). It is reasonable to expect that psychotropic drugs will prove effective for the same psychiatric conditions for which they have an established place in the nonretarded population. However, for the most part this still needs to be established empirically, and the major challenge appears to be reaching consensus on markers of psychiatric disorders in this population. (p. 341).

Although some guidelines have been provided (Reid, 1980; Sovner, 1986; Sovner & Hurley, 1983), it is very difficult to diagnose psychiatric disorders accurately in people with mental retardation (Reid, 1983). In the absence of accurate psychiatric diagnosis, there is at present no satisfactory method for matching patients and medications.

It appears that psychotropic medications are often used not to manage specific psychiatric disorders in people with mental retardation, but rather to deal with relatively discrete behaviors perceived by caregivers as troublesome. For example, a survey conducted by Tu and Smith (1983) in five institutions revealed that the most commonly recorded reasons for pharmacotherapy were aggressiveness (29%), hyperactivity (24%), self-injury (12%), excitability (12%), and anxiety (8%). As Aman and Singh (1991) indicated, "It is clear that none of these constitutes a diagnosis as such, and several of the symptoms are remarkably vague" (p. 348).

The effects of particular drugs and drug classes on specific problem behaviors are complex and do not admit ready summary. But it is important to emphasize that no drug or drug class consistently and specifically controls the kinds of behaviors that typically cause problems for people with mental retardation. This is the case, for instance, with self-injurious behavior, a pernicious and relatively common problem that occasionally, but not consistently, responds to such drugs as thioridazine (Mellaril), lithium carbonate, and naltrexone (Trexan) (Aman et al., 1993; Farber, 1987; Gadow & Poling, 1988). In the absence of compelling evidence of effectiveness for any agent, selection of medication is apt to rest upon a clinician's personal experiences.

Once a decision has been made to prescribe a drug from a particular therapeutic category, a specific agent must be selected. In many cases, all members of a particular drug class are quite similar. For example, with respect to neuroleptic drugs:

No one drug or combination of drugs has a selective effect on a particular symptom complex in groups of psychotic patients; although individual patients appear to do better with one agent than another, this can only be determined by trial and error. . . .Since the choice of a drug cannot be made on the basis of anticipated therapeutic effect, the selection of a particular medication for treatment often depends on side effects. If a patient has responded well to a drug in the past, it should probably be used again... (Baldessarini, 1990, p. 402)

Although many drugs within a therapeutic category produce similar effects, most physicians become familiar with one or two members of each category and (unless there are clear contraindications), use these drugs in preference to other, similar agents. The advantage of this strategy is that a clinician can more easily learn the pharmacological properties (e.g., indications, contraindications, side effects, usual dosage, appropriate schedule of administration, interaction with other compounds) of a few drugs than of many. Being fully aware of a drug's pharmacological properties helps to optimize treatment effectiveness and to avoid errors.

Despite the advantages of regularly employing a limited number of behavior-change medications, there are certainly situations in which newly developed drugs merit application, or, as Sovner (1988) emphasized, unusual usage of established drugs is warranted.

Once a particular drug has been selected, an initial treatment schedule must be delineated. This involves specifying the route of administration, time of administration, and dose. These factors determine the concentration of drug at its sites of action and, hence, the magnitude of its effects across time.

With nearly all behavior-change medications, there is considerable variation in the range of doses commonly prescribed. Treatment characteristically is begun with a dosage described in the literature as low to moderate, administered at appropriate intervals. That dose is increased until the behavioral problem is adequately controlled, side effects become intolerable, or the recommended maximum dose is reached. In dealing with extremely agitated patients, it is sometimes judicious to begin with a high dose, which is titrated downward once initial control of the problem behaviors is gained.

With neuroleptics, in particular, it is common practice to attempt to ascertain the minimum effective dose (MED), which is the least amount of medication that produces the desired effect in a given patient. This dose is desirable because the frequency and severity of side effects generally are related directly to dosage.

One obviously can determine whether a patient benefits from a pharmacotherapeutic agent only if the medication is actually taken at the time and dosage intended, and this must be ensured, not assumed. Perhaps less obvious is the need to specify precisely the kinds of changes in behavior that constitute benefit for a patient, and to determine beyond reasonable doubt whether a drug has produced such changes.

Sprague and Werry (1971) suggested that a small experiment is begun each time a drug is prescribed with the intent of improving behavior. In this experiment, the treatment team hypothesizes that drug administration will produce desired alterations in the client's target behaviors without inducing intolerable side effects. Data that reflect target behaviors and side effects when the drug is and is not administered provide the only real means of testing this hypothesis. As in a formal research project, the data collected in clinical practice should be valid (i.e., reflect the dimensions of concern), reliable (i.e., yield constant scores if behavior does not change), and sensitive (i.e., capable of changing as a function of treatment).

Social Validity, Treatment Acceptability, and the Least Restrictive Alternative

The steps involved in a data-based approach to the pharmacological management of a behavior disorder are comparable to those involved in nonpharmacological management of the same disorder, and the ethical concerns relevant to drug treatment are not fundamentally different from those relevant to other interventions. All interventions merit scrutiny with respect to goals, procedures, and outcomes. These aspects determine the acceptability of a given intervention, which Kazdin, French, and Sherick (1981) defined as the "judgements of lay persons, clients, and others of whether the procedures proposed for treatment are appropriate, fair, and reasonable for the problem or client" (p. 900). It is reasonable to assume that treatments which are judged as highly acceptable by particular individuals are viewed as ethical by those people, although a treatment might be deemed unacceptable for reasons unrelated to ethics (e.g., cost).

A sizeable literature has developed concerning the general acceptability of particular behavioral interventions and the variables that determine acceptability in particular circumstances (e.g., Calvert & Johnston, 1990; Lennox & Miltenberger, 1990; Miltenberger, 1990; Reimers, Wacker, & Koeppl, 1987). Lennox and Miltenberger (1990) proposed that 12 specific factors, which they grouped into four categories (efficacy considerations, secondary effects, social/legal implications, and practical consideration), influence the acceptability of behavioral interventions in a given situation, and offered suggestions for considering these factors in making decisions about proposed and ongoing treatments. The factors that they discuss seem to be as relevant to drug treatments as to behavioral interventions.

Treatment acceptability data represent one type of social validity data (Kennedy, 1992). In general, social validity data reflect feedback from consumers concerning their satisfaction with the goals, procedures, and outcomes of an intervention. "Consumers" are those individuals who are involved in and affected by an intervention. In the case of drug treatment for a mentally retarded patient, they might include the patient (where feasible), parents and guardians, direct care staff, advocates, and physicians.

Social validity data characteristically are collected through interviews, questionnaires, or surveys (Fuqua & Schwade, 1986; Kazdin, 1977; McMahon & Forehand, 1983). They are measures of consumers' verbal behavior and are important insofar as they predict whether a given intervention will be used and, if it is used, whether it will generate undesirable side effects (Hawkins, 1991). In developing useful behavior-change technology it is important to demonstrate that an intervention works in ways that are likely to generate its use in future applications, and a sizeable minority of studies in applied behavior analysis report social validity data (Kennedy, 1992; Schwartz & Baer, 1991). Many behavior analysts believe that social validity data are worth reporting (e.g., Baer, Wolf, & Risley, 1987; Wolf, 1978), even though they can only supplement the objective outcome measures on which evaluation of an intervention ultimately rests (Michael, 1980; Schwartz & Baer, 1991).

The availability of social validity data relevant to the use of psychotropic drugs with mentally retarded people would be useful in determining whether caregivers and patients characteristically are satisfied with particular treatments. If they are not –and the fact that experts point to a generally negative view of drugs (e.g., Aman & Singh, 1991; Sovner, 1988) suggests that this may be so–there is legitimate reason to be concerned with how drugs are being used.

Nonetheless, social validity has been given short shrift in the literature dealing with the psychopharmacology of mental retardation. Exceptions are a recent article by Singh and Aman (1990), who discuss the general importance of social validity measures, and studies in which caregivers rate the acceptability of hypothetical interventions (Singh, Watson, & Winton, 1987; Spreat, Lipinski, Dickerson, Nass, & Dorsey, 1989).

Singh et al. (1987) asked the mothers of mentally retarded children to rate the acceptability of four treatment techniques, differential-reinforcement-of-incompatible behavior (DRI), overcorrection, time-out, and drug therapy, in the context of two clinical case studies. The problem in one case was hyperactivity; in the other, it was aggression. Treatment acceptability was evaluated with the Treatment Evaluation Inventory, which contains 15 Likert-scale items (Kazdin et al., 1981). Participants were given descriptions of each treatment, but details of those descriptions was not provided. Results indicated that the intervention rated as most acceptable was DRI, followed by overcorrection. Time-out and drug therapy were less, and similarly, acceptable.

The study by Singh et al. (1987) is seminal, thereby important. A potential difficulty, however, is its presentation of "drug therapy" as a homogeneous entity. Obviously, many different psychotropic drugs can be used with mentally retarded people, and acceptability may differ according to the specific drug (and dose) under consideration.

The same concern is relevant to a more complex study by Spreat et al. (1989), who used vignette methodology to examine variables that might influence the acceptability of 12 interventions (differential reinforcement, response cost, contingent exclusion, visual screen, overcorrection, aversive taste, water mist, time-out room, psychotropic medication, personal restraint, mechanical restraint, and response-contingent electric shock). These authors, recognizing the importance of the least restrictive alternative principle in the treatment of mentally retarded people, had attendees at a conference on communication training, all of whom were involved in the care and treatment of persons with mental retardation, rate the restrictiveness of the interventions. From least to most restrictive, the interventions were rated in the order that they are listed above (i.e., psychotropic medication was seventh). Ratings did not constitute a simple linear hierarchy, however, and Spreat et al. (1988) proposed a five-tier classification system. In this system, psychotropic medication was classified (with time-out room, and personal restraint) as a Level 4 intervention. Hence, its acceptability was relatively low.

The least restrictive alternative principle is "one of the most widely used, yet least understood, concepts in mental health law" (Johnston & Sherman, 1993, p. 103). It has been especially important with respect to the treatment of persons with developmental disabilities, including mental retardation (Martin, 1979; Turnbull, 1977). As the findings of Spreat et al. (1989) suggest, there appears to be general support for the notion that psychotropic medication is a relatively restrictive intervention. For example, in discussing how the least restrictive principle pertains in a legal sense to educating handicapped children, Martin (1979) emphasizes that:

> Some schools consider placing a medicated child in a regular classroom as the least restrictive alternative. But chemical restraints are highly restrictive. They do not educate, remediate, or habilitate. For some children they eliminate a problem that has an adverse effect on educational performance, but for the vast majority the effect is to interfere with education and also to cause long-term harmful side effects. The reality is that the child is being chemically restrained to meet the needs of staff not trained to deal with certain behaviors, and that is too restrictive. (pp. 85-86)

By any reasonable standard, using a psychotropic drug to induce "chemical restraint" is restrictive and not in the patient's best interest. All psychotropic drug use is not, however, for the purpose of "chemical constraint." Moreover, as Johnston and Sherman (1993) point out, the concept of least restrictive alternative is complex, and does not provide a simple standard for evaluating potential treatments. They note, after Reese (1984), that six criteria may enter into the determination of restrictiveness. They are: a) the public's rating of the acceptability of the procedure; b) the deprivation of liberty necessary to implement the procedure; c) time in the habilitation program; d) amount of risk associated with the procedure; e) amount of discomfort and stress that the procedure produces; and f) degree of irreversibility of expected or unexpected effects (Johnston & Sherman, 1993, pp. 107-108).

Some of these criteria are vague and difficult to apply and problems inevitably arise when attempts are made to create and apply a universal hierarchy of interventions based on their "restrictiveness." As Johnston and Sherman (1993) relate,

> It is of no help to say that LRA [least restrictive alternative] is a legal description of a widespread cultural desire to use as little intervention as possible to accomplish therapy and training objectives for developmentally disabled individuals. What constitutes "intervention" is defined only by contrast to the environments customarily encountered by individuals who are not disabled. A discussion among professionals of what in general is customary, what constitutes an intervention, and what is justifiable under what conditions inevitably leads to significant disagreements. Adding opinions from the full range of interested parties seems to guarantee divisiveness. And yet, because LRA has no meaning independent of such

Table 2: ACDD Standards for Drug Therapy

Establishing the Need for Medication

Except for necessary medical or dental procedures, whenever . . . behavior-modifying drugs . . . are employed to manage maladaptive behavior

492 the individual's record documents than any potentially harmful effects of the [medication] have been weighed carefully against the harmful effects of the targeted behavior, and the interdisciplinary team's decision that the harmful effects of the behavior clearly outweigh any potentially harmful effects of the [medication].

493 When an individual exhibits maladaptive behavior and the systematic efforts of the agency to eliminate the behavior have been demonstrated to be ineffective, the services of a behavior management consultant are obtained.

494 Except for necessary medical or dental procedures . . . drugs for behavior management... are not employed except as an integral part of an individualized written program . . . that is designed by the individual's interdisciplinary team to lead to a less restrictive way of managing, and ultimately to the elimination of the behavior.

Prior to the implementation of a written program incorporating the use of [behavior-modifying drugs]

495 the agency documents that legally adequate consent has been obtained.

496 the program has been reviewed and approved by the agency's behavior management committee.

497 the program has been reviewed and approved by the agency's human rights committee.

498 Each committee established a program review date not to exceed one year.

509 Proposed programs that call for the concurrent administration of more than one drug to manage the behavior of an individual are sent for review to the agency's behavior management and human rights committee accompanied by a statement from a physician or psychopharmacologist not affiliated with the agency substantiating that the use of the drugs is not contraindicated. (*See standards 496 and 497*)

Each program utilizing drugs to manage behavior

510 identifies any potential harmful effects of the drugs in nontechnical terms.

511 specifies provisions for at least a monthly interval for re-evaluating the continued use of the drugs and consideration of the reduction and elimination of the drugs.

Emergency Medication

484 Emergency [medication] used to prevent an individual from inflicting bodily harm may not be repeated more than three times within six months without being incorporated into a written behavior management program that meets the requirements of relevant standards.

Table 2 *(continued)*

486 A report of each use of emergency [medication] is provided to the agency's human rights committee.

Self-administration

452 In accordance with their abilities and needs, individuals are trained to attend to their own health and medical needs by self-administering medications and making medical . . . appointments.

Record Keeping

353 A medication . . . history is documented through interviews and a review of records from previous placements is obtained within thirty calendar days of an individual's admission.

457 The record of each individual receiving medication includes a medication response profile that is updated at least monthly or whenever a medication is stopped. The profile identifies the medications taken and observable responses of the individual that may be indicative of either therapeutic benefit, the presence of side effects, or of adverse reactions. Frequencies of seizures or targeted maladaptive behaviors are indicated on the profiles of individuals who have drugs prescribed for control of seizures or for behavior management.

Medication Storage and Administration

669 The unit dose or individual prescription system is used for all prescription drugs, and, whenever possible, drugs that require dosage measurements are dispensed in a form ready to be administered to the individual.

Pharmacists employed by the agency

670 develop a formulary in consultation with physicians.

671 maintain current pharmaceutical reference material.

672 provide information about drug use and abuse to individuals, parents, guardians, advocates, staff, and members of the behavior management and human rights committees.

673 maintain drug profiles for each individual.

674 review the records of individuals for whom medications have been prescribed.

675 are responsible for the storage and dispensing of routine and emergency medications.

All drugs administered by the agency are

676 stored under lock and key and otherwise secured as required by law.

677 stored separately from non-drug items.

678 stored under proper conditions of temperature, light, humidity, and ventilation.

679 Drugs to be applied externally are distinguishable from drugs to be taken internally by means of packaging and labeling or segregation within storage areas.

680 Discontinued drugs, outdated drugs, and drug containers with worn, illegible, or missing labels are promptly disposed of in a safe manner and in accordance with agency policy.

681 No medication is administered by the agency without a written, or verbal order authenticated within 48 hours, by a physician or other legally authorized person.

682 Each prescription contains a month/day/year stop date, or a review by the prescribing physician at least monthly is documented, unless deviation from this requirement is justified and documented in each case by the prescribing physician.

683 Medications are administered, and administrations are recorded, only by persons authorized to do so.

684 Medications are used only for the individual for whom they were issued.

685 Each drug is identified up to the point of administration.

686 Each administration of a non-prescription drug not administered by means of a unit dose or individual prescription system is recorded.

687 All medication errors are reported in accordance with agency written policy.

881 Serious medication errors and drug reactions are reported to the physician and to the agency's chief executive officer or to a person designated by written policy.

689 Documentation of medication errors and corrective action taken is maintained by the agency.

Note: From *Standards for Services for People with Developmental Disabilities* by the Accreditation Council on Services for People with Developmental Disabilities (ACDD), 1987, Boston: Author. Copyright 1987 by the ACDD. Adapted by permission. The ACDD standards for the use of medication are part of a much larger system of quality assurance, and they should be implemented in conjunction with the other components.

---

views, it cannot usefully guide decision making unless these conflicts are identified and resolved. (p. 108).

Given the problems inherent in applying the least restrictive alternative principle, dismissing all pharmacological interventions as intrinsically restrictive, and therefore of limited use, is an oversimplification, at best.

Legal Standards and Ethical Treatment

As noted previously, legal decisions over the past 20 years have determined, in part, how psychotropic drugs are currently used with mentally retarded people. Although the legal concepts underlying the development of treatment standards are arcane for people who are not attorneys, the effects of what Sprague (1982, 1988) termed "litigation, legislation, and regulations" on the development of clinical standards have been direct and powerful. The standards for drug therapy promulgated by the Accreditation Council on Services for People with Developmental Disabilities (ACDD), summarized in Table 2, provide an example of the kinds of procedures characteristically recommended.

Table 3: Provisions Established as a Result of Litigation, Legislation, and Regulations

1. Specific target behaviors that are to improve as a function of drug treatment should be delineated.
2. Evaluation of the need for medication should be performed by an interdisciplinary team.
3. Written informed consent should be procured before drug treatment is initiated.
4. The minimal effective dose drug dose should be used.
5. Periodic attempts at dosage reduction should be scheduled.
6. Drug treatment should be integrated with behavioral and educational interventions.
7. Periodic, data-based evaluations of drug efficacy should be arranged.
8. Evaluations of drug efficacy should include monitoring for side effects (especially tardive dyskinesia if antipsychotics are prescribed).

(from Kalachnik, 1988)

Although the specific standards developed by different oversight agencies vary in their particulars, most entail eight fundamental provisions (Kalachnik, 1988), which are listed in Table 3. These provisions provide a useful frame of reference for anyone interested in providing effective, and ethical, drug treatment for behavioral disorders in people with mental retardation.

Treatment Decisions and Proxy Consent

It is generally assumed that mentally competent adult patients have a right to be fully informed about proposed medical treatment, and to accept or reject that treatment. When the patient is not judged capable of making decisions and consent is by proxy, significant legal and ethical issues are raised concerning who should be involved in the decision-making process (Drew, Logan, & Hardman, 1992; Shaw, 1977). These issues are relevant, but not unique, to the use of psychotropic drugs. They are also complex and vexing (Drane, 1985; Gaylin & Mackin, 1982).

In some cases, a decision to medicate a mentally retarded person is made unilaterally by a parent or guardian following consultation with a physician. This might occur if, for example, a mentally retarded adult residing in the family home began to exhibit signs of a sleep disorder and was brought to the family physician for treatment. How medications are characteristically used in such cases has not been documented, but personal experience suggests that there may be reason for concern. Specifically, even though parents or guardians have the patient's best interest foremost in mind, they may have insufficient information to make an informed decision. If this is the case, and if the medication recommended by the physician is inappropriate, it is possible for the mentally retarded person to receive medications that do no good, and may do considerable harm. Regardless of the number of people involved in treatment decisions, the likelihood that the patient will benefit from treatment is directly related to the level of knowledge of the decision makers.

Although there are cases where the legal guardian, working in conjunction with a private physician, is responsible for decisions concerning medication, this is unusual. Characteristically, people with mental retardation are involved with a number of service agencies, and treatment decisions reflect inputs from members of an interdisciplinary team. For example, the ACDD Standards for Drug Therapy specify that drugs for behavior management are only to be used as part of an individualized written program that is designed by the individual's interdisciplinary team. In addition, to provide further protections for the patient (and for itself), the agency is required to have the program reviewed and approved by the agency's behavior management committee, and by its human rights committee. Finally, the agency is required to document that legally adequate consent has been obtained. These three requirements go far in ensuring that treatment is arranged in an ethical manner.

The interdisciplinary team should include (or secure input from) the patient (if feasible), parent(s) or legal guardian, other people who are first and foremost concerned with the well being of the patient (advocates), people who are aware of the patient's needs, and people who are knowledgeable concerning alternative ways of meeting those needs, including the prescribing of psychotropic drugs. If such a group reaches consensus that drug treatment should be initiated, it is unlikely that the decision is clearly unethical.

Reviews of the decision by the behavior management and human rights committees provide further protection against abuse. The essence of the protection is consensual validation: If a sizeable number of people, with different specialities and interests, agree that drug treatment is appropriate (and ethical), other people are likely to do likewise.

One person who usually must do so for the initiation of treatment to meet legal guidelines and clinical standards is the person who is legally responsible for the patient (the patient, her or his parents, the legal guardian, or other persons acting on behalf of the parents). That person must formally consent to the treatment before it is begun. The concept of consent is so complex and important that the American Association on Mental Retardation commissioned a special task force to examine the topic (Turnbull, 1977). When considered as a legal concept, three elements must be present if the consent is to be effective, or "informed." Those elements, which are discussed elsewhere (Turnbull, 1977), are capacity, information, and voluntariness.

It is conceivable that drug treatment could proceed legally without parental (or similar) consent, because precedent establishes that parents cannot block needed services for handicapped individuals and that such individuals have a right to effective treatment (Martin, 1979). To my knowledge, however, there is no case in which a court of law has ordered that a psychotropic drug be used with a mentally retarded patient despite parental objections.

The Essence of Ethical Drug Use

I am no ethicist. My recollections of the writings of John Stuart Mill, Immanual Kant, Herbert Spencer, and other philosophers dimly remembered from undergraduate courses provide no guidance for discussing how psychotropic drugs ought to be used. From my somewhat naive perspective, it appears that well-informed people who act in agreement with the clinical standards that have arisen out of litigation, legislation, and regulations are apt to provide pharmacological treatments in a manner that most professionals and lay people find ethically acceptable. Such people will provide drug treatments that have three general characteristics, discussed below. If these characteristics are present, ethical problems are apt to be minimized, although they can never be eliminated.

The Goals of Treatment Are Clear and in the Patient's Best Interests

A persistent problem in scientific studies and everyday clinical practice is the use of psychotropic drugs to treat vague and ill-defined disorders. The problem has three aspects. One is that failure to specify precisely what signs and symptoms a drug is to improve makes it difficult to pick an appropriate medication. A second is that it is impossible to know whether a drug produced the desired effect unless one knows precisely what the desired effect entails. A third is that it is unclear whether the goals of treatment are in the patient's best interest unless those goals are specified in terms of precise changes in behavior. Accurate assessment of the behavioral disorder at hand is a necessary prerequisite to the wise use of psychotropic drugs.

Many different techniques can be used to assess behavior along quantitative and qualitative dimensions. These include self-reports, global clinical evaluations, standardized tests, behavioral checklists and rating scales, and direct observation. Techniques that are appropriate for evaluating drug effects in people with mental retardation are discussed elsewhere (e.g., Aman, 1991; Aman & White, 1986; Kalachnik, 1988; Gadow & Poling, 1986).

Once the alleged behavioral disorder has been assessed and expressed in terms of quantified observations, concerned individuals can make an informed decision as to a) whether any intervention is needed, b) what the intervention is intended to accomplish (i.e., treatment goals), and c) whether pharmacotherapy is appropriate in light of these goals. As discussed earlier, these decisions are apt to be ethically appropriate if they are made by an interdisciplinary team of informed individuals.

Treatment Decisions Are Made on the Basis of Real Drug Effects

As a rule, the within-subject, direct observation strategies that behavior analysts characteristically use to evaluate nonpharmacological interventions are well suited to clinical drug assessments (Poling & Cleary, 1986a, 1986b; Singh & Beale, 1986). Consider, for example, a study conducted by Marholin, Touchette, and Stewart (1979), who used a withdrawal (B-A-B) design to examine how chlorpromazine affected four mentally retarded adults. (A fifth person also was studied under a similar but more complex withdrawal design; for simplicity, this subject will not be

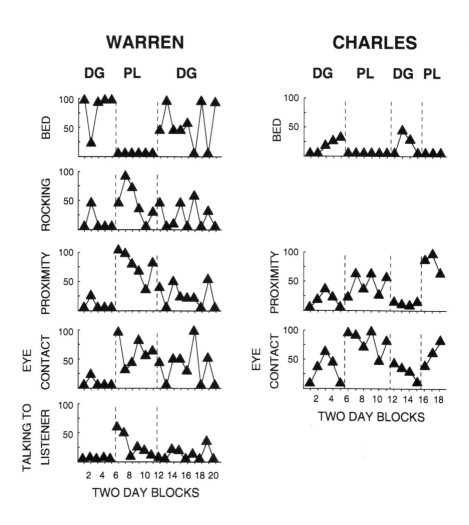

Figure 3. Percentage of intervals during which a variety of social behaviors occurred during chlorpromazine (DG) and placebo (PL) conditions.
Figure is modified from Marholin, D., Touchette, P. E., & Stewart, R. M. (1979).
Withdrawal of chronic chlorpromazine medication: An experimental analysis. Journal of Applied Behavior Analysis, 12, *150-171. Copyright 1979 by the Society for the Experimental Analysis of Behavior. Reproduced by permission.*

considered here.) Several behaviors were carefully measured by direct observation in workshop and ward settings, among them compliance to verbal requests, accuracy and rate of performance of workshop tasks, time on task, eye contact, talking to self, talking to others, standing, walking, being within three feet of others, being in bed, approaching others, and touching others. During the first 19 days of recording, chlorpromazine was given. This was followed by a 23-day drug-free (placebo) phase and a 25-day period in which drug treatment was reinstated.

Some of the data collected by Marholin et al. are shown in Figure 3. The effects of withdrawing chlorpromazine differed appreciably across subjects, but some desirable behaviors did emerge when the drug was withdrawn. Certainly the medication was not producing consistently beneficial effects: "Changes in the behavior of these severely retarded adults which we attributed to chlorpromazine were diverse and generally of no clear relevance to the patients' well being, access to the environment, or physical or psychological comfort" (Marholin et al., 1979, p. 169). Because Marholin et al. provided a quantitative analysis of a range of behaviors under controlled conditions involving the alternate presence and absence of drug, they were able to make such an assertion with relative confidence. Given their findings, further use of chlorpromazine with any of the patients could not be justified on ethical or practical grounds. Because drug treatment inevitably poses a risk, it is always inappropriate to expose a person with mental retardation to a psychotropic drug unless there is clear evidence that the drug produces therapeutic benefit for that individual.

While the absence of therapeutic effects is sufficient reason for changing or ceasing treatment, the presence of therapeutic effects does not necessarily justify continued drug treatment. Even when obvious benefits are observed, adverse side effects must be considered in evaluating the acceptability of treatment. Such effects include somatic complaints and impairment of adaptive behavior. Although a several useful assessment devices are available (see Aman, 1991; Aman & White, 1986; Kalachnik, 1988), it is difficult to be sure that all side effects will be detected, especially if the patients are nonverbal. A major ethical concern is that the patients with mental retardation may suffer undetected, and significant, harm as a result of drug therapy. This concern can be countered, but only partially, by carefully monitoring for side effects and, if they are detected, modifying treatment to alleviate them. Techniques for managing side effects include reducing dosage, prescribing a collateral medication, and switching to another psychotropic agent.

In some cases, however, it is impossible to reduce side effects significantly, and one must ask whether the benefits associated with treatment outweigh its costs to the patient. No simple metric provides an answer; perhaps the best that can be done is to abide with the decision reached by a well-informed interdisciplinary team.

In addition to weighing observed costs against observed benefits, members of such a team must consider possible long-term adverse reactions that are not presently evident. Here, their task is to evaluate short-term gains relative to long-term losses, the certainty and severity of which cannot be predicted accurately. Tardive dyskinesia induced by long-term use of neuroleptics is the prime example of a serious and delayed side effect. These involuntary movements, which include tics, grimacing, lip smacking, and tongue thrusting, occur in a significant number of mentally retarded people who take neuroleptics (Golden, 1988; Schroeder, 1988).

It is impossible to predict with confidence whether a given patient will develop tardive dyskinesia, although the probability of this occurring appears to be related to the specific agent used and the cumulative lifelong dose received (Gadow & Poling, 1988). The disorder usually does not appear until drug treatment has gone on for at least one or two years, frequently is masked until the drug is withdrawn or the dosage is reduced, and may be irreversible (Golden, 1988). The seriousness of tardive dyskinesia is such that neuroleptic drugs should not be used for trivial reasons and, when they are used, care should be taken to minimize risks. Even when this is done, the use of neuroleptics always poses a significant risk to the patient. It is for this reason, in large part, that many people construe drug treatment as relatively restrictive, to be used only when other, less harmful, treatments have failed.

The adverse effects of neuroleptics are real, serious, and common enough to constitute a major concern that should never be ignored, regardless of the kind of patient being treated (Baldessarini, 1990). Nonetheless, it is important to recognize that:

1. Other drug classes do not produce the same adverse reactions as neuroleptics. For example, stimulant drugs at moderate doses usually produce few serious side effects and are generally considered to be very safe (Gadow & Poling, 1988). It is unfair to consider all drug treatments to be equally harmful.

2. Some people do not suffer significant side effects from neuroleptic drug treatment. These drugs have been prescribed for millions of patients, many of whom tolerate them well (Baldessarini, 1990).

3. Some persons with mental retardation derive benefits from neuroleptic (or other) drugs that cannot be equalled through nonpharmacological interventions.

Given the foregoing, it is critical that decisions concerning psychotropic drug use with mentally retarded people are individualized and data-based to the fullest extent possible. Because we can never know a priori precisely how a given person with mental retardation will respond to medication, we must always determine what the medication is intended to do and whether this goal is accomplished. Moreover, we must take care to ensure that observed benefits are evaluated relative to real and possible costs to the patient, and that all decisions are made in her or his best interests. If this is done, treatment is rational and ethical as well.

Drug Therapy Is Flexible and Integrated with Nonpharmacological Interventions

Drug treatment alone will not meet the needs of people with mental retardation. Relative to other behavior-change interventions, psychotropic medications are cheap and easy to administer. Moreover, should they fail to produce desired changes in behavior, responsibility for the failure does not obviously rest with direct care staff. Finally, even when they do not produce the desired therapeutic effect, they may make troublesome patients easier to manage (e.g., through sedation). For these reasons, there is a temptation to offer pharmacological interventions as a substitute for a comprehensive and individualized habilitative program. This practice fails to maximize quality of life for the patient, benefits only caregivers, and cannot be justified. Pharmacological treatments may render patients more sensitive to nonpharmacological interventions (Hersen, 1986), but the former cannot replace the latter. There is no substitute for comprehensive planning and programming to maximize the capacity of people with mental retardation to function in, and derive pleasure from, their worlds.

Of course, neither the people nor the worlds in which they function are static. Although Sovner (1988) is correct in emphasizing the foolishness of repeatedly trying to reduce medication in a person who is responding favorably when drug is present and has consistently deteriorated when drug was withdrawn in the past, it is equally foolish to assume that a person's need for, and response to, medication will not change over time. Appropriate use of medication requires constant monitoring and evaluation; there is no status quo in psychopharmacology. Singh and Aman (1990) provide an interesting discussion of several kinds of variables, many complex and interactive, that may influence how a person with mental retardation responds to drug therapy.

Concluding Comment

There is no doubt that some persons with mental retardation have suffered substantially as a result of inappropriate use of psychotropic drugs. In particular, neuroleptic drugs historically were overprescribed in institutional settings, to the detriment of residents. The worst abuses have ended, in part as a result of litigation brought forth on residents' behalf. Nonetheless, although useful general clinical standards have been developed on the basis of court decisions, the legal system should not be construed as a safeguard against unethical practices. As David L. Bazelton, a Court of Appeals Judge for the District of Columbia, cautioned, "Although courts may be able to respond to and highlight society's most serious abuses, their remedial efficacy is severely constrained. . . . Moreover, courts are by nature backward-looking institutions, called upon to resolve problems only after they have arisen. Unfortunately, this often means that courts cannot and do not become involved until the time for the best solution has passed" (1979, p. 542).

Ultimately, responsibility for the ethical use of any intervention resides with those individuals responsible for its use. I have argued here that responsibility for appropriate use of psychotropic medications rests not just with physicians, but with all people concerned with the well being of the patients in question. If those people are well informed and constantly strive to ensure that patients receive appropriate treatment, only persons with mental retardation who clearly need and benefit from psychotropic drugs will receive them. Using drug therapy with such persons will, in all likelihood, be deemed ethically acceptable by most members of society.

References

Aman, M. G. (1987). Guest editorial. Overview of pharmacotherapy: Current status and future directions. *Journal of Mental Deficiency Research, 31*, 121-130.

Aman, M. G. (1991). *Assessing psychopathology and behavior problems in persons with mental retardation: A review of available instruments.* Rockville, MD: U.S. Department of Health and Human Services.

Aman, M. G., & Field, C. J. (1985). Pharmacological management. In N. N. Singh & K. M. Wilson (Eds.), *Mental retardation in New Zealand: Provisions, services, and research* (pp. 223-249). Christchurch, NZ: Whitcoulls.

Aman, M. G., Hammer, D., & Rojahn, J. (1993). Mental retardation. In T. H. Ollendick & M. Hersen (Eds.), *Handbook of child and adolescent assessment* (pp. 321-345). Boston: Allyn and Bacon.

Aman, M. G., & Singh, N. N. (1980). The usefulness of thioradizine for treating childhood disorders - Fact or folklore? *American Journal of Mental Deficiency, 84*, 331-338.

Aman, M. G., & Singh, N. N. (1983). Pharmacological intervention. In J. L. Matson & J. A. Mulick (Eds.), *Handbook of mental retardation* (pp. 317-337). New York: Pergamon Press.

Aman, M. G., & Singh, N. N. (1986). A critical appraisal of recent drug research in mental retardation: The Coldwater studies. *Journal of Mental Deficiency Research, 30*, 203-216.

Aman, M. G., & Singh, N. N. (1988a). Patterns of drug use, methodological considerations, measurement techniques, and future trends. In M. G. Aman & N. Singh (Eds.), *Psychopharmacology of the developmental disabilities* (pp. 1-28). New York: Springer-Verlag.

Aman, M. G., & Singh, N. N. (1988b). *Psychopharmacology of the developmental disabilities.* New York: Springer-Verlag.

Aman, M. G., & Singh, N. N. (1991). Pharmacological intervention. In J. L. Matson & J. A. Mulick (Eds.), *Handbook of mental retardation* (2nd. ed., pp. 347-372). New York: Pergamon Press.

Aman, M. G., Singh, N. N., & White, A. J. (1987). Caregiver perceptions of psychotropic medication in residential facilities. *Research in Developmental Disabilities, 8*, 449-465.

Aman, M. G., & White, A. J. (1986). Measures of drug change in mental retardation. In K. D. Gadow (Ed.), *Advances in learning and behavioral disabilities* (Vol. 5, pp. 157-202). Greenwich, CT: JAI Press.

American Psychiatric Association. (1987). *Diagnostic and statistical manual of mental disorders, third edition, revised.* Washington, DC: Author.

Baer, D. M., Wolf, M. M., & Risley, T. D. (1987). Some still-current dimensions of applied behavior analysis. *Journal of Applied Behavior Analysis, 20*, 313-327.

Baldessarini, R. J. (1990). Drugs and the treatment of psychiatric disorders. In A. G. Gilman, L. S. Goodman, T. W. Rall, & F. Murad (Eds.), *The pharmacological basis of therapeutics* (pp. 383-435). New York: Macmillan.

Bazelton, D. L. (1979). Preface, Symposium - Mentally retarded people and the law. *Stanford Law Review, 31*, 541-544.

Beyer, H. A. (1988). Litigation and the use of psychoactive drugs in developmental disabilities. In M. G. Aman & N. N. Singh (Eds.), *Psychopharmacology of the developmental disabilities* (pp. 29-57). New York: Springer-Verlag.

Bruininks, R. H., Hill, B. K., & Morreau, L. E. (1988). Prevalence and implications of maladaptive behaviors and dual diagnosis in residential and service providers. In J. A. Stark, F. J. Menolascino, M. H. Albareli, & V. C. Gray (Eds.), *Mental retardation and mental health: Classification, diagnosis, treatment, services* (pp. 3-29). New York: Springer-Verlag.

Calvert, S. C., & Johnston, C. (1990). Acceptability of treatments for child behavior problems: Issues and implications for future research. *Journal of Clinical Child Psychology, 19*, 61-74.

Drane, J. F. (1985). The many faces of competency. *Hastings Center Report, 15*, 17-26.

Drew, C. J., Logan, D. R., & Hardman, M. L. (1992). *Mental retardation: A life cycle approach.* New York: Macmillan.

Farber, J. M. (1987). Psychopharmacology of self-injurious behavior in the mentally retarded. *Journal of the American Academy of Child and Adolescent Psychiatry, 26*, 296-302.

Fuqua, R. W., & Schwade, J. (1986). Social validation of applied behavioral research: A selective review and critique. In A. Poling & R. W. Fuqua (Eds.), *Research methods in applied behavior analysis: Issues and advances* (pp. 265-292). New York: Plenum Press.

Gadow, K. D., & Poling, A. (1986). *Methodological issues in human psychopharmacology.* Greenwich, CT: JAI Press.

Gadow, K. D., & Poling, A. (1988). *Pharmacotherapy and mental retardation.* Boston: College-Hill Press.

Gaylin, W., & Macklin, R. (1982). *Who speaks for the child: The problems of proxy consent.* New York: Plenum Press.

Golden, G. S. (1988). Tardive dyskinesia and developmental disabilities. In M. G. Aman & N. N. Singh (Eds.), *Psychopharmacology of the developmental disabilities* (pp. 197-215). New York: Springer-Verlag.

Greiner, T. (1958). Problems in methodology in research with drugs. *American Journal of Mental Deficiency, 64*, 346-352.

Hawkins, R. P. (1991). Is social validity what we are interested in? Argument for a functional approach. *Journal of Applied Behavior Analysis, 14*, 205-213.

Hersen, M. (1986). *Pharmacological and behavioral treatment: An integrative approach.* New York: Wiley.

Johnston, J. M., & Sherman, R. A. (1993). Applying the least restrictive alternative principle to treatment decisions: A legal and behavioral analysis. *The Behavior Analyst, 16*, 103-115.

Kalachnik, J. E. (1988). Medication monitoring procedures: Thou shall, here's how. In K. D. Gadow & A. Poling (Eds.), *Pharmacotherapy and mental retardation* (pp. 297-312). Boston: College-Hill Press.

Kazdin, A. E. (1977). Assessing the clinical or applied importance of behavior change through social validation. *Behavior Modification, 1*, 427-452.

Kazdin, A. E., French, N. H., & Sherick, R. B. (1981). Acceptability of alternative treatments for children: Evaluations by inpatient children, parents, and staff. *Journal of Consulting and Clinical Psychology, 49*, 900-907.

Kennedy, C. H. (1992). Trends in the measurement of social validity. *The Behavior Analyst, 15*, 147-156.

Lawless, E. W., Jones, M. V., & Jones, R. M. (1986). Methods for comparing the risks of technology. In V. T. Covello, J. Menkes, & J. Mumpower (Eds.), *Risk evaluation and management* (pp. 157-182). New York: Plenum Press.

Lennox, D. B., & Miltenberger, R. G. (1990). On the conceptualization of treatment acceptability. *Education and Training in Mental Retardation, 25*, 211-224.

Lipman, R. S., DiMascio, A., Reatig, N., & Kirson, T. (1978). Psychotropic drugs and mentally retarded children. In M. A. Lipton, A. DiMascio, & K. F. Killam (Eds.), *Psychopharmacology: A generation of progress* (pp. 1437-1449). New York: Raven Press.

Marholin, D., Touchette, P. E., & Stewart, R. M. (1979). Withdrawal of chronic chlorpromazine medication: An experimental analysis. *Journal of Applied Behavior Analysis, 12*, 150-171.

Martin, R. (1979). *Educating handicapped children: The legal mandate.* Champaign, IL: Research Press.

Matson, J. L., & Barrett, R. P. (1982). *Psychopathology in the mentally retarded.* New York: Grune & Stratton.

McMahon, R. J., & Forehand, R. L. (1983). Consumer satisfaction in behavioral treatment of children: Types, issues, and recommendations. *Behavior Therapy, 14*, 209-225.

Meinhold, P. M., & Mulick, J. A. (1990). Risks, choices and behavioral treatment. *Behavioral Residential Treatment, 5*, 29-44.

Meinhold, P. M., & Mulick, J. A. (1993). Social policy and science in the treatment of severe behavior disorders: Defining and securing a healthy relationship. *Clinical Psychology Review, 12*, 585-603.

Menolascino, F. J., Levitas, A., & Greiner, C. (1986). The nature and types of mental illness in the mentally retarded. *Psychopharmacology Bulletin, 22*, 1060-1071.

Michael, J. L. (1980). Flight from behavior analysis. *The Behavior Analyst, 3*, 1-22.

Miltenberger, R. G. (1990). Assessment of treatment acceptability: A review of the literature. *Topics in Early Childhood Special Education, 10*, 24-38.

National Institute of Mental Health (1987). *Final report investigation of alleged scientific misconduct on grants MH-32206 and MH-37449.* Bethesda, MD: Author.

Plotkin, R., & Gill, K. R. (1979). Invisible manacles: Drugging mentally retarded people. *Stanford Law Review, 1979*, 637-679.

Poling, A., & Bradshaw, L. (1993). Psychopharmacology. In M. Hersen & A. Bellack (Eds.), *Handbook of behavior therapy in the psychiatric setting* (pp. 113-132). New York: Plenum Press.

Poling, A., & Cleary, J. (1986a). The role of applied behavior analysis in evaluating medication effects. In A. Poling & R. Fuqua (Eds.), *Research methods in applied behavior analysis: Issues and advances* (pp. 299-312). New York: Plenum Press.

Poling, A., & Cleary, J. (1986b). Within-subject designs. In K. Gadow & A. Poling (Eds.), *Methodological issues in human psychopharmacology* (pp. 115-136). Greenwich, CT: JAI Press.

Poling, A., Gadow, K., & Cleary, J. (1991). *Drug therapy for behavior disorders: An introduction.* New York: Pergamon Press.

Reese, R. M. (1984). Ensuring the right to minimally adequate habilitation: A proposed role for human rights committees. *Mental Retardation, 22,* 142-146.

Reid, A. H. (1980). Diagnosis of psychiatric disorder in the severely and profoundly retarded patient. *Journal of the Royal Society of Medicine, 73,* 607-609.

Reid, A. H. (1983). Psychiatry of mental handicap: A review. *Journal of the Royal Society of Medicine, 76,* 587-592.

Reimers, T., Wacker, D., & Koeppl, G. (1987). Acceptability of behavioral interventions: A review of the literature. *School Psychology Review, 16,* 212-227.

Schroeder, S. R. (1988). Neuroleptic medication for persons with developmental disabilities. In M. G. Aman & N. N. Singh (Eds.), *Psychopharmacology of the developmental disabilities* (pp. 82-100). New York: Springer-Verlag.

Schwartz, I. G., & Baer, D. M. (1991). Social validity assessments: Is current practice state of the art? *Journal of Applied Behavior Analysis, 24,* 189-204.

Shaw, A. (1977). Dilemmas of "informed consent" in children. In D. J. Horan & D. Mall (Eds.), *Death, dying, and euthanasia* (pp. 75-90). Washington, DC: University Publications of America.

Singh, N. N., & Aman, M. G. (1990). Ecobehavioral analysis of pharmacotherapy. In S. R. Schroeder (Ed.), *Ecobehavioral analysis and developmental disabilities: The twenty-first century* (pp. 182-200). New York: Springer-Verlag.

Singh, N. N., & Beale, I. L. (1986). Behavioral assessment of pharmacotherapy. *Behavior Change, 3,* 34-40.

Singh, N. N., Watson, J. E., & Winton, A. S. W. (1987). Parents' acceptability ratings of alternative treatments for use with mentally retarded children. *Behavior Modification, 11,* 17-26.

Sovner, R. (1986). Limiting factors in the use of DSM-III criteria with mentally ill/mentally retarded persons. *Psychopharmacology Bulletin, 22,* 1055-1059.

Sovner, R. (1987). Behavioral psychopharmacology. In J. Stark, F. J. Menolascino, M. Albarielli, & V. Gray (Eds.), *Mental retardation and mental health: Classification, diagnosis, treatment, services.* New York: Springer-Verlag.

Sovner, R. (1988). Foreword. In K. D. Gadow & A. Poling (Eds.), *Pharmacotherapy and mental retardation* (pp. vii-xii). Boston: College-Hill Press.

Sovner, R., & Hurley, A. D. (1983). Do the mentally retarded suffer from affective illness? *Archives of General Psychiatry, 40*, 61-67.

Sovner, R., & Hurley, A. D. (1984). Discontinuing psychotropic drug therapy: Rationale, guidelines, and side effects. *Psychiatric Aspects of Mental Retardation Reviews, 3*, 41-44.

Sprague, R. L. (1982). Litigation, legislation, and regulations. In S. E. Breuning & A. Poling (Eds.), *Drugs and mental retardation* (pp. 377-414). Springfield, IL: Charles C Thomas.

Sprague, R. L. (1988). Litigation about psychotropic drugs. In K. D. Gadow & A. Poling (Eds.), *Pharmacotherapy and mental retardation* (pp. 297-312). Boston: College-Hill Press.

Sprague, R. L., & Werry, J. S. (1971). Methodology of psychopharmacological studies with the retarded. In N. R. Ellis (Ed.), *International review of research in mental retardation* (Vol. 5, pp. 147-219). New York: Academic Press.

Spreat, S., Lipinski, D., Dickerson, R., Nass, R., & Dorsey, M. F. (1989). A paramorphic representation of the acceptability of behavioral programming. *Behavioral Residential Treatment, 4*, 1-13.

Tu, J. B., & Smith, J. T. (1983). Factors associated with psychotropic medication in mental retardation facilities. *Comprehensive Psychiatry, 20*, 289-295.

Turnbull, H. R., III. (1977). *Consent handbook.* Washington, DC: American Association on Mental Deficiency.

Turnbull, H. R., III. (1981). *The least restrictive alternative: Principles and practices.* Washington, DC: American Association on Mental Deficiency.

Werry, J. S. (1988). Conclusions. In M. G. Aman & N. N. Singh (Eds.), *Psychopharmacology of the developmental disabilities* (pp. 239-245). New York: Springer-Verlag.

Wolf, M. M. (1978). The case for subjective measurement, or how behavior analysis is finding its heart. *Journal of Applied Behavior Analysis, 11*, 203-214.

Wyatt v. Stickney, 344 F.Supp. 373 (M.D.Ala., 1972).

Discussion of Poling

The Ethics of Pharmacotherapy: Simply a Case of Stimulus Control?

Debra W. Fredericks

University of Nevada

Poling has provided a comprehensive treatment of ethical pharmacotherapy, a difficult undertaking due to the scope of the subject. He proposes valuable suggestions for all phases of behavioral drug treatment and raises several considerations regarding research. Without doubt, consumers of pharmacotherapy services will benefit if contingencies support treatment teams keeping abreast of the issues outlined by Poling.

The ethical practice of pharmacotherapy, according to Poling, entails stimulus control engineered by legislation and carried out by well informed, professionally diverse treatment teams. This discussion offers an alternative approach to the understanding of ethical behavior. Three significant issues raised in Poling's paper will be elaborated upon within the context of an interbehavioral perspective. These are: social validity, characteristics of ethical treatment, and the concept of "well informed" teams. Let us begin by summarizing how ethical behavior may be conceptualized within interbehavioral field theory.

Ethics as Cultural Interbehavior

Ethical behavior, Poling asserts, is a case of stimulus control. On the surface, this definition appears to be parsimonious and practical. There are standards and provisions set forth by different organizations which generally reflect and promote legislative action. The behavior of individuals responsible for providing treatment interventions for persons with mental retardation are constricted within boundaries established by such legislation. However, this analysis is problematic in two areas: the unit of analysis and rule governance.

Unit of Analysis

Although the study of ethics is concerned with individual behavior, our analysis is likely to be more effective when commenced at the level of the group. Simply stated, what we are talking about when we refer to "ethics" are the actions of groups, specifically, psychological collectivities.

Psychological collectivities are groups of individuals with shared stimulus and response functions; they have something in common and that something" is a psychological interbehavior, conventionally referred to as "attitudes", "beliefs", and "ideas" (Kantor, 1982; Kantor & Smith, 1975). Any particular individual's behavior, therefore, is deemed ethical or unethical only by contrast to the prevailing cultural response functions of the dominant collectivity. Therefore, ethical treatment must be defined within the context of a dynamically evolving interaction between collectivities and cultural stimulus objects over time. What constitutes ethical behavior may be quite different for the same collectivity over time and between collectivities at the same time. An example is the widespread use of chloropromazine (Thorazine) in early years after its discovery. It was often utilized in a way which would not be considered ethical today, namely as a chemical restraint. Nevertheless, by virtue of shared stimulus and response functions of the dominant cultural collectivity of the time, those pharmacologic practices, by definition, were ethical by definition. The practices of less dominant collectivities, particularly those which advocated for the rights of vulnerable populations, functioned to gradually change the definition of ethical pharmacotherapy. Consequently, stimulus functions of vulnerable persons and response functions of groups interested in providing treatment were altered. Thus, the definition of ethical treatment evolved, and in fact, continues to evolve to this day.

Rule Governance

Ethical treatment decisions go beyond the stimulus control provided by legislation. Laws and provisions become institutionalized as cultural stimulus objects. The enactment of laws necessarily involves the linguistic interbehavior of members of collectivities. In addition, the ethical behavior of individuals is rule-governed in the sense that rules are derived at a personal level. They are acquired as shared responses of a psychological collective, which, in turn, influence the stimulus functions of cultural objects, such as laws and provisions. Proactive behaviors on the part of groups in changing existing laws, and in enacting new laws, result. As an aside, it should be noted that if the individuals are well-informed, as Poling advocates, it is probably less likely that myths will participate in rule derivation.

In summary, persons behaving ethically are behaving verbally, therefore an analysis of individual rule-governance is required. In this regard, however, the analysis of rule governance in terms of verbal operant behavior may be problematic (Hayes, 1987).

Social Validity

As indicated by Poling, social validity has not received the attention it warrants. Social validity measures may be an effective means of identifying the shared stimulus-response functions which define a collectivity. Researchers, treatment providers, advocates, family members, and persons with mental retardation may or may not belong to the same collectivities. Effective action between those with an interest in ethical practices requires shared goals. However, differential responding with respect to goals is indicative of persons belonging to different collectivities. Progress toward ethical pharmacotherapy would thus be impeded by incompatible response functions of various collectivities.

The ethical provision of treatment may be facilitated by social validity measures in two ways. First, social validity measures are useful indicators of the acquired group rules in that they reflect the prevailing attitudes of the collectivity to which an individual belongs. Goal directed behavior of treatment teams may be facilitated by consideration of incompatible attitudes within the team. In addition, if social validity measures suggest the participation of myths as rules, efforts can be made to disperse the controlling influence of such myths by education and training procedures.

Secondly, the approval of drug research protocols may be expedited by researchers first obtaining social validity measures prior to writing the proposal. The type of linguistic repertoire which supports the various advocacy groups and committees involved in approval may be incorporated into the proposal. Concerns and criticisms of drug research common to certain collectivities may be anticipated and answered prior to submission. In addition, the execution of approved research may be facilitated by identifying sources of social invalidity.

Characteristics of Ethical Pharmacotherapy

Poling clearly outlines what contemporary ethical pharmacotherapy involves. This material is provided in Tables 2 and 3 of his chapter under the heading, *The Essence of Ethical Drug Use*. The single most important contribution to the actualization of ethical pharmacotherapy practices is the application of single subject experimental design strategies in the applied setting (Barlow, Hayes, & Nelson, 1990).

Unfortunately, single subject design strategies are often carelessly and ineffectively utilized by treatment teams (Fredericks, Hayes, Radcliffe, & Collins, 1992). In order to understand the prevailing stimulus control for this behavior, the analysis, again, needs to be at the level of cultural interbehavior. For example, although an analysis of individual behavior may indicate that contingencies maintain practices inconsistent with single subject design strategies, it is the influence of cultural institutions which maintains such behavior across individuals as members of psychological collectivities over time. If the goal is to change the behaviors of treatment teams toward more effective application of single subject design strategies, intervention may need to target the monolithic, institutionalized stimulus functions operating within the medical establishment which favor large group designs, inferential statistics, and ignores persons with mental retardation and their families.

Producing Well-Informed Treatment Teams

Poling asserts that "well-informed" treatment teams are more likely to engage in ethical pharmacotherapy. As previously mentioned, well informed-teams are probably less likely to base decisions on myths. However, exactly what constitutes "well-informed teams" raises some question.

According to Poling, poorly informed treatment teams are those who are inadequately trained and who have no exposure to the data base. The implication is that training and providing information will produce ethically behaving teams.

It is yet to be established, however, what types of procedures for training and education will be most effective.

Several factors are worthy of attention. First, research indicates an over-willingness of health care providers to depend upon invalid and unreliable data, even when they have access to valid and reliable measures (Fredericks et al., 1992). Second, research on judgement heuristics demonstrates an often intractable resistance to information which challenges preconceived opinions (Nisbett & Ross, 1980; Tversky & Kahneman, 1974). Third, the research on health education has often shown an ineffective impact of traditional educating methods on individual behavior change (Glanz, Lewis, & Rimer, 1990). In short, just because members of a treatment team know what they are supposed to do does not mean they will do it.

The study of education and training strategies must also integrate a study of cultural interbehavior. Cultural institutions may be the source of counter-controlling contingencies. For example, the medicalization of behavior may be one such institution that supports differential stimulus functions for members of a treatment team, especially when the team includes a diversified representation of professionals, paraprofessionals, and laypersons. Though the team may function as a single psychological collectivity, the functions of many conflicting collectivities may also be actualized in the various individual members of the team. Truly effective training and education procedures therefore must be responsive to the variety and complexity of cultural interbehaviors with respect to those being educated and the many cultural institutions having arisen from our medical system.

Summary

Ethical pharmacotherapy involves obligations on the parts of those involved to provide the most effective treatment available, confidently ascribe change to that treatment, and to objectively evaluate the treatment as beneficial. This can be achieved through the judicious use of social validity measures, through the application of single subject experimental design strategies in the applied setting, and by establishing well-informed treatment teams. Needless to add, more research is called for on the influence of culture and rule-governance on ethical behavior. Effective training procedures for treatment teams need to be established. It is recommended that the resulting analyses be made within the context of medical treatment as institutionalized cultural stimuli.

References

Barlow, D. H., Hayes, S. C., & Nelson, R. O. (1990). *The scientist practitioner*. New York: Pergamon Press.

Fredericks, D., Hayes, L., Radcliffe, D., & Collins, J. (1992, May). *Behavioral data and pharmacotherapy: Real concerns regarding illusory beliefs*. Paper presented at the International Association of Behavior Analysis conference, San Francisco.

Glanz, K, Lewis, F. M., & Rimer, B. K. (Eds.). (1990). *Health behavior and health education: Theory and practice*. San Francisco: Jossey-Bass.

Hayes, L. J. (1987). Rule-governed behavior: An implicit analysis of reference. In A. C. Catania & S. Harnad (Eds.), *B. F. Skinner, Consensus and controversy* (pp. 265-276). London, U. K.: Falmer Press.

Kantor, J. R. (1982). *Cultural psychology*. Chicago: Principia Press.

Kantor, J. R., & Smith, N. (1975). *The science of psychology: An interbehavioral survey*. Chicago: Principia Press.

Nisbett, R., & Ross, L. (1980). *Human inference: Strategies and shortcomings of social judgment*. Englewood Cliffs, NJ: Prentice-Hall.

Tversky, A., & Kahneman, D. (1974). Judgment under uncertainty: Heuristics and biases. *Science, 185*, 1124-1131.

Chapter 10

Social Responsibility: Genetics and the Developmentally Disabled

Gregory J. Hayes
University of Nevada, Reno

The concept of social responsibility, of obligations to the population that we serve, in my experience is not a common theme in the training of professionals who provide services to persons with developmental disabilities. In medicine, for example, while the need to inculcate some sense of the professional's role in broader social issues has been discussed and written about since at least the 1950s (Bruhn & Smith, 1972), and while for the first time the majority of medical schools now have some measure of training in subjects such as medical ethics, social issues have nevertheless taken a back seat the clinical here-and-now: the concept that social obligations may be inherent in the role of the professional has remained for the most part undiscussed.

In confronting the issue of social responsibility, I have chosen in this paper to focus on important changes on the horizon in the field of genetics, which will profoundly impact both the population at large and persons with developmental disabilities in particular. Both current and pending advances in genetic research provide us with a picture of the types of social issues we will need to confront in the not-to-distant future. To understand the potential problems such scientific advances in genetics may generate, it is useful to draw first on the past by reviewing key aspects of the eugenics movement of the last century, then juxtapose this information against the current trends in genetic research, in particular the multi-billion-dollar Human Genome Project now underway.

The Early Eugenics Movement

Francis Galton, building on his cousin Charles Darwin's natural selection theory and on discussions then in vogue of selective manipulation of desirable plant and animal attributes, proposed a systematic attempt to influence the evolution of the human species to which, in 1883, he attached the term "eugenics," from the Greek meaning "well born." Galton asked: "Could not the race of men be similarly improved? Could not the undesirables be got rid of and the desirables multiplied?" (Pearson, cited in Gregorios, 1991, p. 146).

Galton, as was true of the philosopher Herbert Spencer before him, also believed there was a hierarchy of races and that members of each racial group were likewise hierarchically arranged. He believed that the order of races and the order of classes or groups within a race was permanently determined by genetic inheritance.

Galton's notion of eugenics was to improve the races through careful attention to marriage practices, emphasizing the mating of healthy individuals with particularly desirable traits in an effort to decrease and theoretically eliminate a constellation of disorders thought to be inherited. This effort, he felt, should include limiting large family size among the lower classes and expanding the generally smaller family size of the upper classes.

By the early 20th century Galton's concept of eugenic progress had grown considerably in popularity in the United States. Public advertisements declared: "How long are we Americans to be so careful for the pedigree of our pigs and chickens and cattle, and then leave the ancestry of our children to chance, or to 'blind' sentiment?" (Gregorios, 1991, p. 146). His concept had also been expanded by this time to include a strategy of involuntary sterilization as a means of preventing those exhibiting "undesirable" traits from reproducing at all. Traits deemed undesirable were, of course, the value judgments of those in power, or, in the words of one author, "white, Anglo-Saxon, Protestant gentlemen" (Gallagher, 1989, p. 17), and came to include an every widening litany of intellectual, social, and physical defects, including many conditions we would now include under the heading "developmental disabilities."

Eugenics in America

The argument for mass sterilization of certain classes of individuals (always replete with racist overtones) was fueled by reportedly scientific genealogical studies of the family trees of defective persons. In America, Henry Goddard's 1912 study on the "heredity of feeble-mindedness," purported to demonstrate that the family tree of a woman with mild mental retardation was riddled with this same "high grade" defectiveness, thus proving the hereditary nature of the problem. (Goddard was, by the way, responsible for the term "moron" in reference to this type of individual, whom he found to be seriously deficient morally, intellectually, and socially.) Similar studies were used to show that a wide array of physical, psychological, and sociological problems were demonstrably hereditary in nature and should be forcefully and unhesitatingly addressed for the good of society.

These various studies were widely accepted by many influential scientists of the day. In fact, in some cases, it was not until many years later that the methodology of these purportedly scientific efforts was definitively scrutinized. Goddard's highly influential study, for example, although increasingly suspect for decades, was not fully exposed as a sham until 1985 (Smith). Goddard, an ardent believer in the hereditary basis of physical and mental diseases, had in fact constructed the data necessary to prove his point, while the family he studied—presented through the use of a pseudonym and thus difficult for others to independently investigate—in fact, exhibited the typical wide range of intellectual and social achievements common to most family trees.

Goddard's study and others were oriented from the outset to the maintenance of Caucasian purity and the elimination of what the investigators felt to be the negative effects of certain elements of the population on the population at large. In particular this effort concentrated on the poor, the socioeconomic group which, among other things, appeared to include the greatest percentage of persons with what we now term developmental disabilities. The common eugenic view was that the poor were poor because of their poor heredity, that the poor exhibited flaws, defects, and disease in greater abundance because of this heredity, and that the poor thus needed to be removed from the gene pool supplying future generations (Smith, 1993). The studies thus promoted and subsequently prompted the institution of aggressive, involuntary sterilization efforts in the public interest. In fact, by the early 1930s, more than 27,000 persons had been involuntarily sterilized in the United States and fully thirty states had enacted sterilization legislation which allowed "compulsory sterilization of the criminally insane and other people considered genetically inferior" (Lifton, 1986, p. 22).

Eugenics and Nazi Germany

Nazi Germany was greatly inspired by America's efforts to protect the human gene pool and, in particular, the white race (although they would have preferred this to be further limited to the Nordic or Aryan group, which they referred to as a "race" as well). Within six months of Hitler's rise to power in 1933, sterilization laws were enacted. The Nazi government moved swiftly: the initial compulsory sterilization project numbered more than 400,000 persons.

While the protection of the Aryan race was the key reference point, this did not exclude persons of Nordic extraction from the list of the "hereditarily sick" (Lifton, 1986, p. 25). The categories of individuals comprising this first sterilization effort were the congenitally feebleminded or mentally retarded, schizophrenics, manic depressives, individuals suffering from hereditary blindness or deafness, and individuals with grave bodily malformations, epilepsy, Huntington's chorea, and what was described as hereditary alcoholism. Franz Lenz, an influential German physician-geneticist, even recommended a more radical step, fortunately never implemented: the sterilization of all persons exhibiting the slightest hint of mental problems of any sort, a group he felt totaled about 20 percent of the German population (Lifton, 1986).

Numerous American eugenicists applauded the Nazi's effort, especially the pace at which Nazi words were being translated into action. Included in this American group was the physician Foster Kennedy, who, writing in the *American Journal of Psychiatry* in 1942, advocated the killing of profoundly retarded children. From the outset, the German eugenics effort was substantially more zealous than the American version. With the blessing of the government, which moved to protect physicians and other professionals from legal liability, the project passionately escalated into an all-out war against those who would contaminate the German *Volk*. "German society in the 1930s was swept by a kind of demented idealism," emphasizing and glorifying health, youth, and sport (Gallagher, 1989, p. 18). Illness was viewed as a "disgrace"—a misery that could "only be removed from the world by [the] painless extermination of the miserable" (Lifton, 1986, p. 44). The destroying of "life unworthy of life" was viewed as a morally necessary "healing work" (Lifton, 1986, p. 46).

The desire to protect the health of the German people was so intense that sterilization came to be viewed as an incomplete and, thus, unsatisfactory solution. Sterilized persons were viewed as a continued drain on society. They took up precious bed space in institutions and hospitals. They consumed substantial public resources. Most importantly, they offered society nothing in return; they were felt to be, in a word, useless. Accordingly, influential German administrators "declared that sterilization was insufficient: psychopaths, the mentally retarded, and other inferior persons must be isolated and killed" (Lifton, 1986, p. 48). One German officer was even more succinct: "The solution of the problem of the mentally ill becomes easy if one eliminates these people" (Lifton, 1986, p. 50). What then followed came to be known as the euthanasia or mercy killing project.

The program was quietly begun in late 1938 or early 1939, when the war effort was expected to dampen any religious concern or opposition. Robert Lifton, an American psychiatrist who has extensively investigated the participation of German doctors during the Nazi era, captures the program's beginnings:

> The occasion for initiating the actual killing of children, and of the entire "euthanasia" project, was the petition for the "mercy killing"...of an infant named Knauer, born blind, with one leg and part of one arm missing, and apparently an "idiot...." In late 1938 or early 1939, Hitler ordered Karl Brandt, his personal physician and close confidant, to go to the clinic at the University of Leipzig, where the child was hospitalized, in order to determine whether the information submitted was accurate and to consult with the physicians there. Brandt reported that the doctors were of the opinion 'that there was no justification for keeping [such a child] alive'; and he pointed out...that in maternity wards in some circumstances it was quite natural for the doctors themselves to perform euthanasia in such a case without anything further being said about it. (1986, p. 50-51)

With Hitler's blessing then the child was euthanized. Similar cases followed in rapid succession, beginning with deformed and mentally deficient infants and young children.

As the euthanasia project moved into high gear, the pretext of obtaining permission was dropped. "The children were generally kept for a few weeks in the institution in order to convey the impression that they were being given some form of medical therapy" (Lifton, 1986, p. 55). Records were then falsified to indicate other, more conventional causes of death such as pneumonia, ruptured appendix, and so forth. Families were kept in the dark as to the true nature of the project. Individuals seen as candidates for the euthanasia program quickly came to include both adults and children. A variety of methods for killing were utilized and scientifically evaluated. These methods included various types of lethal injections, starvation, and the first uses of gas, the latter garnering a reputation as the most efficient and humane of all the various methods employed. In addition, the first Nazi gas chambers and crematoria were constructed for the euthanasia program and lessons learned from this experience were subsequently applied to the mass exterminations of "the final solution."

Criticisms of Eugenic Strategies

In Nazi Germany, the eugenics movement, initially similar to that of the United States, rapidly deteriorated into a program of mass murder, ultimately killing, as we are all painfully aware, millions of Jews, and hundreds of thousands of other supposedly undesirable, nonproductive members of society, as well as antisocial elements in disagreement with the government, and many prisoners of war.

The following critical comments apply generically to the subject of eugenics. For those interested, Lifton's *The Nazi Doctors: Medical Killing and the Psychology of Genocide* provides an extensive analysis of the Nazi experience.

Eugenics is in essence a manifestation of our desire to control our own destiny. Indeed, as the bioethicist Ruth Macklin (1977) has observed, the desire to improve the human population by increasing its positive attributes (what we would now call positive eugenics) is ancient: it was clearly articulated, for example, by Plato in the *Republic*. Positive eugenics has had its modern incarnation in strategies such as the saving of the semen of respected, intellectually exceptional men for use in artificial insemination, with the goal of widely dispersing the positive characteristics of these individuals throughout the population. No doubt many persons donating to sperm banks harbor similar if less grandiose motivations.

There are, however, problems with positive eugenics strategies, at least at present. First and foremost, "it is difficult to imagine that we would all agree on what traits we would like to see increased in the human species" (Munson, 1992, p. 421). Further, any such process would be fraught with error. While in theory efforts at positive eugenics *might* have positive effects, the chances are greater that unexpected negative effects would result. Macklin (1977), for example, makes several important points in this regard. First, a particular genetic trait can only be determined to be positive within the context of its interaction with its environment. That is to say, the phenotypic manifestation of the genotype may prove advantageous in some environments, neutral in others, and disadvantageous in still others. Secondly, transmitting positive traits to future generations is further complicated by our relative ignorance. For example, if we had been able to place Abraham Lincoln's frozen sperm into use, a great deal of suffering would have been inadvertently produced, for we are now aware that Lincoln, certainly among our most respected historic figures, suffered from Marfan's syndrome, a serious, often life-limiting, genetically based disease not even discovered until a generation after his death (Macklin, 1977). Similar unexpected problems lurk around every genetic corner. Thirdly, and perhaps most importantly, most desirable traits appear to have strong environmental components. The direct, genetic aspects of these traits often pale in comparison to the profound impact of a person's life experience.

A critique of what we term negative eugenics, that is the effort to eliminate undesirable characteristics in a population such as through the sterilization efforts previously described, is more complex. In brief, apart from the obvious infringements on personal choice, efforts at negative eugenics are not likely to make much of a difference in the prevalence of a particular problem in a population. There are several reasons why this is so. First, there is again considerable evidence that the early eugenic assumption that most disease is fundamentally genetic in origin is often wrong. For example, even among physicians no more than 10% of mental retardation is regarded as primarily genetic in origin (some professionals active in the developmentally disabled field would find even this percentage excessive). Secondly, even if a disease is primarily genetic in nature, negative eugenic strategies would still be of little value to the population as a whole, because most genetically linked diseases are recessive in nature. This means that the manifestation of the disease requires that two, generally asymptomatic carriers of the recessive gene must first mate. Thus, the elimination of the disease in a population is not possible without the elimination of all the carriers of the genetic trait. Since carriers are generally unaffected or minimally affected by the one recessive gene they carry, their identification can only be achieved through massive, population-wide genetic screening programs. Such mass screening projects, apart from their significant cost, carry with them the added problem of the false positive. In fact, the less prevalent the carrier state or disease is in a population, the more likely a positive screening result will be falsely positive. This difficulty adds a requirement of multiple testing of each sample to avoid the false positive, a costly addition which also ironically diminishes the ability to find the true positive, the actual carrier of the genetic trait in question (i.e., the false negative rate unavoidably increases with the use of multiple tests.)

In the case the carrier state there is an added twist: carriers may receive *positive* benefits from the recessive gene they carry, benefits which would be lost if carriers were eliminated. For example, the carriers of the recessive gene for sickle cell disease have been found to be relatively immune to the effects of malaria–an extraordinarily positive benefit in those areas of Africa where the gene and malaria is particularly common. A second example is found in cystic fibrosis. One in 25 persons harbors a single recessive gene for this disease–an extremely high prevalence rate. Evolutionary biologists feel that such a high carrier rate would not be observed if there were not positive benefits from it. Exactly what these positive benefits are is not yet known, but the point is clear: eliminating carriers is not simply the ridding of unwanted material from the gene pool.

Eliminating all carriers of undesirable genetic traits is particularly nonsensical for another reason: each and every one of us is now estimated to carry from five to eight recessive genes for various abnormalities. Thus a consistently applied program of negative eugenics would ultimately allow no one to survive at all!

Further, eugenics is first and foremost a value-laden system in which the dominant group, the "powers that be," select which traits are desirable and which are not, which persons or classes of persons are of value to society and which are not. It is presumptuous for any group to attempt to determine what is best for the larger population in such fundamental ways. Accordingly, it should not be surprising that ethical analyses based on most major bioethical theories view both positive and negative eugenics strategies in a negative light. Utilitarianism, however, which seeks to maximize the positive benefits of an action for the greatest number of people and which is therefore the most commonly held orientation of public policy makers, would theoretically support a positive eugenics effort *if and when* it could be shown with reasonable certainty that the consequences would truly be, on balance, positive. Given the muddiness of that possibility at present, most utilitarians would defer judgment. Regarding negative eugenics, most utilitarians would limit their support to efforts at the individual level only in which women or couples considering children or already expecting a child would potentially benefit by improved genetic counseling regarding genetically linked conditions. Even at this level, however, the waters are far from clear. Most bioethicists, including utilitarians, remain exceedingly wary. They ask such questions as: What diseases or conditions are legitimately viewed as genetic in origin? To what degree is the expression a genetic abnormality linked to environmental factors? How then should we view genetic condition that is expressed only in particular environments? How accurate is the information provided by genetic screening? Do genetic counselors allow real choices by presenting value-neutral and non-coercive information?

The Human Genome Project

Eugenics has fallen into disfavor since the excesses of the 1930s. Subsequent criticisms such as those just summarized have further isolated any serious pursuit of eugenic dreams to individuals who are for the most part on the radical fringe of society.

The Human Genome Project, however, may alter this reality, opening the doors yet again to future evolutions of eugenic strategies. The Genome Project seeks to map the genetic material contained in a full set of human chromosomes—the genome. Once the project is completed in an estimated 10 to 15 years, geneticists will be able to see firsthand the sequencing of the three billion base pairs or linked nucleotides which form the information chain of the DNA molecules in each human being. This multi-billion dollar project will be accomplished through the combined efforts of scientific groups in both the United States and abroad. The map it will produce will then be used to point the way to an unprecedented explosion of genetic research, which will in turn systematically determine the markers and specific nucleotide sequences responsible for or contributory to thousands upon thousands of diseases, conditions, and traits. In so doing, the project will over time profoundly impact society and societal values, changing how genetic information may legitimately be utilized and indeed our very understanding of what it is to be human.

The Human Genome Project and the research efforts it will spawn will generate truly massive amounts of new knowledge. The application of this knowledge will yield extraordinary power. "The ethical problem is not the acquisition of this power, but in its wise use" (Gregorios, 1991, p. 150). There is no doubt this new information will produce a multitude of positive interventions, but just as likely—perhaps even more so, given the lessons of human history—it will produce at least the potential for massive abuse done in the name of genetic well-being. For all the excitement the Human Genome Project generates, a very dark side of the project looms menacingly ahead.

To the project's credit, in recognition of the difficult dilemmas to come, fully three percent of its budget will be used for the evaluation of ethical and policy issues. Nevertheless, we may well find that the knowledge generated is, like the genie in the lamp, too overwhelming in its effects to entirely control. As professionals we must take note: the genetic explosion to come will be no less dramatic than the explosive force with which we unlocked the secrets of the atom. The dangers are many, the potential risks to persons with developmental disabilities among the most clear.

Without minimizing the potential for the positive uses of this new knowledge, we must concentrate first on the potential negatives of the Genome Project. While some of the concerns I will express need not come to pass, it *is* clear that the new genetics will dramatically alter society's perception of disease and what it means to be "normal."

What we regard as normal has changed dramatically over the last 100 years. Common human problems once accepted as part of the aging process only a few generations ago, for example, are now considered intolerable abnormalities which must be repaired or replaced. The change in perception is sometimes extreme. Today, joint pain in a knee or a hip following a game of tennis, once a reality we simply lived with, may be grounds for aggressive therapies which may even include a total joint replacement (Gaylin, 1993). In this same way, the Genome Project will unavoidably change what human traits and conditions we consider acceptable and desirable. Genetic markers will likely be found in abundance for all types of conditions, including conditions with strong behavioral or environmental components such as schizophrenia and most forms of mental retardation (Nolan, 1992). With apparently solid genetic information available, the temptation will be strong to focus on these "known" explanations for particular conditions rather than on often less defined environmental ones.

This emphasis on inherited factors in response to the new, post-Genome Project genetics may produce a variety of problems. Changing definitions of normalcy will be particularly threatening to the developmentally disabled. Genetic markers will be used to add more precise definition to specific disabilities. Normalcy will then be more precisely defined as the absence of particular genetic sequences judged "defective." This increased genetic focus on normalcy will tend to yield a new emphasis on the labeling of those harboring "defective" genes. Labeling of conditions based on genetic information such as we have seen, for example, in Down

Syndrome with its obvious extra chromosome will most likely become true for most conditions currently viewed as developmental disabilities.

The concerns regarding the labeling of individuals have been long discussed by bioethicists and others. Labeling, while at times of pragmatic value, tends to produce discrimination and to generate self-fulfilling prophesies by pigeonholing individuals in particular categories from which there is often no escape (Gaylin, Thompson, Neville, & Bayles, 1978). The use of the increasingly vast array of genetic information to legitimize these labels will make such categorizations appear more solid and objective, and will lend support to those who wish to engage in discriminatory practices.

The influence of the new genetics on public perception will, for example, make the truly perfect baby appear possible, even realistic, for the first time. A "normal" baby will therefore, at least in the public view, have no known genetic "flaws." Public expectations will be propelled to new heights. Yet perfection will still, in reality, remain impossible: unexpected abnormalities will be observed in offspring from time to time in spite of genetic screening and other efforts to the contrary. There is thus the danger that in this age of new genetic expectations, persons manifesting conditions which in the public view should have been prevented will be deemed outcasts, unacceptable mistakes, and will be stigmatized to a greater degree than we have yet experienced. Such a concern may appear excessively pessimistic in light of significant gains in recent years for persons with disabilities and such progressive pieces of legislation as The Americans With Disabilities Act. But societal norms can change over time. And in the wake of the Human Genome Project there is a definite risk that the current sensitivity to the needs of the developmentally disabled group will diminish dramatically.

The new genetics will be seductive. The public will want to believe that perfection can indeed become the norm and they will be susceptible to pronouncements of what is imperfect or undesirable, pronouncements which, while often value judgments at their root, will be cloaked in the objectivity of the genome. The new genetics will ultimately make it possible to eliminate many conditions deemed unacceptable. These new found abilities, while potentially useful, will also provide an adequate genetic rationale for a new wave of eugenicists who may well try again to rid the world of particular traits or conditions which in their view are "unworthy of life".

The definition of normal may well become so narrow, that the "yearning to control the life course" may negate the value of chance in every day life in the public view (Bonnicksen, 1992, p. S10). Such a constricted view of normalcy will work against the significant gains made for persons with developmental disabilities. For example, in the quest for perfection genetic screening will probably become the norm; ultimately, in fact, it may even be made mandatory. The responsibilities of good citizenship will probably then require that each person gain knowledge about his or her genetic inheritance. This knowledge, for all its benefits, may become a Pandora's box. Such data, for example, will be difficult if not impossible to keep confidential (Draper, 1992). Once in the hands of those who wish to use it to their own ends, many individuals who today consider themselves healthy and normal will find themselves labeled in unexpected ways. We may learn, for example, that we are carriers of recessive genes for undesirable conditions or that we actually harbor a particular coded sequence that may produce demonstrable disease some day. Based on this new data, the discriminatory practices of the future may touch a shockingly large percentage of the population.

Information from genetic screening will, of course, be used to assure a more normal offspring. For cystic fibrosis, in fact, this goal is already a reality. Screening can currently identify the carriers of the cystic fibrosis gene. As we have noted, carriers of this recessive gene are particularly common. Accordingly, once the potential to screen for this trait became available, the insurance industry and certain employers were quick to press for its widespread use. National screening programs were discussed. In this case, bioethicists and others expressing concerns regarding confidentiality and coercion thwarted all such strategies. But changing norms and views on the uses of genetic information may make the identification not only of cystic fibrosis carriers but the carriers and the potentially diseased of thousands of other apparently genetically linked conditions commonplace in the future.

For insurance companies or employers, the desire to know more about their clients or employees is perhaps expected. Insurance companies want to assess risk and to charge accordingly or deny coverage as they see fit; employers want to hire healthy persons who will take little sick leave, who will not drive insurance costs up excessively, and who will not be an unusual risk in specific job settings. Such useful information is also, however, a potent tool for discrimination. In the cystic fibrosis example it became quickly obvious how at least some insurance companies might make use of their new-found knowledge. To lower risk, insurance companies appeared hopeful of influencing parental decisions regarding future offspring. If, for example, a couple wished their offspring to be covered by an insurance policy, the insurance company would probably require that the embryo or fetus be screened and the information gained be applied appropriately in their view. What this appeared to mean was the aborting of defective fetuses. Those couples for whom abortion was unacceptable and who chose for whatever reason to keep their child would do so with the knowledge that the child would be uninsurable and that all medical costs would be their own responsibility. In the case of cystic fibrosis this scenario did not take place and our current health reform effort may well "solve" the fiscal aspects of the example. Nevertheless, it is a harbinger of things to come, demonstrating that genetic information could easily be put to coercive use. In the future, given a more genetically oriented society, pressures to eliminate embryos and fetuses exhibiting a wide variety of socially undesirable traits or conditions can be expected. These conditions will certainly include many developmental disabilities. Besides once again the obvious infringement on choice and personal rights, the dangers are several. First, the information gained from genetic screening may or may not be accurate. Secondly, the apparent genetic abnormality may not translate into significant disability. Genetic screening will focus at first on those conditions which are strongly genetically determined, profoundly detrimental, and manifested under all environmental conditions. Over time, however, screening may come to include conditions in which genetic abnormalities are manifested only given certain environmental stimulations and those in which genetics plays but a minor role. Genetic counseling, already suspect to some observers (Rothman, 1992), can be expected to assume the values of the society in which it functions. A stronger emphasis on genetic variables will lead parents to seek counseling because of "new felt obligations" and the fear of allowing a child to be born with a condition that could and should have been prevented. Fear will render parents increasing risk-averse, and will tend to make their decisions increasingly conservative. What this may well translate to is the elimination of embryos and fetuses in essentially all conditions to which a genetic factor is linked in any way. Many parents, over time, will tend to become more and more unwilling to take any chance of a problem arising in their offspring, however remote.

The enthusiasm for what is possible through genetics will also affect how we allocate resources. The focus will be on genetics and other social programs may suffer accordingly. Instead of addressing our environmental problems, be they pollution or dysfunctional families, the temptation will be to focus our efforts on genetic research in the hope, as the respected bioethicist George Annas relates, "that we will someday find a 'genetic fix' to permit humans to 'cope' with these unhealthy conditions" (1993, p. 155). An editorial in *Science* expresses this very type of emphasis in stating that the Human Genome Project may in fact help to solve the homeless problem by providing treatment answers for the significant percentage of homeless who are mentally ill, a disease which may have significant genetic determinants (Koshland, 1989).

"In a strikingly different approach to public health, the health of a population [may be] maintained not by preventing the members of that population from becoming sick, but by keeping potentially sick people out of the population..." (Rothman, 1992, p. S14). Those who are "potentially sick" may come to include an ever-increasing list of defects, flaws, traits, and conditions judged unacceptable if not by the scientific community than by politicians, policy makers, and the population at large. The slippery slope of who may be included on this list of undesirables is uncomfortably reminiscent of the Nazi experience.

At the very least the enormous database of the new genetics will fuel the possibility of a more modern version of the eugenics movement. Those advocating positive eugenics, for example, will become increasingly confident they can truly identify the "best" individuals whose genetic material should be widely disseminated. Highly value-laden, what is "best" will be defined in crisp, scientific, genetic terms, a stream of specific nucleotide sequences deemed positive and an equally lengthy list of absent undesirable genetic sequences and markers. Still other researchers will probably seek to employ genetic engineering techniques to repair particular defects in otherwise meritorious genes (removing, for example, the

Marfan's Syndrome defect in some latter-day Abe Lincoln). Thoughts of the "Superman" and a "Brave New World" cannot be far away.

Future negative eugenics efforts, should they occur, will acknowledge the practical impossibility of removing all carriers from the population and will instead concentrate on preventing the birth of all persons manifesting the negative traits or conditions of the carrier state. The goal will be to prevent the occurrence of all potential disease and may, as we have noted, come to include conditions in which genetics is of little predictive value. In addition, authors on the subject have observed:

> Prenatal or preconception diagnosis could [also] be encouraged ... [simply] to avoid long-term costs to the State. This rationale, disguised as responsible planning and priorities of resource allocation, could lead to the most dangerous and subtle form of eugenics, economic eugenics (Knoppers & Laberge, 1991)

Minimizing the Negative

Some of the potential negatives of the Human Genome Project should remain the "worst case scenarios" of skeptical and cautious professionals. If this is to be so, however, our involvement in the social process that the Genome Project will precipitate is paramount.

The dangers are very real and repeatedly acknowledged in the literature (Annas, 1993; Knoppers & Laberge, 1991). In addition, as bioethicists have often observed, there is in the medical profession a general tendency to view new developments as beneficial (Nolan, 1992), and medicine will play a particularly powerful role in the utilization of the information of the new genetics. It is therefore imperative that other professions and advocacy groups with other perspectives and concerns insist on their participation in the process, particularly at the policy level, to buffer the medical enthusiasm that will otherwise drive the process.

"The tools of molecular genetics are poised for an attack on human disease with an efficiency unprecedented in the history of medicine" (Friedmann, 1991, p. 137). We must now consider how we can assure that this revolution is reasonably contained and positively utilized. Although the time frame is uncertain, public perceptions *will* change. The influence of genetic information *will* increase. Increased allocation of resources toward genetic goals *will* take place. But with our active involvement we can do much to assure that the hard-fought gains achieved in the interest of persons with developmental disabilities will not be lost to future generations.

Involvement in these social issues by professionals providing services to the developmentally disabled is not only required but, in my view and that of most philosophic traditions common to bioethics, truly imbedded in the very notion of being a professional. That is to the good for we are in essence presented here with an opportunity. Whereas the atomic energy revolution and development of weapons of mass destruction proceeded for many years without public knowledge, discussion, or debate, the genetics revolution is unfolding much more openly and is actively seeking the input of concerned professionals and advocacy groups. The Human Genome Project is attempting to proceed responsibly in funding significant efforts to engage the difficult policy and ethical issues. If these efforts to minimize the potential negative impacts of the new genetics are to bear fruit, however, it is crucial that these discussions not be one sided. Other points of view must be heard.

Further, we must assure that a public education process is begun and aggressively continued. And we must assure these educational efforts present more than the geneticists' perspective, a perspective strikingly summarized in the words of James Watson, co-discover of the structure of DNA and the former head of the Human Genome Project, who in reference to the project once said: "How can we not do it? We used to think our fate is in our stars. Now we know, in large measure, our fate is in our genes" (Jaroff, 1989, p. 62). The public must be made aware of other points of view. The public must know that there are many who strongly believe that "the person is not the gene or disease" (Knoppers & Laberge, 1991, p. 51). The public must be made aware that there are dangers, that all that glitters is not gold. As Wexler has noted:

> We must remember that World War II was not so long ago—and that Fascism is with us today. We cannot permit concentration camps, literal or figurative, for the ill or genetically stigmatized. We are embarking upon an experiment in improving health in the midst of a world of fragile peace, a world suffocating with sufficient nuclear weaponry to rob any disease of its target. Technological developments and the Human Genome Project are providing us with unparalleled opportunities to understand hereditary disease, but we must remember the camps and never pretend to not see (1991, p. 90)

In the final analysis, only an informed and active citizenry cognizant of both the potential benefits and the risks of this brave new genetic world can make a difference. As professionals serving the developmentally disabled we must be part of that process.

References

Annas, G. (1993). *Standard of care: The law of American bioethics.* New York: Oxford University Press.

Bonnicksen, A. (1992). Genetic diagnosis of human embryos. *Genetic grammar,* Special Supplement, *Hastings Center Report, 22*(4), S5-S11.

Bruhn, J. G., & Smith, D. C. (1972). Social ethics for medical educators. In M. B. Visscher (Ed.), *Humanistic perspectives in medical ethics.* Buffalo, NY: Prometheus Books.

Draper, E. (1992). Genetic secrets: social issues of medical screening in a genetic age. *Genetic grammar,* Special Supplement, *Hastings Center Report, 22*(4), S15-S18.

Friedmann, T. (1991). Some ethical implications of human gene therapy. In E. Bankowski & A. M. Capron (Eds.), *Genetics, ethics and human values: Human genome mapping, genetic screening and gene therapy. Proceedings of the XXIVth Council for International Organizations of Medical Sciences Conference* (pp. 132-138). Geneva: CIOMS/World Health Organization.

Gallagher, H. G. (1989). Genetic engineering--the new eugenics? Evolving medical attitudes towards the quality of life. In B. Duncan & D. E. Woods (Eds.), *Ethical issues in disability and rehabilitation* (pp. 17-25). New York: World Rehabilitation Fund.

Gaylin W. (1993, October). Faulty diagnosis: Why Clinton's health-care plan won't cure what ails us. *Harpers*, pp. 57-64.

Gaylin, W., Thompson, T., Neville, R., & Bayles, M. (1978). Sterilization of the retarded: In whose interest? *Hastings Center Report, 18*(3), 28-41.

Goddard, H. H. (1912). *The Kallikak family: A study in the heredity of feeble-mindedness.* New York: Macmillan.

Gregorios, P. (1991). Ethical reflections on human gene therapy: Toward the formulation of a few questions and some answers. In E. Bankowski & A. M. Capron (Eds.), *Genetics, ethics and human values: Human genome mapping, genetic screening and gene therapy. Proceedings of the XXIVth Council for International Organizations of Medical Sciences Conference* (pp. 143-153). Geneva: CIOMS/World Health Organization.

Jaroff, L. (1989, March 20). The gene hunt. *Time*, pp. 62-67.

Kennedy, F. (1942). The problem of social control of the congenital defective: education, sterilization, euthanasia. *American Journal of Psychiatry, 99*, 13-16.

Knoppers, B. M., & Laberge, C. M. (1991). The social geography of human genome mapping. In E. Bankowski & A. M. Capron (Eds.), *Genetics, ethics and human values: Human genome mapping, genetic screening and gene therapy. Proceedings of the XXIVth Council for International Organizations of Medical Sciences Conference* (pp. 39-55). Geneva: CIOMS/World Health Organization.

Koshland, D. (1989). The molecule of the year. *Science, 246*, 1541.

Lifton, R. J. (1986). *The Nazi doctors: Medical killing and the psychology of genocide.* New York: Basic Books.

Macklin, R. (1977). Moral issues in human genetics: Counseling or control? *Dialogue, 16*, 386-396.

Munson, R. (1992). *Intervention and reflection: Basic issues in medical ethics.* Belmont, CA: Wadsworth Publishing.

Nolan, K. (1992). First fruits: Genetic screening. In *Genetic grammar*, Special Supplement, *Hastings Center Report, 22*(4), S2-S4.

Pearson, K. (1914). The life, letters, and labours of Francis Galton. Cambridge: Cambridge University Press. Cited in Gregorios, P. (1991). Ethical reflections on human gene therapy: Toward the formulation of a few questions and some answers. In E. Bankowski & A. M. Capron (Eds.), *Genetics, ethics and human values: Human genome mapping, genetic screening and gene therapy. Proceedings of the XXIVth Council for International Organizations of Medical Sciences Conference* (pp. 143-153). Geneva: CIOMS/World Health Organization.

Rothman, B. K. (1992). Not all that glitters is gold. In *Genetic grammar*, Special Supplement, *Hastings Center Report, 22*(4), S11-S15.

Smith, J. D. (1985). *Minds made feeble: The myth and legacy of the Kallikaks*. Rockville, MD: Aspen Systems.

Smith, J. D. (1993). *The eugenic assault on America: Scenes in red, white, and black*. Fairfax, VA: George Mason University Press.

Wexler, N. (1991). Presymptomatic testing for Huntington's disease: Harbinger of the new genetics. In E. Bankowski & A. M. Capron (Eds.), *Genetics, ethics and human values: Human genome mapping, genetic screening and gene therapy. Proceedings of the XXIVth Council for International Organizations of Medical Sciences Conference* (pp. 80-92). Geneva: CIOMS/World Health Organization.

Discussion of G. Hayes

Remembering the Past

Thomas Scully

University of Nevada School of Medicine

"Those who cannot remember the past are condemned to repeat it."
George Santayana,
The Life of Reason, Vol. I, 1905

Dr. Hayes, in his paper "Social Responsibility," reminds us of the past abuse of human subjects in the name of science, research and medical therapy. One only need read the morning paper or watch the evening news to be similarly reminded: the use of radiation in research and treatment programs involving vulnerable populations without their consent took place in the United States, under government sponsorship, within the past 40 years—and this after the Nuremberg trials, the world's condemnation of the German experiment of the 1930s and the establishment of Institutional Review Boards under the auspices of the federal government.

Other examples, such as the syphilis studies of black men in Tuskegee, Alabama and hepatitis studies in the institutionalized mentally retarded at Willowbrook School in New York City, challenge us to be ever vigilant against sliding down the "slippery slope" and once again repeating the tragic mistakes of the past.

Dr. Hayes, in his very moving talk, well received by the audience, exhorted us to approach the rapid advances being made in the Genome Project and genetic engineering with caution, especially in light of the tremendous scientific and technological advances which are expected to relieve much human suffering in the foreseeable future.

Since many developmental disabilities arise from genetic diseases, it can be anticipated that much of the research in genetics will, of necessity, involve children with developmental disabilities or the potential of developing them. This prospect raises the inevitable ethical question: Is it ever morally permissible to engage children with developmental disabilities in research to which they cannot give informed consent--and if so, under what circumstances?

Society's enthusiasm in the past for new scientific and technological advances has resulted in the medical profession being granted enormous power to influence patient's decisions or, in the case of children, those of their guardians. Research positivism has often swayed the consent process toward favoring new developments. A tendency to generalize from the specific has led to the extrapolation of results from one small study in a limited group to larger and often dissimilar groups resulting in the application of therapeutic techniques to groups of patients in whom the techniques were neither adequately studied nor proven efficacious.

One need only cite the examples of oxygen and chloroamphenicol therapy in the newborn, DES and Thalidomide in pregnant women, and coronary bypass and cardiopulmonary resuscitation in adults. In these instances, treatments studied and proven efficacious in one group of patients were applied to other groups of patients in which the results were at best neutral and at worst dangerous and harmful, in some cases leading to blindness, death, cancer, or severe congenital birth defects.

All too often "new" treatments are presented to patients or their guardians as "accepted," as the "standard of care," or as the "state of the art" when, in fact, the recommended treatments are unproven, experimental, and the real nature of the medical and scientific uncertainty is neither acknowledged nor fully explained prior to obtaining consent.

But in addition to these comments about full disclosure of any diagnostic or therapeutic procedure prior to obtaining or giving consent, there are the ethical concerns regarding privacy and confidentiality raised by the development of the Genome Project. It is reasonable to anticipate that some day soon, based on the study of one or a few cells, much of our past history and future prospects for disease or disability will be laid out in a computer printout for all to see! Such is the risk of some proposed genetic screening projects designed to help but which may, in fact, do more harm than good.

As society's enthusiasm for eliminating many genetic *conditions* deemed unacceptable is rewarded with positive and acceptable results, we must be vigilant that a similar enthusiasm for eliminating many *people* deemed unacceptable does not develop.

And who is to decide which genetic conditions are unacceptable and in need of elimination? And how will such decisions be made in such a way as to avoid discriminatory practices against certain groups or individuals based on the knowledge of their genetic code?

The definitions of "normal" and "defective" are likely to change over time as new "objective" genetic data legitimizes decisions which are really judgments based on the values of the majority. "Labeling" someone "abnormal" may well lead to self-fulfilling prophecies, a phenomenon all too recently seen in this century. Dr. Hayes does a service to ethics and the developmentally disabled person in his thoughtful, articulate and well presented paper. We who attended the conference are grateful to him.

Concluding Discussion

Bringing Professional Behavior Under Control

Marcia L. Bennett
Sierra Regional Center

The papers and discussions so far have demonstrated clearly the complexity of our task: from a behavior-analytic perspective, can we come to a general understanding of ethical issues as they relate to the lives of people with developmental disabilities? For the purpose of the present discussion, I will try to tie together what I see as common threads emerging at this conference. I will also bring up questions and issues that I believe require further analysis.

We have been talking about ethics and people with developmental disabilities in a number of ways. First, we have examined what counts as *ethical behavior*. We have examined the characteristics of ethical behavior and the histories of reinforcement and current contextual variables relevant to its occurrence. Secondly, we have discussed *values*. This approach leads us to articulate rules that we can agree upon (as members of a verbal community) about services for people and the direction these services should take. Finally, we have determined that the notion of *control* is central to an examination of ethics.

In identifying a range of behaviors that we would identify as "ethical," we are developing and describing a *class*. Our activities here are similar to Skinner's recommended approach to operational definition (Skinner, 1945), by which the meaning of a psychological term is clarified by looking at the circumstances under which the term arises as verbal behavior. The circumstances that lead us to describe behavior as "ethical" are of interest here. Several approaches may assist us in clarifying the term. The behavior of professionals and decision makers can be examined directly, as recommended by Van Houten and Healey. This inquiry would give us information on the environmental contingencies operating to support (or hinder) "ethical" practices within a service delivery system. Or, the behaviors of people with developmental disabilities can be our focus, with an interest in developing the verbal repertoires that support ethical conduct. Steve Hayes has recommended the utility of this approach. The behavior of others (parents, family members, program staff, teachers, peers) who have direct influence on the quality of life of individuals with developmental disabilities can be looked at. The utility of this approach is that the context of people's lives may be changed to have beneficial results, for example, by exposure to relevant learning experiences that can maximize competence, health, and access to needed supports. Bijou and Ghezzi have advocated for the importance of this work. Finally, Luke and Collins and Linda Hayes remind us of the importance of taking into account the broader context found in our social institutions and cultural practices to come to a better understanding of ethical behavior.

We can begin to generally describe the nature of the contingencies that operate in the control of ethical (and unethical) behavior. An example may be helpful here. Decisions are sometimes made by groups designed to "watchdog" ethical behavior, such as ethics committees in government. Such decisions usually involve judgements about what has motivated people who are charged to behave in the best interests of others. When the person appears to have made personal gains at the expense of the welfare of people subject to his or her control, we would say that the individual has violated rules of ethics.

Behavior brought "under the control of the welfare of others" is the subject of the paper by Steve Hayes and Greg Hayes. Their analysis points to the importance of verbal repertoires and rules in establishing the effectiveness of complex relational contingencies. It would be important to look at how the behavior of institutional or program staff, family members, teachers, therapists, and others can be brought under the influence of certain "values" or rules having to do with the future welfare of people in their charge, rather than being reinforced by more personal, idiosyncratic, consequences.

Professional behavior is brought under the control of relevant contingencies through a reliance on *data* and the activities of science. The discussion has emphasized the importance of data to drive our decision-making about services for people with disabilities. Behavior-analytic research on complex social contingencies involved in the provision of effective and humane services for people with disabilities is scarce. Nevertheless, there are a variety of data available, in the form of group studies, surveys, and descriptions of program outcomes, that may be useful to us as we proceed.

Another way professional behavior may be brought under the control of relevant contingencies is the recent emphasis on *outcome measures* for evaluating service delivery systems (Accreditation Council On Services for People with Disabilities, 1993). By emphasizing how services impact the behavior of individuals with disabilities rather than the structure of service agencies—review committees, meeting schedules, policies and procedures—our attention is focused on the actual practices of agencies that make a difference for people. The current move toward utilizing outcome measures to justify funding, for example, can only be helpful in this regard.

As we struggle with the question of ethics, we continue to talk about what it is we *value*. We have mentioned the importance of a lack of personal coercion, the value of diversity in behavioral repertoires and environments, freedom of movement, enriched access to sources of both positive and negative reinforcement, the importance of allowing for preference and choice, among others. It may be that a notion of "full community inclusion" is important just because it grossly describes some of the complex contingencies that are consistent with more behavior-analytic values around behavioral diversity and reinforcement. For example, providing services within a community context (as opposed to a segregated, institutional context) may allow people to come into contact with a wide range of potentially reinforcing events that are not otherwise readily available. Such "inclusionary" environments may also allow for more diversity in behavior, as events are less structured and predictable. Histories of reinforcement with respect to a wide array of stimulus conditions are therefore generated. In addition, behavior is more likely to come under the control of more "natural" contingencies, rather than the contrived contingencies generated in institutional or sheltered programs.

The third way we have looked at what it means to behave in "ethical" ways is to examine issues of *control*. People with disabilities are often practically and legally in situations in which their behavior is conspicuously controlled by others. When treatment teams and behavior analytic consultants decide to intervene to change a particular behavior, a complex set of controlling conditions are usually constructed and put into place. These conditions may bear little relation to the contingencies that normally prevail in the various contexts in which the person lives. Additional contingencies are then sometimes constructed to assure that staff "follow the treatment plan" or that "generalization" of behavior to other environments occurs. While effective procedures that develop more adaptive skill repertoires can be extremely helpful, we need to ask ourselves questions about when we should step in with our procedures to control or change prevailing contingencies. What kinds of ethical questions should be asked when behavior change procedures are being considered?

In addition, control is an issue when rights are removed or restricted, such as when a legal guardianship is established. Guardianship is established partially as a countercontrol measure to the ability of agencies to act in ways that compromise the rights of the individual, yet it has its own set of problems. Guardians may not make decisions based on the welfare of the person in their charge, and the preferences (expressed verbally or nonverbally) of the person with a disability may be overruled or disregarded in lieu of a guardian's opinion. The notion of "empowerment," in which people with developmental disabilities are seen as the locus of control for decisions affecting their lives and the nature of the services they receive, maps onto these issues of control.

We are dealing with a wonderfully complex set of issues in our deliberations of ethics and people with developmental disabilities. Resulting actions must be based on examining the bedrock of contingencies operating in the control of the behavior of ourselves and others who work on their behalf.

References

Accreditation Council On Services for People with Disabilities. (1993). *Outcome based performance measures*. Landover, MD: Author.

Skinner, B. F. (1945). The operational analysis of psychological terms. *Psychological Review, 52,* 270-277, 291-294.

Concluding Discussion

Agreeing on Working Assumptions

Donald A. Jackson
Sierra Regional Center

Despite the fact that we represent broadly different perspectives, some directions and themes are beginning to emerge. It appears that we are already agreeing on some working assumptions about ethical practice in developmental disabilities. Since they have a major impact on how we make decisions about our ethical professional behavior, these points are worth reviewing.

We all seem to agree that when Ron Van Houten says clients have a right to a therapeutic living environment, it means the goal for people with developmental disabilities should be *full community membership*. We quickly embrace the idea that a lifestyle similar to our own is appropriate for our clients. This perspective reflects an important paradigm shift. We have moved beyond the era of institutional reform, and even beyond deinstitutionalization. (In terms of education, similar shifts have occurred: school reform, mainstreaming, and now full inclusion.)

Despite unanimous support from a room full of behavior analysts, the goals of full inclusion and full community membership are derived only vaguely from data. They are primarily goals resulting from political or legal perspectives rather than research, reflecting our collective values that emanate from societal views on basic personal liberties.

We do not know a lot about the effects of settings on skill development. Yet many professionals and many parents agree that full community membership or full inclusion is appropriate. Nor do we know much about how to be sure a person benefits from training in more normal environments. Other rights reviewed by Van Houten (to behavioral assessment, treatment that teaches functional skills, effective treatment) do not necessarily flow from full inclusion. Bill Healey pointed out the dilemma we as educators and practitioners can face, of choosing between what is politically correct and what is effective. Public Law 94-142 required that handicapped children be provided with the least restrictive school environment; whereas the most appropriate treatment would be found in the least restrictive *effective* environment.

Similarly, we appear to be rallying behind the notion that there is dignity in risk. Measuring success against this rule, clients should be afforded a reasonably normal lifestyle even if problem behaviors are less likely in a more restrictive living or treatment milieu. Dave Luke and Jackie Collins spoke to this issue in their comments about ethical decision making in advocacy efforts. From the performance engineering perspective they presented, it might be considered unethical to misuse available resources in serving clients. So, if improvements in a client's functioning in an undemanding or tolerant environment do not generalize to more demanding, normal environments, we may have demonstrated very little about useful, effective treatment.

In federally funded agencies, perspectives are slowly changing. Luke and Collins pointed out that minimum compliance standards (focusing on the adequacy of facilities and services) are being replaced by outcome performance measures (focusing on the client's needs and satisfaction). Such a functional approach is rather new. Only a few years ago, federal reviewers of ICF/MR developmental centers required the creation of hierarchical rankings of behavioral interventions based solely on subjective judgments of aversiveness. As Van Houten pointed out, we know now the aversiveness of a restrictive intervention must be individually determined, taking into consideration such things as the amount of time it takes for an intervention to be effective, and the consequences of delaying an intervention.

A third assumption we have accepted here is that clients have the right to treatment decisions that are based on good data. In many circumstances, it would be unethical for a behavior analyst to prescribe interventions without conducting a meaningful functional analysis, or to continue treatments without conducting ongoing evaluations of effectiveness. But it is incorrect to assume that trained behavior analysts will always be ready and able to make important decisions about clients' lives. Indeed, much decision making comes from personal valuing through the stating of preferences for one procedure over another. We as intervention specialists often have little or no information about how such decisions are made. We can only conjecture about the personal histories, social influences, or other contingencies we do not control.

A vivid example of the role of individual preferences over data was discussed earlier today: a hearing impaired person's personal decision to not have a cochlear implant, even though this procedure would greatly improve the ability to hear, because not hearing is normal in the deaf community. Even when preferences—developed for whatever reason—are articulated only vaguely, they can easily outweigh information from well-controlled research. This can present the behavior analyst with difficult ethical decision points. For example, how do we deal with a client who makes a decision we disagree with, especially when it involves the expenditure of limited resources? And how do we respond when a person with developmental disabilities makes decisions without exposure to alternatives? An individual might agree to stay in group care in part because of a lack of exposure to community living alternatives.

In his comments, Van Houten recommended that we address the need for more well-trained behavior analysts who can provide effective treatments. If we are to base treatment decisions on good data, however, we must avoid the appearance of allegiances and be more concerned with good outcomes. It is an issue that has deep roots. In discussing the ethical preparation of professionals and paraprofessionals twenty years ago, Todd Risley raised the controversial point that we should certify procedures, not people (Risley, 1974). Certifying procedures, he argued, is necessary because we must identify effective approaches before we can rationally certify people. The point is relevant here in that we still need to be reminded to avoid guild issues (pulling for the home team) when instead we need to focus on effective and ethical methods and desired outcomes, the hallmark of behavior analysis.

The assumptions discussed here reflect a different perspective on people with developmental disabilities. Context becomes increasingly important. Disability from this perspective is viewed in terms of a person's functioning within specified environments and needed systems of support. A disability is truly a disability only when we are unable as a community to provide the supports necessary for acceptable supported community living. Poor vision is not often considered a disability because it is easily corrected. Being deaf is not a disability if you consider deafness to be normal and the ability to communicate as a deaf person unimpeded.

This view affects how we work and what is considered ethical and unethical. It is reflected in the American Association on Mental Retardation's new approach to defining mental retardation. AAMR stresses the use of a process for determining what support is needed by the person in a variety of specific areas of adaptive functioning. When this approach is taken, intelligence (or that which is commonly measured by IQ tests) is less relevant, or perhaps not relevant at all. Instead the focus is put on the assets and liabilities of the person's environment and the types and intensities of supports being received. This approach puts less emphasis on a person's condition and functioning level (i.e., mild, moderate, severe, or profound retardation) as the independent variable. Rather, more emphasis is given to the environmental conditions and support structures as independent or intervening variables and the person's functioning level, living or employment status, or level of satisfaction as the *dependent variable* (American Association on Mental Retardation, 1992).

Behavior analysts are faced with a variety of ethical challenges in how they approach their work. The papers in this volume help us to begin to understand how, in the real, practical world of applied work, ethical professional behavior must be derived from an understanding of the many forces that impinge on day-to-day decision making.

References

American Association on Mental Retardation. (1992). *Mental retardation: Definition, classification, and systems of supports* (9th ed.). Washington, D.C.: Author.

Risley, T. R. (1974). Certify procedures not people. In W. S. Wood (Ed.), *Issues in evaluating behavior modification: Proceedings of the first Drake conference on professional issues in behavior analysis* (pp. 159-181). Champaign, IL: Research Press.